CHANGING HUMAN NATURE

CHANGING HUMAN NATURE

Ecology, Ethics, Genes, and God

James C. Peterson

William B. Eerdmans Publishing Company
Grand Rapids, Michigan / Cambridge, U.K.

Published 2010 by
Wm. B. Eerdmans Publishing Co.
2140 Oak Industrial Drive N.E., Grand Rapids, Michigan 49505 /
P.O. Box 163, Cambridge CB3 9PU U.K.

Printed in the United States of America

15 14 13 12 11 10   7 6 5 4 3 2 1

Library of Congress Cataloging-in-Publication Data

Peterson, James C., 1957-
    Changing human nature: ecology, ethics, genes, and God / James Peterson.
        p.   cm.
    Includes bibliographical references and index.
    ISBN 978-0-8028-6549-6 (pbk.: alk. paper)
    1. Christianity — Psychology. 2. Theological anthropology — Christianity.
    3. Nature and nurture. 4. Human beings. 5. Persons. 6. Human behavior.
    I. Title.

BR110.P43   2010
233′.5 — dc22

                                                              2010017948

www.eerdmans.com

For my daughters Laura and Noelle

Contents

Contents

Introduction: Our Changing Nature

At 8:32 A.M., Pacific Daylight Time, May 18, 1980, a 10,000-foot mountain in the Cascade Range exploded. About 425,000 tons of rock and ash roared east parallel to the ground at 425 miles an hour. Fifteen minutes later, what were once 54,000 acres of pine tree woods were open plain, a mile-long lake appeared that remains to this day, and a river shifted course and destination. Nature, the material world around us, is constantly changing. The changes are sometimes sudden, sometimes so slow that they are almost imperceptible to our life span, but always, relentlessly ongoing. Most changes are not as abrupt as the eruption of Mount Saint Helens, but over time there is little in the material world that stands still. There are underlying patterns at the deepest levels that are so consistent that we call them laws, such as that electrons are attracted to protons, but nature as the combination and interaction of these forces is constantly moving in seemingly infinite variety.

Some of the change is cyclical: night and day, the phases of the moon each month from full to dark and back again, seasons of winter to spring, spring to summer, summer to fall, and fall back to winter. On longer cycles glaciers extend and retreat. Volcanoes create land that erodes from wind and tide. There is also linear change. We see streams oxbow to a new course. River deltas form land in the sea where there was none. The universe is expanding. Every star that we can see is moving away from us. Projected into the future, all movement in the material universe will eventually run out of the finite energy that it is dispersing and cease in total entropy. Much of what was, will not be again, and what is yet to come has not always been before.

1

Introduction

A few moments ago all the stars of the universe were closer together. Projecting that movement back into the past indicates that there was a time when all energy was gathered in just one place. The singularity exploded out, in part concentrating in pockets to form stars and planets. Life began, became more complex, developing awareness, consciously choosing, growing in understanding and ability to shape the environment on into the future. The novelist Arthur C. Clark, the Jesuit priest and paleontologist Teilhard de Chardin, and modern transhumanists such as Ray Kurtweil all celebrate this narrative. They relish evident trends over time such as that more recent organisms tend to have fewer offspring but invest more in them.[1] Such a progression, like the direction of a rising tide with waves ebbing and flowing but overall gradually advancing, has been celebrated by Howard J. Van Till as a "fully gifted creation."[2] He writes that the Creator endowed the material universe with existence and characteristics needed to develop over time wondrous variety and conscious appreciation.[3] B. B. Warfield, the Princeton professor best remembered in some circles for his argument for the inerrancy of Christian Scripture, argued just as vigorously for a mutual reinforcement between classic Christian doctrine and a developing creation. How the existence of God as Creator fits with the data of a long history of change has continued to draw theories, such as Michael Behe's and William Dembski's ideas of intelligent design revealed in punctuated intervention.[4] By their view, God uses evolution over time, but intervenes as needed to keep it moving on God's intended course. Others have joined in with sophisticated critiques of the neo-Darwinism that extends Darwin's thought to a materialistic philosophy. Darwin himself did not see atheism as a necessary corollary to his theory.[5] For these

---

1. While this strategy is increasingly prominent among more recent creatures, there is still more total biomass in the world among creatures that do not invest concentrated resources in individual progeny, so the trend is not eliminative. Jeffrey P. Schloss, "Divine Providence and the Question of Evolutionary Directionality," in *Back to Darwin: A Richer Account of Evolution*, ed. John B. Cobb Jr. (Grand Rapids: Eerdmans, 2008), pp. 339-50.

2. Howard J. Van Till, *The Fourth Day* (Grand Rapids: Eerdmans, 1986).

3. Such theological hope does not offer calculated assurance; rather it recognizes direction. Schloss, "Divine Providence," p. 349.

4. Michael Behe, *Darwin's Black Box: The Biochemical Challenge to Evolution* (New York: Free Press, 2006); William Dembski, *The Design Inference: Eliminating Chance through Small Probabilities* (Cambridge: Cambridge University Press, 2006).

5. The book *Back to Darwin*, cited in note 1, gathers an august array of scholars to critique neo-Darwinism and offer salient alternatives to it.

theologians, God may well have used change over time to create the world as we presently know it. Genetic, paleontological, and geological evidence does coordinate and indicate overwhelmingly that the earth has existed over aeons.[6] If it has not, God has created the world like an instant towering oak tree with a multitude of tree rings inside. The tree rings would seem to show the amount of annual growth over many seasons. The tree would appear to have a history that it did not. The observational evidence on a global scale is that continents have shifted, mountains have risen, canyons have eroded into existence, and life-forms have changed. The world looks as if the Creator, who decided that a material universe would exist rather than not, who could intervene in that process repeatedly or allow it to unfold from the original gift, at least chose that creation would develop over time.

What the Christian Scriptures state clearly is that the one true God created all that is. There are detailed discussions among those who are convinced that the Christian Scriptures are reliable, as to what they do and do not teach about *how* God created.[7] For example, seventeen hundred years ago Saint Augustine was convinced that Genesis 1 does not describe God creating the world in six (twenty-four-hour) days. He saw the point of the text as quite different from a description of the process used to make a finished creation. He saw in Genesis that God endowed creation with the capacity to develop. In his commentary *The Literal Meaning of Genesis*, Augustine describes the world as created like a seed to grow and develop over time.[8] Denis Lamoureax argues to the same end that the first chapters of Genesis indicate that they are using ancient science language about the earth.[9] The references to a solid sky or firmament holding back waters above, reflect the accepted understanding and terminology of the days when Genesis was first written. For God to have

6. See, for example, the accessible *Language of God: A Scientist Presents Evidence for Belief*, by Francis Collins (New York: Free Press, 2006).

7. James R. Moore, *The Post-Darwinian Controversies: A Study of the Protestant Struggle to Come to Terms with Darwin in Great Britain and America, 1870-1990* (Cambridge: Cambridge University Press, 2003); David N. Livingstone, *Darwin's Forgotten Defenders: The Encounters between Evangelicals and Evolutionary Thought* (Grand Rapids: Eerdmans, 1984).

8. Augustine, *The Literal Meaning of Genesis* 5.23.44, *The Works of St. Augustine*, vol. 13, trans. Edmund Hill, ed. John E. Rotelle (Hyde Park, N.Y.: New City Press, 2002), p. 299.

9. Denis O. Lamoureux, *I Love Jesus and I Accept Evolution* (Eugene, Oreg.: Wipf and Stock, 2009), pp. 43-87.

explained fusion or stellar mass would have been incomprehensible to readers and have obscured the essential revelation of God's existence, being one, who speaks, who cares. . . John H. Walton argues a complementary case that the first chapter of Genesis is describing the God-assigned functions of different parts of creation, not a step-by-step account of the way creation was formed.[10] Meredith Kline as well, also for exegetical reasons, sees the first chapters of Genesis describing the order God has given to the world, not the chronology of its creation.[11] Each of these scholars is arguing that Genesis tells the reader a great deal about God and God's plan for creation. The text uses numbers, in different sequences in chapters 1 and 2, to reveal God and what God has made, not how God made it. Finding a description of creation method in Genesis is reading into the text ideas that were not intended. When interpreters use Genesis to insist on a creation six thousand years ago or to rule out species change over time, they are not defending Scripture, they are defending their misunderstanding of Scripture. Genesis does not say that the world is old or young, or whether all living creatures are related by common descent or not. Neither is the point of the text.

Henry Morris has argued passionately on the contrary that the first two chapters of Genesis must be read as a description of God's method of recent creation. He states that "If God's purpose was the creation and redemption of man, as theistic evolutionists presumably believe, it seems incomprehensible that he would waste billions of years in aimless evolutionary meandering before getting to the point."[12] Six themes can begin a response. (1) God seems to have a broader purpose for creation than just to support human beings. Rodney Scott, a scuba diver and Wheaton College professor of biology, has pointed out that most of the earth's diversity and beauty is under water, where few human beings ever experience it.[13] God's creativity and delight are not just in regard to human beings. There is no reason to assume that any time before human beings was therefore wasted. (2) In the biblical tradition, God is often

10. John H. Walton, *The Lost World of Genesis One: Ancient Cosmology and the Origins Debate* (Downers Grove, Ill.: InterVarsity, 2009).

11. Meredith G. Kline, "Space and Time in the Genesis Cosmogony," *Perspectives in Science and Christian Faith* 48 (1996): 2-15.

12. Henry M. Morris, *Scientific Creationism* (Green Forest, Ariz.: Master, 1985), p. 219.

13. Rodney Scott, annual meeting of the American Scientific Affiliation, Baylor University, Waco, Texas, August 3, 2009.

described as sovereignly choosing to develop over time great movements from the most intimate beginnings. God starts a covenant people with a special mission, whose number will be as the stars in the sky, with one couple, Abram and Sarai. God sets the people of Israel free in the exodus by first addressing one shepherd named Moses. The church that now numbers two billion members was begun with the birth of one person, Jesus of Nazareth. (3) The second letter of Peter declares that a thousand of our years is as a day for God. Summer feels endless to a five-year-old, as it is a major portion of her life. To an adult, summer slips by like a three-day weekend. The infinite God's experience of time is probably quite different from ours. (4) Is the sheer variety and abundance of life a waste or is it characteristic of God's lavish generosity? God welcomes wide diversity of life through creation and bids it in Genesis 1:22 to be fruitful and multiply. (5) We could find comfort in the patience God shows for creation so gradually unfolding. That bodes well for God's patience with our own slow maturing.[14] (6) Life developing over time from common ancestors gives us a point of identification and belonging with all the life that God has made. Granted, evolution can be described as a vicious competition, red with tooth and claw, but it may rather be characterized in the following way:

1. Individuals of a species vary; some of these variations are inherited.
2. More individuals within each species are produced than will live to grow up and to reproduce.
3. Individuals with certain traits are more likely to survive and to reproduce than those with other traits. A key adaptive advantage has been found in varieties of cooperation.[15]

This latter description emphasizes working together more than competition. "All the great transitions of biological history involve greater levels of cooperativeness — the origin of cells, the formation of symbiotic relationships that then produced eukaryotic cells, the generation of multicellular organisms, and the origin of sexual reproduction."[16]

14. Rebecca Flietstra, "Rooting Evolution in Grace," in *Divine Grace and Emerging Creation*, ed. Thomas Jay Oord (Eugene, Oreg.: Pickwick, 2009), p. 159.
15. Flietstra, "Rooting Evolution in Grace," p. 164.
16. Flietstra, "Rooting Evolution in Grace," p. 168.

While theories of evolution emphasize the dynamic changing of nature from past deep time, it is another study to explore and test all the evidence for it and to think through possible challenges and insights that it might provide.[17] Theologians such as John Haught have focused on the implications of evolution if it is indeed God's chosen method of creation.[18] It is not necessary to this book, however, to resolve the means God used to create the world. Readers who accept an evolutionary description are fundamentally convinced that nature (the material world) changes. For readers who have not adopted that reading of the evidence, it is more than enough for the purpose of this book to acknowledge the shifting combinations of matter and energy that we have already seen in just the thousands of years of recorded human history. Our environment is constantly moving between hot and cold, wet and dry. In moments or years earthquakes create ridges and lakes, rivers flood and change their channels, hurricanes erode coastlines. Over just decades glacial ice melts, river deltas extend or recede, and climate shifts. Over the centuries of recorded human history, lava pours out across parts of New Mexico, woolly mammoths cease to live in North America, potatoes from South America grow worldwide, and human population groups spread and mix around the globe. Cyclical and linear change is measurable and characteristic of our planet. Our physical world moves.

Awareness of constant change in nature is not a recent discovery. In the first full century after Jesus Christ, the church father Irenaeus described creation as good but not yet complete.[19] Irenaeus saw Genesis describing God creating on the first day and declaring it good, only to return to the task the next day and again declare it good. God creates on the third, fourth, fifth, and sixth days, each time adding, shaping, refining, and declaring the day's change good. The rest on the seventh day Sabbath is a celebration, not an eternal refrain from further work or creation. The established pattern is a rhythm of creation, development, celebration, and more creation. God is not finished yet. The world as we know it is a work in progress with most yet to come. C. S. Lewis

---

17. For example, Gaymon Bennett et al., eds., *The Evolution of Evil* (Göttingen: Vandenhoeck & Ruprecht, 2008).

18. John F. Haught, *God after Darwin: A Theology of Evolution* (Boulder, Colo.: Westview Press, 2007), chapter 9.

19. Irenaeus, *Against Heresies* 4.38; 5.8-22, particularly 8, 10, and 15. See Gregory of Nyssa as well.

carried on this theme when he wrote, "God, from the first, created her (Nature) such as to reach her perfection by a process in time. He made an Earth at first 'without form and void' and develops the earth from that point."[20]

Not only does nature change, but one part shapes another. Volcanoes build mountains from the ocean floor to emerge as new land. Surtsey Island stands now off Iceland where there was only water in 1962. Glaciers carve valleys. New species replace old ones. Nature is interactive and dynamic. As part of this world, people too change and shape one another and the world. This is most evident in culture. People have adapted to perennial ice in the Arctic and to the desiccating heat of the Namibian desert. The underlying physical laws are consistent, but how they come together in human life is amazingly varied. Our human nature includes the ability to speak, yet globally we converse in at least 42,000 distinct languages.

Human change includes our physical nature. Most human beings today live markedly longer than the generation of their great-grandparents. Current adult stature is so much taller than generations ago that medieval armor for champion warriors looks as if it was designed for children. Ron Green observes that

> five or six thousand years ago, human populations in northwestern Europe became heavily dependent for survival on whole milk derived from domesticated cattle. Throughout history, most human beings stopped drinking milk soon after being weaned from their mothers, and the genes that permitted them to digest milk sugar (lactose) were turned off. Around the world in cultures that are not milk-dependent the turning off of these genes still produces adult lactose intolerance. But in northern Europe (and in some cattle-raising regions of Africa), the opposite occurred: people with mutations in lactose-digesting genes survived and those that could not process this essential food died.[21]

Now for the millions of their descendants, milk, cheese, and ice cream are relished as central to daily food, while discomforting to most adult

20. C. S. Lewis, *Miracles* (San Francisco: Harper, 2001), p. 195.
21. Ronald M. Green, *Babies by Design: The Ethics of Genetic Choice* (New Haven: Yale University Press, 2007), p. 13.

7

human beings in the world. It is reported that also about 5,800 years ago at another corner of the globe, a gene mutation occurred that increased human brain size. That mutation was so advantageous that it spread quickly throughout all the peoples of the world. Human beings became markedly more intellectually able due to a relatively recent and traceable genetic change.[22] Even within the relatively brief frame of recorded human history, our cultures and physical bodies are substantially different from what preceded.

Saint Irenaeus noted that the first command of God to human beings in the book of Genesis was to "be fruitful and multiply" (Gen. 1:28). These are terms of development.[23] In fact, Irenaeus reads Adam and Eve as children in the garden. That they were naked and not ashamed implies to Irenaeus that they had not yet gone through puberty. They had to grow up before they could multiply.[24] God created Adam as good, but not mature.[25] The whole of humanity is foreshadowed in this good start and intended growth. For Irenaeus, humanity is declared good from the start, but not complete. Part of what it means to be human for individuals and humanity is to grow over time at every level of human life. "The love for God which is the life of man cannot emerge *ex nihilo* in full bloom; it requires to grow with experience."[26] The rabbinic discussion parallels Irenaeus at this point. The question was raised as to why, if God wants males to be circumcised, they are not born circumcised. Rabbinic consensus was that God created the world, including male anatomy, in need of further development so that human beings could have a part in that development.[27] Participating in that process is part of being human, of becoming who God would have us to be. There is discovery ahead. As creatures, human beings individu-

---

22. Nitzan Mekel-Bobrov et al., "Ongoing Adaptive Evolution of ASPM, a Brain Size Determinant in Homo Sapiens," *Science* 309 (September 9, 2005): 1720-22.

23. Irenaeus, *Against Heresies* 4.11.1.

24. M. C. Steenberg, *Irenaeus on Creation: The Cosmic Christ and the Saga of Redemption* (Leiden: Brill, 2008), pp. 142-45, expounding Irenaeus's *Demonstration of Apostolic Preaching* 12, 14.

25. Irenaeus, *Against Heresies* 4.38.

26. Douglas Farrow, "St. Irenaeus of Lyons: The Church and the World," *Pro Ecclesia* 4 (1995): 348.

27. Elliot N. Dorff, citing *Genesis Rabbah* 11:6 and *Pesikta Rabbati* 22:4, "Judaism and Germline Modification," in *Design and Destiny: Jewish and Christian Perspectives on Human Germline Modification*, ed. Ronald Cole-Turner (Cambridge: MIT Press, 2008), p. 37.

ally and corporately thrive in growth.[28] God's creation is to be fulfilled in and through time. It is not finished yet.

For Irenaeus, because the first human beings who knew God were young, inexperienced, and immature, they had only one command to obey. They were responsible for one command, which they should have followed. They were welcome to eat widely in the garden, but not from one particular tree.[29] Humanity had the opportunity to grow in knowledge, and the first step was to follow God's direction, to recognize and act on the priority that God comes first.[30] That God's design for human beings, including love for God, is to be developed through experience over time "is what makes the fall such a devastating affair. In the fall man is 'turned backwards.' He does not grow up in the love of God as he is intended to. The course of his time, his so-called progress, is set in the wrong direction."[31] Human beings will change. In human rebellion, the potential for positive growth is instead turned to increasing degradation. The direct disobedience in eating of the tree when God had forbidden it began the journey in the wrong direction, away from God rather than toward God. Irenaeus continues that the Fall, the loss, death, is mostly a loss of what human beings could have become, not what they already had. It is not that maturity is taken away, rather that they stop growing toward maturity. They were like an infant that through some injury became incapable of speech before realizing that potential.[32] Such was a devastating loss of what should have become.

We still make choices that shape ourselves and the material world for good or for ill. We inhabit an infinitesimal corner of an expanding universe and influence just a fragment of that, but our corner is different because of what we do. Our human physical form is shaped by our decisions, as is the rest of nature. Medical interventions have saved many lives. Often patients who in the past would have died are now able to have children of their own, and the deleterious condition that we treated becomes more common.[33] Zebra mussels introduced to the

---

28. Irenaeus, *Against Heresies* 4.11.2.
29. Steenberg, *Irenaeus on Creation*, p. 164.
30. Irenaeus, *Against Heresies* 4.38-39.
31. Farrow, "St. Irenaeus of Lyons," p. 348.
32. Steenberg, *Irenaeus on Creation*, pp. 167-69.
33. Eric T. Juengst, "Altering the Human Species? Misplaced Essentialism in Science Policy," in *The Ethics of Inheritable Genetic Modification*, ed. John Rasko, Gabri-

Great Lakes by oceangoing ships through the Saint Lawrence Seaway are cleaning the water by their filter feeding, but crowding out native species. Such human impact on the material world is not just a modern phenomenon. The fantasy projection that the earliest human beings were in a steady renewable relationship with nature is not what the anthropological record indicates. For example, it seems to be more than coincidence that in North America the woolly mammoths died out shortly after human beings arrived on the continent.

We not only shape nature unintentionally. We cannot survive unless we shape nature deliberately. Few of us live on tropical islands with no need of shelter and with abundant food at hand that can be eaten raw. As soon as we form branches into a roof to shed the rain, catch a fish with a hook, or cook the fish over a fire on a sharpened stick, we are changing our environment. That is our God-given nature. If we are to survive, we shape nature by the combination and application of the underlying givens. The question is not whether we will shape our surroundings; it is whether we will do so consciously and conscientiously. Our past and present give us a starting point but not a goal. The key guide is not what we have been, but what we should be. We are from the dust and to dust we shall return, but in the meantime what shall we be and how does that contribute to God's plan for our part in creation? There can be rich insight from our past concerning how we came to be this way in this place, yet as we continue to walk, the more important question is where we will go and how we will take the next step. Nature is constantly changing as it shapes nature and us. Consciously intended or not, human beings are constantly changing as we shape nature and ourselves. Simply saying no to any change is both impossible and unfaithful. The question before us is not whether we will shape nature and ourselves but whether we will be aware that we are doing so, and choose well how we do so and to what purpose.

The philosopher Hans Jonas once exhorted the theologian James Gustafson to "use your surplus and give us the real article! The skeptical hedgings we will supply, but first we want the full blast of your strongest guns. For we well know that immanent reason . . . has not the last word on ultimate questions of our being and at some point must borrow from sources of light beyond itself, or at least consider their

---

elle O'Sullivan, and Rachel Ankeny (Cambridge: Cambridge University Press, 2006), p. 124.

witness."[34] Writing as a theologian, I will seek to respond to that request with my best reading of the Christian tradition on our place in a universe of constant change. While theological conviction may seem as boldly contrasting to the spirits of our times as Jonas suggests, I will still seek to point to and articulate that transcendent light.

Since no human being knows all and sees all, each of us directs our attention and interprets what we see from a perspective. I have found the varied Christian tradition to be the most comprehensively coherent way of understanding the world. It would be a different study to explain why I am thus convinced. At this point I will simply defer to the contemporary work of philosophers such as Alvin Plantinga and Richard Swinburne; historians such as Paul Rhodes Eddy and Gregory A. Boyd, F. F. Bruce, and Colin Hemer;[35] and apologists such as William Lane Craig, Alister McGrath, Clark Pinnock, and John G. Stackhouse Jr. They and others ably present aspects of the case that Jesus the Christ can be known through trustworthy accounts from his time, his ongoing work among his people to this day, his direct address to those open to his presence, and his sheer sense-making presence. "I believe in Christianity as I believe that the Sun has risen: not only because I see it, but because by it I see everything else."[36] In this work, I will gladly listen to and learn from other perspectives, but I will not try to abstract out an essentialist view that everyone will agree to. That is simply not possible. A Christian perspective should be of interest to the two billion people who call themselves Christian, those who work with them, and truth seekers interested in understanding a view so widely held.

Part I of this book will explore the God-given call to shape what is entrusted to us. Chapter 1 of part I works out our responsibilities in

34. Hans Jonas, "Response to James M. Gustafson," in *The Roots of Ethics: Science, Religion, and Values*, ed. Daniel Callahan and H. Tristram Engelhardt Jr. (New York: Plenum, 1981), p. 210.

35. See, for example, *Knowledge of God* by Alvin Plantinga and Michael Tooley (Oxford: Wiley-Blackwell, 2008). Most recent of many fine works by Richard Swinburne, *Was Jesus God?* (Oxford: Oxford University Press, 2008). Paul Rhodes Eddy and Gregory A. Boyd, *The Jesus Legend: A Case for the Historical Reliability of the Synoptic Jesus Tradition* (Grand Rapids: Baker Academic, 2007); F. F. Bruce, *The New Testament Documents: Are They Reliable?* (Leicester: InterVarsity; Grand Rapids, Eerdmans, 1988); Colin Hemer, *The Book of Acts in the Setting of Hellenic History* (Tübingen: J. C. B. Mohr, 1989).

36. C. S. Lewis, "Is Theology Poetry?" in *The Weight of Glory and Other Addresses* (San Francisco: HarperSanFrancisco, 2001), p. 140.

11

tending the world as God's garden. Then in chapter 2 the means of technology are considered. Chapter 3 makes the case that the creation entrusted to our intentional shaping includes ourselves, ourselves include our bodies, and our bodies include our genes. My approach will not be anthropomonistic, as if only human beings matter, nor anthropocentric, as if all creation exists only for human use.[37] My intent is to be theocentric, centering in what God has designed and intended for human beings and the rest of creation. Human beings play an assigned role, but we are not the sum of all that God cares about. In part II, each of three chapters will address a commonly proposed guide for shaping human nature that offers helpful caution, but inadequate and sometimes even misleading direction. When these guides are elevated to absolute prohibitions, as they often are, they end up forbidding things that we *should* do. In part III, I will propose four standards that should be considered when shaping human nature. Part IV will address the crucial question of who applies these standards.

Francis Fukuyama has noted with appreciation that "Religion provides the clearest grounds for objecting to the genetic engineering of human beings, so it is not surprising that much of the opposition to a variety of new reproductive technologies has come from people with religious convictions."[38] In contrast, in this book I will listen carefully to religious and other objections, learn from them, and propose a theological approach, rooted and thriving in the historic Christian tradition, that is nuanced and substantially positive about our calling to shape our environment and ourselves, including our genes.

37. Lukas Vischer, "Listening to Creation Groaning," in *Listening to Creation Groaning: Report and Papers*, ed. Lukas Vischer (Geneva: Centre International Reforme John Knox, 2004), pp. 21-22.

38. Francis Fukuyama, *Our Posthuman Future: Consequences of the Biotechnology Revolution* (New York: Picador, 2003), p. 88.

I Called to Shape What Is Entrusted to Us

1 God's Garden

The Nature of God and the God of Nature

The only God, as the Trinity, was complete and everlasting without us, but chose to extend the love of God in making a material universe. In that world created where nothing was before are creatures who can love God, each other, and all else that God has made. Indeed, the world is filled with contingencies that in the slightest variance would have left no physical place for conscious beings. The Cambridge University physicist Sir John Polkinghorne cites as an example the exquisitely balanced forces that hold nuclei together yet can allow them to decay. Such stability yet recombination is necessary for the existence of physical life. He has joined others in describing these surprising circumstances as examples of "the anthropic principle" that holds that the physics of the material universe looks as if it was designed to make life possible.[1]

One of the most quoted sentences in the Bible is found in the third chapter of John. "God so loved the world that he gave his only Son, so that everyone who believes in him may not perish but may have eternal life" (John 3:16). The text does not say that God so loved people; rather it says that God loves the world (the cosmos), which is everything that God has made. The cosmos includes people, but it is not just people. God cares about all that God has made. God the Son

1. John Polkinghorne, "A Potent Universe," in *Evidence of Purpose*, ed. John Marks Templeton (New York: Continuum, 1994), pp. 105-15.

came to live in that world in the person of Jesus Christ for the sake of that whole creation. It is this Christ, God with us, who is described as having made the world even before being incarnate within it (John 1:10-12). It is this Christ who is described as sustaining the world to this day (Heb. 1:3). It is this Christ who is proclaimed as the one who will eventually fulfill creation's purpose, reconciling everything in him (Col. 1:15-20). People matter, but apparently so does the rest of God's creation. In Genesis God blesses the fish and birds (Gen. 1:22). When the flood comes, God remembers Noah, but also each type of animal on the ark (Gen. 8:1). The covenant that follows is with every living thing (Gen. 9:9-10). As Job describes, God knew and cared for the world long before humans (Job 38–39). Jesus speaks of God's care for the plants and birds (Matt. 6:26). Sallie McFague goes further than these biblical texts when she describes the earth as "the body of God."[2] On the contrary, only God is God. The creation is what God has made, not God, but it is appropriate for God's people to love the world as something that God loves and, in a sense as McFague argues, to "love nature for the same reason that we love God and our neighbor: because it is valuable in itself and deserves our love."[3] Everything that God has made has value, particularly every living thing, as Holmes Rolston has argued.[4]

Romans 8:19-24 is often quoted:

> For the creation waits with eager longing for the revealing of the children of God; for the creation was subjected to futility, not of its own will but by the will of the one who subjected it, in hope that the creation itself will be set free from its bondage to decay and will obtain the freedom of the glory of the children of God. We know that the whole creation has been groaning in labor pains until now; and not only the creation, but we ourselves, who have the first fruits of the Spirit, groan inwardly while we wait for adoption, the redemption of our bodies. For in hope we were saved.

2. Sallie McFague, *God's Body: An Ecological Theology* (Minneapolis: Fortress, 1993), p. xi.

3. Sallie McFague, *Super, Natural Christians: How We Should Love Nature* (London: SCM, 1997), p. 177.

4. Holmes Rolston III, *Environmental Ethics: Duties to and Values in the Natural World* (Philadelphia: Temple University Press, 1988).

God cares about all creation and has a plan to bless it.[5] The futures of human beings and the rest of nature are intertwined. Parallel to the advocacy of deep ecology, ecofeminism, and biocentric egalitarianism, nature has its own part to play.[6] We human beings are just part of God's creation that God has declared to be good. God is the one who has all dominion. The earth is the Lord's (Exod. 9:29; John 1:1-3; 1 Cor. 10:26; Col. 1:16).

Strikingly, although God is the source and sustainer of all, and although a right relationship with God is the fulfillment of what it is to be a human being and for every other part of creation, God has created the world in such a way that human beings can live for a while as if God does not exist. God is the fundamental and pervasive reality. God is the center, what T. S. Eliot called "the still point of a turning world," yet God can be functionally ignored for a time. Nature does indicate that God is, but does not show it undeniably, let alone show what God is like (Rom. 1:20). Nature, whether understood as affected by human rebellion against God, not yet finished, or both, is too ambiguous. If one starts with nature, does one posit God as the one whose design and priorities are revealed in the parasite or the platypus? By the light of nature alone, is God vicious, whimsical, or quite something else? Yet if one knows God, it is possible to see a fit between nature and Christian revelation.[7] A Christian understanding of nature sees a world that resonates with the comprehensive coherence of the Christian tradition, hence providing confirming data for that worldview.[8] Further, God can use nature to reveal God's self. The primary revelation of God is through the incarnation into the natural world. "And the Word became flesh and lived among us" (John 1:14). The Creator can communicate through the creation, but nature of itself does not irresistibly lead to such insight.

5. Cheryl Hunt, David Horrell, and Christopher Southgate, "An Environmental Mantra? Ecological Interest in Romans 8:19-23 and a Modest Proposal for Its Narrative Interpretation," *Journal of Theological Studies* 59, no. 2 (2008): 546-79.

6. For a widely used gathering of influential texts on this line, see Michael E. Zimmerman et al., *Environmental Philosophy: From Animal Rights to Radical Ecology*, 4th ed. (Englewood Cliffs, N.J.: Prentice-Hall, 2004).

7. This is the approach, for example, of Alister McGrath in the Riddell Lectures of 2008 and in his book *The Open Secret: A New Vision for Natural Theology* (Oxford: Blackwell, 2008).

8. John Polkinghorne made this case in *Science and the Trinity: The Christian Encounter with Reality* (New Haven: Yale University Press, 2004).

This strange situation is a gift. Human beings are designed to live in fellowship with God, but it is an intimacy founded on invitation. If it was forced it would not be the same relationship. It is by choice, not by overwhelming fact or fiat. Directly confronted with God's presence as Isaiah was at his calling, we would be struck with terror. Like a shadow before a spotlight, our sheer, faint existence would be overwhelmed in God's unshielded presence. Instead, God has created a physical world where we can recognize and value God's presence or not. God reveals more to those who seek God, and allows those who do not to carry on for a brief time as if alone. The physical world with all its beauty and terrors, sunsets and tornadoes, directs us to seek God from admiration and fear and the sheer surprise that the world is at all, yet allows us to live for a time as if there were no God. That choice is essential to the quality of the relationship. The hiddenness of God has a high price in that some human beings never turn to know the One who makes human life most worthwhile, but those who do, experience a relationship with God and a quality of life that surpass a sometimes puzzling or stressful start.

Part of relationship with God is to live well with one another, yet this too is by invitation. The social nature and dependence of human beings encourage us to know and enjoy one another. The material world pushes human beings to band together to survive, but we can separate ourselves. The physical world grants sufficient physical space that we can live in a hermit's isolation or even in urban crowds as if no other human beings existed. There is a high cost to living with others, though not as high as living without others. Part of the beauty and intensity of loving others is because it is chosen, not required. Human beings can also be right with the rest of the material world, but this too is a decision. We can rapaciously destroy what we touch or we can nurture our part of the world. God's revealed intent is that each human being should freely welcome being right with God, fellow human beings, and the world we have received. We can fulfill the two great commandments to love God and one another, or turn to isolation and death. We can choose whether to care for the world we have received or not.

The Image of God

The second chapter of Genesis depicts the first human couple as gardeners in God's garden. There they were to care for God, one another, and all else in their assigned place. A garden is more ecologically complex than a wilderness. As with a wilderness there is an intricate interrelationship of life-forms and energy, but a garden has the added dimension of the gardener's intent. Human beings are placed in a unique position of being part of the earth. We are from the dust and to dust we shall return. Yet human beings are uniquely created in God's image (Gen. 1:27-31). There have been long debates over what "God's image" precisely entails. Three definitions have been dominant. One emphasizes that human beings have capacities that are uniquely God-like, such as the ability to reason and the freedom to make choices.[9] Most human beings will hence be in God's image in that sense. However, Martin Luther noted that Satan also would be in God's image if capacities such as reason were sufficient.[10] A second interpretation focuses on carrying out God's delegated dominion as much as possible in the way that God would. This view takes particular note that the command to rule the earth immediately follows the description of being made in God's image. This calling is a task and a representation. "Just as powerful earthly kings, to indicate their claim to dominion, erect an image of themselves in the provinces of their empire where they do not personally appear, so man is placed upon the earth in God's image, as God's sovereign emblem."[11] A third sees the image of God in relationships with God and other human beings. As John Calvin suggests, a mirror cannot reflect something unless it is in oriented relationship with it.[12] It may be that each view is correct in part. God's image includes capacity, calling, and relationship. All three aspects need to be present to bear fully the image and likeness of God. They are deeply interrelated. Reflecting God's image has to do with both the capability to carry out and the actual carrying out of choices as God would. One needs certain capacities such as reason to carry out the calling to stewardship of the world in a Godly way, but one will only be able to achieve that way of life if one is in an empowering relationship with God. One is reflecting God's image only if one is sufficiently oriented to God to reflect his presence. Jesus Christ is the only one who has fully reflected God's image (Col. 1:15).

9. Douglas John Hall names this view as the most dominant in the church up through the time of Thomas Aquinas. *Imaging God: Dominion as Stewardship* (Grand Rapids: Eerdmans, 1986), pp. 92-93.

10. Hall, *Imaging God*, pp. 100-101.

11. Gerhard von Rad, *Genesis*, p. 58, quoted by Noreen Herzfeld in *Technology and Religion* (West Conshohocken, Pa.: Templeton Press, 2009), pp. 11-12.

12. Hall, *Imaging God*, p. 104.

The degree to which we each reflect God's image develops by grace over time. There may be a threshold in reflecting God's image from mainly in potential to in some sense present, but at no point in this life is it complete. Those rebelling against God by act or apathy would not be reflecting God's image. What then of Genesis 9:6, that the death penalty is required for shedding the blood of human beings because they were made in God's image? Also the New Testament letter of James warns against cursing human beings that were made in God's image (James 3:9). These protections may not be limited only to those well reflecting God's presence. The reference to God's image may refer to the potential for each human being to bear that image even when it is not being acted out. *To fulfill* the image of God includes a unique capacity to know God and one another, living out a calling, and a right relationship with God, God's people, and the rest of creation.

Capacity

Contrary to Plato, Marcion, and others, there is nothing distasteful about matter. Human beings are not trapped in bodies. Human beings are embodied beings, our God-given bodies being essential to what and who we are. In the second chapter of Genesis, Adam is described as being made from the earth. The very name Adam is a play on the original language's word for clay. Human beings are of the earth. We use the same genetic system as other creatures on earth; we require food, we respire, and we have progeny. The human body of bone, sinew, and opposing muscles is the same basic system as used by other animals. We share many emotions and motivations with fellow creatures.[13] But human beings are not just animals. At the cellular level, nematodes and human beings have much in common, but that baseline commonality does not describe adequately all that is human. Washoe the chimpanzee can use 250 signs from American Sign Language. That is not Shakespeare. There is a point where a quantitative difference in skill transitions to a qualitative difference in emergent capability.[14]

---

13. Temple Grandin and Catherine Johnson, *Animals Make Us Human: Creating the Best Life for Animals* (Boston: Houghton Mifflin Harcourt, 2009).

14. James C. Peterson, "The *Imago Dei* as More Than Capacity," *Toronto Journal of Theology* (forthcoming).

Human life cannot be fully described by what happens at lower levels of complexity such as physics. Physicists sometimes refer to their pursuit of "the theory of everything," that is, trying to understand how the most basic particles and forces interact. In a sense that would then be a theory of everything in that everything material, including the human body, is based upon such interaction. But because one can describe an event at an atomic level does not capture the complexity of reality at higher levels. A chemist may say yes, you have described the involved atoms, but together they are forming a molecule of glucose. Glucose has structure and characteristics more than just its constituent parts. Then a biochemist approaches and says she appreciates all the chemist has learned about the glucose molecule, but there is a further level of reality not yet described. The glucose is being converted to lactic acid to generate ATP. A physiologist arrives to explain that this ATP is being released to power the contraction of a muscle attached to a vocal cord. A neurologist adds that the contraction is not random, but is rather at the command of the brain. A musician explains that the brain is triggering change in pitch to accomplish singing. Now an economist arrives to appreciate that physics, chemistry, biochemistry, physiology, neurology, and music may all be true descriptions, but says they are incomplete. Part of the reality being described is that the musician is singing for pay. It always comes back to money. But a sociologist steps in and says there are lots of ways to earn money. This musician has chosen to sing in this chorus in part to be with her friends. Then a theologian observes that all the former is quite true, but the chorus they are singing is from the oratorio *Messiah*. The singer is quite intentionally worshiping God through the soaring words and music. Describing the human world at the simplest level of physical phenomena can be insightful, but so often remains incomplete. Human motivation is too ambiguous and complex for what has been called "nothing buttery."[15] "Nothing buttery" is when an action is described as "nothing but" a manifestation of some elemental part. There are often multiple levels to phenomena that cannot be reduced to the most elemental.[16] Examining only one aspect at a time to better understand its contribution can be a helpful exercise, but such

15. Donald MacKay, *Human Science and Human Dignity* (London: Hodder and Stoughton, 1979). Again in Malcolm A. Jeeves, *Human Nature at the Millennium: Reflections on the Integration of Psychology and Christianity* (Leicester: Apollos, 1997).

16. Michael Polanyi, *Knowing and Being* (London: Routledge and Kegan Paul, 1969).

is quite different from declaring the whole merely the sum of its smallest parts. The more complex the phenomenon, often the more important the emergent properties that cannot be atomized. Each level of description can contribute understanding within its area of expertise, but cannot claim more than it actually provides.

The highest levels of complexity are unique to human beings. The opening of Genesis describes human beings as of the earth, yet the only creatures in-breathed with God's spirit. This refers to a unique capacity to enter into relationship with God, but not to exhaust it. God is accessible, yet vastly beyond what human beings could even begin to comprehend. Rabbi Jay Holstein tells the story of walking along a Florida beach and seeing a little girl industriously running into the surf with her pail, filling it with seawater, hauling it back up the beach, and pouring the water down a hole. From a nonthreatening distance he asked her what she was doing. She proudly explained that "today I am going to empty the ocean with my pail." She knew what the brine tasted like on her tongue. She knew how the surf tugged at her feet. She could smell the salt in the air. She knew the ocean with the fullness of all her senses. Yet she knew nothing of undersea volcanoes and canyons, blue whales and barracuda, icebergs and tropical islands, water stretching from where she stood all the way to the African coast. We too can know God with everything that we are, but we cannot begin to comprehend all that God is. That may be a task for eternity. Human beings can have the capacity to be uniquely related to God and can change the environment we live in far more than can any other species. Our capability and responsibility are far greater.

Calling

As God nurtures and develops us in relationship with God, we are to nurture and develop the small part of creation that God has entrusted to us. When by God's initiative we freely yield to God, God nurtures our relationship with God, one another, and the rest of creation that all might flourish. While we cannot begin to imagine all that God is leading us to become and to do, it involves the fulfillment of this creation. That includes transcending it both now and in the future while living it. Matter *matters* for what it is, for what it will be, and for the people we are becoming in how we live within it. The physical world is a God-given place to do this, to choose and to care about God, others, and God's world entrusted to us.

We sojourn on God's land then as temporary tenants (Lev. 25:23), but some dominion is delegated to human beings bearing God's image in our limited physical sphere. It is not an unqualified dominion. Lynn White Jr.'s often-quoted charge that current ecological damage is rooted in the Genesis idea of absolute dominion does not accurately engage the text.[17] The granted dominion is not to pillage for any human intent. It is to carry out God's direction to care for God's garden. There are limits to what human beings may do with the physical world entrusted to them. For example, they may use part of it for food, and not other parts (Gen. 1:27-29). The granted dominion is one of ruling the creation as God's representatives. That requires that human beings care for creation as God does and remember that it is still God's creation. This is the particular world God made. It is God's choice out of all possible contingencies. It deserves respect and preservation as the work of God's hands. Nature does not exist only for human use. Creation is not anthropocentric any more than human beings should be. The material world and human beings are to be theocentric. The cosmos is God's. God is its founder, sustainer, and purpose. It is in God that we "live and move and have our being" (Acts 17:28).

This earth is generously given to human beings to live in for a time. Sunlight. Oxygen. Fresh water. We can wreck these endowments, but they initially come to us as a gift. Yet the garden is needy. It requires tending. Human beings are uniquely created in God's image to make a difference to the good in the planet garden. If we are to follow God, to reflect God's image, that includes extending God's creative action. As God develops us, we are to take part in developing his ongoing creation. God has created, is creating, and will create. This material world will someday be transformed into a new heaven and a new earth (Rev. 21:1). God creates, redeems, and transforms not only the human beings of his creation, but also all the rest of his creation.

17. Lynn White Jr., "The Historical Roots of Our Ecological Crisis," *Science* 155, no. 3767 (March 10, 1967): 1203-7. Richard T. Wright offers a rebuttal in "Responsibility for the Ecological Crisis," *BioScience* 20 (1970): 851-53. Michael S. Northcott passionately points out recent examples of abusing the concept of dominion in "The Dominion Lie: How Millennial Theology Erodes Creation Care," in *Diversity and Dominion: Dialogues in Ecology, Ethics, and Theology*, ed. Kyle S. Van Houtan and Michael S. Northcott (Eugene, Oreg.: Cascade Books, 2010), pp. 89-108.

God's plan for creation has been described primarily in four ways. They are not all mutually exclusive. It may be that God created the world in its highest state of perfection. God is perfect and would only make that which is perfect. Redemption then is to return to the world as given before it was harmed by human rebellion. Origen and Augustine discuss it in this way. A second possibility is to see human sin as a wrenching yet positive and necessary step toward what God intends for us. This is the view of supralapsarianism. God ordained the fall into sin as part of his purpose before the world was even created. The Fall was not a tragic mistake. At its deepest levels it was part of God's design. Romans 8:22 describes creation groaning in travail. If that is a reference to childbirth, it could be read as a sinfully stressed but natural course leading to desired birth. Yet Isaiah 24 talks about the curse of sin on the land, the earth defiled by its people. Such a description leaves us with a contradiction or at least a mystery if sin is ordained by God. A third view seeks to explain sin and material corruption as caused for a time by created spiritual forces in rebellion against God.[18] A fourth view sees the creation as good, as God declared it to be, yet not complete. It would have been bettered by Adam and Eve successfully passing their time tending the garden as they should have. They could have learned what it was to experience the difference between good and evil, by choosing the good, not the evil. Instead, to their detriment and ours, they chose badly. God has since graciously intervened to bring about redemption rather than simply starting over. Redemption restores our pre-Fall opportunity to grow toward God and into what we should be. The good creation is the starting point, not the finale we seek to regain. In all four of these traditional perspectives, however, we came to be in our present situation; things are not the way they should be and God chooses to work through us to address that.

As originally God's handiwork, the world might be expected to be perfect. Yet being perfect does not mean something cannot grow or develop or be improved. The classic tradition describes Jesus Christ as always perfect, wholly and completely God among us, yet he is also described in Luke as growing in wisdom and stature (Luke 2:52; see also Heb. 5:8-9). It may be that the world is quite good but not yet finished. It

---

18. For a recent appropriation see Gregory Boyd, *God at War: The Bible and Spiritual Conflict* (Downers Grove, Ill.: InterVarsity, 1997), or his chapter "Evolution as Cosmic Warfare: A Biblical Perspective on Satan and 'Natural Evil,'" in *Creation Made Free*, ed. Thomas Jay Oord (Eugene, Oreg.: Pickwick, 2009), pp. 125-45.

may be incomplete. As stated in the introduction, Irenaeus, and also other early church fathers such as Clement of Alexandria and Saint Gregory of Nazianzus, reasoned that God intentionally created human beings and our natural world as less than they would be eventually.[19] Room to grow would not be a lack of ability on God's part any more than it was when at the end of the third day of the Genesis creation story the earth still had no life, yet God declared it good. It was not God's intent to complete it yet. The point is that God sovereignly chooses to create over time and has designed us and our world to do the same. The first command, "Be fruitful and multiply, and fill the earth" (Gen. 1:28), requires development over time to fulfill. Where we started was good. What we will be, will be better. The Eastern Orthodox tradition goes so far as to speak of *theosis*, divinization, in reference not just to human beings, but to the material earth as well. In the incarnation, God lived among us in the person of Jesus Christ. This has begun bringing human beings and the material world into a union with God for which they were intended.[20] Human beings, part of God's creation, are called to have a part in further development. The present world is not all that it can be. That it could be better is clear. That we are to make it better is as well.

In this regard, Donald MacKay appeals to several biblical texts, such as the proverb "He that knoweth to do good and doeth it not, to him it is a sin" (James 4:17), and says, "this teaching runs throughout the Bible, indicating that although there is indeed a sense in which everybody and everything owes its being to God as Creator, it is simply bad theology to conclude from this that God places an embargo on taking our share of responsibility for the way things turn out next."[21] Fully recognizing human limitations, human beings are called to pursue the Creator's priorities. Human beings are given the world as stewards to fulfill their God-given purpose. The human being is singled out as one who has an explicit task. The human being is to "have dominion."[22] It would

---

19. John Hick, *Evil and the God of Love* (San Francisco: HarperSanFrancisco, 1977), pp. 211-18.

20. Thomas Sieger Derr, "The Complexity and Ambiguity of Environmental Stewardship," in Calvin B. DeWitt, *Caring for Creation: Responsible Stewardship of God's Handiwork* (Grand Rapids: Baker, 1998), p. 78.

21. Donald M. MacKay, *Human Science and Human Dignity* (Downers Grove, Ill.: InterVarsity, 1979), p. 58.

22. The Qur'an states that all the heavens and earth have been subjected to human beings (Sura 45:12-13), and warns that humans can abuse that authority (33:72).

seem that humans alone among their fellow creatures will be held accountable for the management — or mismanagement — of the resources at their disposal. For the biblical writers, the world is not merely something to be enjoyed or admired — though it is both — but something to be explored and developed by humanity in a spirit of thankful and responsible stewardship, for the benefit of fellow humans and to the glory of God. With all their limitations, human beings have enough likeness to the Creator to be called upon to accept and pursue the Creator's priorities. This — no less — is their destiny and their dignity.[23]

But human beings have often chosen disastrously. We have often failed to care for God, our fellows, and the world entrusted to us. Our relationship with God, one another, and the physical world has been deeply broken. Because we have chosen not to care for others and God as we should, the material world is not all that it could be. Nature is often crushed under our step. Healing it includes restoration and the relief of suffering. Does such intervention thwart suffering that God ordained? This raises the problem of theodicy. To many, it seems that when the innocent suffer, either God cares but cannot stop it, or God can stop it but does not care. Process theology affirms the first description. God always wishes the best for his creatures but simply does not have the power to set all things right. Human beings are in a joint struggle with God to relieve suffering. For Augustine, John Calvin, and Martin Luther, God is quite capable of controlling everything, and does. That the good and holy God causes evil such as pain is mysterious. This is just another part of reality that human beings do not yet understand. Someday they will.[24] In response, while it is quite right that God may do as God wills, and of course there is much that God does that mere creatures do not understand, I find more persuasive the approach of scholars such as Bruce Reichenbach and Richard Swinburne that God could determine everything, choosing the intensity and duration of each creaturely pain, but chooses not to.[25] God has

---

23. MacKay, *Human Science*, p. 13. The definition of "human dignity" is something of a Rorschach test for philosophical systems. It is used with many different meanings. See, for example, Edmund D. Pellegrino, Adam Schulman, and Thomas W. Merrill, eds., *Human Dignity and Bioethics* (South Bend, Ind.: Notre Dame University Press, 2009).

24. Augustine, *City of God* 12.4.

25. See, for example, Richard Swinburne's *Providence and the Problem of Evil* (Oxford: Oxford University Press, 1998) or Bruce Reichenbach, *Evil and a Good God* (New York: Fordham University Press, 1982).

sovereignly chosen to create creatures with genuine freedom, and hence to self-limit himself in creation and incarnation. Suffering, at root, is a direct result of God giving creatures space to make genuine choices. That becomes a high price for God and creation when ill choices are made, but worth the risk.

The present state of nature then cannot tell us what it will be, or more importantly, what it should be. It is natural in our world to be crippled by parasites, to be killed by disease, and to die at an early age. Nature may be misdirected by sin as well as misinterpreted by our finite and fallen perception of it. Even when perceived accurately, the starting point one apprehends may not yet be complete. The material world can be better. Human beings are assigned as God's agents to garden Earth, to make this world better. Sometimes theologians have described us as pilgrims just passing through this land. The pilgrim metaphor staves off harming the land because it assumes not changing it at all.[26] Avoiding harm is well to affirm, but just living off the land, not tending it, is irresponsible if we are also called to garden while we are here. Gardening rightly understood is not destructive to the land; rather it frees the land to its potential. Calvin DeWitt points out that God's mandate to Adam includes that Adam should "till" the garden. When the word "till" appears in other scriptural contexts, it is most often translated as "to serve." A famous example is that of Joshua challenging the people of Israel to choose whom they will serve. "As for me and my household, we will serve the LORD" (Josh. 24:15). The word translated in Joshua as "to serve" the Lord is what Adam is instructed to do in the garden. Changing the context to agriculture can certainly change the meaning of the word, but DeWitt may be right that in the Genesis context "to till" the garden continues in the sense that it is to serve the garden, to cherish it, to help it to reach its proper end, not to rend or destroy it. This would fit with the paired word to "keep" the garden. Adam is to "till and keep" it. The word translated as "keep" is the same word found in the classic blessing given by Aaron, "The LORD bless you and keep you" (Num. 6:24).[27] Both words in this context and parallel use elsewhere imply

---

26. Margaret Atkins, "Flawed Beauty and Wise Use: Conservation and the Christian Tradition," *Studies in Christian Ethics: Ethics and Ecology* 7, no. 1 (1994): 1-16.

27. DeWitt, *Caring for Creation*, pp. 44-45.

the authority and ability to care for the garden, not to destroy it.[28] The guarding and tending of Genesis 2 regulate the filling and subduing of Genesis 1. Human beings will answer to the owner for how they keep his garden. The model is one of stewardship, not exploitation.[29] Bearing God's image and mandate in that sense, human beings are to nature as God is to human beings.[30] God chooses to care for us, and so should we for nature. Nature is still God's, and we, as God's stewards, are answerable for how we nurture it (Luke 12:41-43; 1 Cor. 4:1-2). "The church performs its distinctive redemptive calling within, and in the service of, the general call of God upon humanity to be stewards of the whole earth God loves."[31]

Yet, some theologians have argued that because the physical world is God's creation, intervening in its natural course is rebelling against God's intent for it and us. Changing the natural course is arrogantly trying to outdesign God. Since God has created the world as it is, it should remain as it is.[32] Its current state is the standard for the good and simple reason that this is how God created the world to be.[33] Cardinal Karol Wojtyla, who became Pope John Paul II, put this theme this way: "this understanding and rational acceptance of the order of nature — is at the same time recognition of the rights of the Creator. Elementary justice on the part of man towards God is founded on it. Man is just towards God the Creator when he recognizes the order of nature and conforms to it in his actions."[34]

---

28. This is contrary to the charge of ecofeminists such as Rosemary Ruether and Sallie McFague that Genesis 1 calls for the exploitive domination of creation.

29. The Au Sable Institute and the Evangelical Environmental Network are examples of advocates for this stewardship model.

30. John Passmore, *Man's Responsibility for Nature: Ecological Problems and Western Traditions* (New York: Scribner, 1974), p. 29.

31. John G. Stackhouse Jr., *Making the Best of It* (New York: Oxford University Press, 2008), p. 237.

32. For a description and critique of this view in regard to genetics, see Thomas A. Shannon, "Genetics, Ethics, and Theology: The Roman Catholic Discussion," in *Genetics: Issues of Social Justice*, ed. Ted Peters (Cleveland: Pilgrim Press, 1998), pp. 144-79.

33. Paul Ramsey, *Fabricated Man: The Ethics of Genetic Control* (New Haven: Yale University Press, 1978), p. 160.

34. Cardinal Karol Wojtyla, as quoted by Thomas A. Shannon, *Made in Whose Image? Genetic Engineering and Christian Ethics* (Amherst, N.Y.: Humanity Books, 2000), p. 36.

While fully recognizing God as the Creator, conforming to nature raises at least three major problems. As we describe them, note that we are not critiquing the philosophical tradition of "natural law." The natural law tradition attempts to reason from the recognition of intrinsic goods for human flourishing without appealing to God or nature as authoritative. It is the appeal to present nature as a standard that I am addressing here.

1. The cardinal's statement is that the standard is not simply the surface of nature. It is to understand and accept "the order of nature." One is to see the underlying, God-given intent of the natural order, but how does one recognize the intent built into nature?[35] Nature is varied and needs interpretation to discern purpose. How does one read the natural intent God has designed into earthquakes, hurricanes, the Black Plague, and malaria? God's intent in nature is not immediately obvious. Proposed interpretations have been myriad. The convictions and commitments one uses to recognize what is "the natural order" may be the actual standard.[36]

2. Even if one could clearly discern a natural order, why consider that a pure expression of God's will? Sin has warped our perceptions and tainted our physical world. The natural order is not currently all that it should be. We cannot assume that what we currently observe is the original intention. The 1984 Panel for Bioethical Concerns of the National Council of Churches asks rhetorical questions to affirm that technology should be used "in harmony with the natural environment and responsible care for it."[37] They describe this as reflecting the Christian responsibility to "eco-ethical stewardship." Yet in the same document the panel also states that "all creatures great and small thus share the total phenomenon of life, with its endless complexity, its tragic wastefulness, and

---

35. This problem is noted as well in Hans-Martin Sass, "A Critique of the Enquete Commission's Report on Gene Technology," *Bioethics* 2, no. 3 (1988): 270, and Jean Porter, "What Is Morally Distinctive about Genetic Engineering?" *Human Gene Therapy* 1 (1990): 421.

36. Michael Banner recognizes this in the midst of his appeals to the authority of the created order of nature. "While Christian sexual ethics must assert the existence and authority of the created order, knowledge of the form and character of that order may be reckoned to be irreducibly theological." *Christian Ethics and Contemporary Problems* (Cambridge: Cambridge University Press, 1999), p. 286.

37. National Council of Churches of Christ USA, Panel on Bioethical Concerns, *Genetic Engineering: Social and Ethical Consequences* (New York: Pilgrim Press, 1984), p. 25.

its often dubious purposes."[38] If they are correct that the natural order includes "tragic wastefulness" and "dubious purposes," why consider it an authoritative, unchangeable standard?

In 1848 Matthew Arnold wrote a poem "to an independent preacher who preached that we should be in harmony with nature."

> "In harmony with Nature?" Restless fool,
> Who with such heat dost preach what were to thee,
> When true, the last impossibility . . .
> Know, man hath all which Nature hath, but more,
> And in that *more* lies all his hopes of good . . .
> Man must begin, know this, where Nature ends . . .
> If thou canst not pass her,
> rest her slave![39]

Jeremy Rifkin has been effective in publicizing his objection to changing nature. Ted Peters summarizes Rifkin's advocacy this way. "He appeals to a vague naturalism, according to which nature itself claims sacred status. He issues his own missionary's call: 'the sacralization of nature stands before us as the great mission of the coming age.'"[40] In contrast, the Christian tradition worships God, not his creation. The creation is to be received with appreciation and cared for as God's handiwork entrusted to us, but it is not God. We have learned from the study of ecology that nature is intricately interrelated. This garden is unimaginably complex and interactive. Our fastest supercomputers can only begin to model effectively just portions of it. Any choices should be incremental and if possible reversible. Vigilant care is needed in changing the finite world we depend upon. What has worked in delicate and intricate balance should be changed only with caution, yet there should be change. The physical world for which we are grateful can be better. The world is a better place without smallpox. The scourge of that disease was eradicated only after years of systematic human effort. Developing the world rightly is part of our call-

38. National Council of Churches of Christ USA, *Genetic Engineering*, p. 23.

39. *The Essential Matthew Arnold: Poems, Critical Essays, Political Writings, Letters* (London: Chatto and Windus, 1949), pp. 52-53.

40. Ted Peters, *Playing God: Genetic Determinism and Human Freedom* (New York: Routledge, 1997), p. 13, quoting Jeremy Rifkin, *Algeny* (New York: Viking Press, 1983), p. 252.

ing. Colin Gunton calls this "movement toward an end that is greater than its beginning."[41]

According to Romans 8:19-24, quoted earlier, the whole creation is groaning in travail, in bondage to decay and subjected to futility, yet in hope. Is the groaning the waiting for human beings to fulfill their part? Mount Denali is not disturbed by the presence, absence, or activities of humans, but the intended whole of creation is sighing until human beings are right with God and creation, like an orchestra that is playing a concerto quite well but is unsatisfied until the featured solo instrument plays its part to attain what it is meant to be.[42] Creation is good but waiting for more. Whether the standard is what was before the Fall or an eschatological standard of what is to be, change is needed. The final judgment will transform some of the world to eternal use and reject some to an appreciated end.

3. What then is God's intent for nature and our lives in it? Craig Gay articulates what seems to be a widely felt concern: "The point is not simply that we have lost a kind of natural simplicity or innocence. Rather, what has been lost, in abstracting away from immediate nature, is the possibility of encountering something outside of ourselves which might discipline — and thus give order to — human making and willing. In the absence of such discipline, modern machine technology seems destined to be destructive of nature, of living human cultures, and indeed of living human beings."[43] We do need guidance, but nature of itself is not adequate to give it. According to Thomas Aquinas, there is a biological basis for our inclinations toward morality, but such desires can conflict or mislead.[44] From wider nature, why follow the lead of tornadoes and parasites? Such a view assumes that the natural order as we find it was created by God as the pinnacle of all that it could be. Any change would be a detraction. Accepting the premise that God created the natural world, one could still welcome it as a right and good starting point, not intended yet as a complete fulfillment. Just because it is natural does not mean it is yet best. It may be indifferent or worse.

41. Colin E. Gunton, *The Triune Creator: A Historical and Systematic Study* (Grand Rapids: Eerdmans, 1998), p. 12.

42. C. E. B. Cranfield, as cited by R. J. Berry, *God's Book of Works: The Nature and Theology of Nature* (London: T. & T. Clark, 2003), p. 232.

43. Craig Gay, *The Way of the (Modern) World; or, Why It's Tempting to Live As If God Doesn't Exist* (Grand Rapids: Eerdmans, 1998), p. 99.

44. Thomas Aquinas, *Summa Theologiae* I.II.94.2.

If either, it may be changed for the better. Better is whatever supports what God has revealed of God's purposes and our calling. It may be that the standard is not where we start, but where we are supposed to be going.

Part of the growth planned for us is to change the natural course. We could not survive if we did not. Far beyond survival, we change the natural course of extreme heat in the summer months by air-conditioning. We eat with knife and fork when it would be more natural to tear the meat directly with our incisors made for that purpose. The knife and fork make eating less messy and some tougher foods more accessible, yet in switching to knife and fork we lose some spontaneity and direct sensual contact with our food. This is sometimes described as a significant loss in countries where one directly takes food in hand. In changing the natural course there are wins and losses. The issue is not that the natural course has been changed. We are part of nature and change it naturally. Beavers build a dam across a stream to create a lake to protect their lodges and make trees more accessible for food. They transform the ecosystem in which they live. That is their nature. Human beings build a dam across a river to protect their homes and provide easier access to water and irrigated food crops. That is part of our nature. Our actions can be destructive of ourselves and the rest of God's world, but they are not inherently destructive or unnatural simply because they bring about change. Nature is to be appreciated and responsibly cared for, yet it is not to be unchangeable and final. I am not suggesting this as a radical new concept for the Christian tradition. It has been articulated by the early church fathers as cited above and is found in Judaism. The long-held commitment of the tradition is to "*tikkun olam,* the mandate to be an active partner in the world's repair and perfection."[45] God is the maker of nature, not its product or captive.

In an attempt to act with efficiency and due humility, some Christian circles emphasize that there is no point in trying to guide technology or any other society-wide concern. By this view, prophecy has revealed that the world will become more violent and decadent until Christ returns to establish his kingdom by force. This is a popular interpretation of the premillennial tradition that Christ returns before the

---

45. Laurie Zoloth-Dorfman, "Mapping the Normal Human Self: The Jew and the Mark of Otherness," in *Genetics: Issues of Social Justice,* ed. Ted Peters, Pilgrim Library of Ethics (Cleveland: Pilgrim Press, 1998), p. 190.

millennium, a thousand years of God's reign on earth. The conclusion then is to focus on what can be done, not lost causes. If the material world and human culture are the *Titanic*, focus on getting people into the lifeboats, the salvation of the gospel. There is no point in rearranging deck chairs. The ship is going down. This view is often tempered in the practice of premillennialists by the recognition that Jesus clearly and repeatedly called for concern for human physical needs.

Human beings are to make their choices as the only earthly beings uniquely in God's image. Our priorities are to reflect God's. This coincides with the command to care for the earth. Stewardship does not mean that the earth has to be kept exactly as it is found. Nature struggles within itself. The earth itself appears to have changed dramatically many times before human beings arrived. Ice age glaciers leveled ancient forest ranges across much of the northern plains that are now part of Canada and the United States. Ninety-nine percent of the species in the fossil record were extinct before widespread human influence. To nurture one part often means restraining another. Supporting the rosebushes often means war on the aphids. It is fitting for human beings to appreciate and care for an intact forest. As stewards understanding the natural cycles, we are still faced with choices. Should we allow a fire to burn part of a forest to the ground as a process that encourages other parts of nature to thrive in the resulting meadows? If a forest begins to succumb to a fungus, should we make the choice as stewards to favor and save the trees or the fungus? Nature has many manifestations. We might also choose to transform some of the trees into paper for books if that is the way you are reading these words now — a worthy use! The physical world is to be appreciated as God's creation, cared for, healed, and transformed as best fits God-given priorities.

Matthew 25 has several themes directly applicable to this calling. In it Jesus tells his disciples what to do in the time from his resurrection until his return at the last day of judgment. That time in between is the period in which we live. The chapter contains three stories. Each one raises issues answered by the next one. The first story is of ten maidens watching into the night for the coming of the bridegroom. The wait was long enough that five of them ran out of oil for their lamps. While they were away buying more, the bridegroom came and they missed the wedding feast. The story reminds us to be always ready for the promised return of Jesus Christ. It could be before the completion of this sentence. On the other hand, it may be a long time. For those who first heard Jesus tell this story, it has already been almost two thousand years. One must have the foresight to prepare for the long haul (bringing enough oil) and the perseverance to endure. So what then are we supposed to do in the meantime?

The story that immediately follows answers that question. It tells of a master who left five "talents" with one servant, two with another, and one with a third servant, giving to each according to his ability. When he returned he was pleased to see that the first servant had doubled his talents to ten and the second had doubled his to four. The master was outraged, however, to discover that the third servant had simply buried the entrusted resource in order to return exactly what he had received. He had failed in his responsibility to multiply the resources the master had given to him. The first story warns that we should always be ready, but we may have to wait some time before the second coming. The second story tells us that the intervening time should be spent faithfully in God's service, investing wisely what he has entrusted to us. We are responsible to multiply and employ our God-given resources. In other words, we are to have our suitcases packed and ready to go, but we are not merely to hang out at the airport. So what would be a godly multiplication and use of resources?

The third story answers that question. It is description of the last day of judgment. Jesus returns on his throne and his angels separate his people from those who are not. His people are recognized by how they cared for the needs of others. Technology can be of great service in fulfilling that mandate. There was a time when polio crippled countless children. If the disease progressed far enough to weaken or paralyze breathing, all that could be offered was an iron lung. In that procedure, all but the child's head was laid inside a massive machine that pumped air in and out to collapse and expand the child's lungs repeatedly. The technology was primitive, costly, and severely limiting. Better technology, namely, the polio vaccine, was developed over years of concentrated effort. A simple oral dose or single shot prevented the child from ever having a case of the disease. This superior technology was inexpensive and freeing. When cars are sliding off a mountainside road, it is admirable to start an ambulance service, but even better to install guardrails.

Paul Santmire argues that our calling is aptly depicted in the metaphor that the mature Augustine used of migration to a good land that will be fecund. That is better context and guidance for our attitude toward nature than delivery from it, a theme found in ascent metaphors.[46] We are not trying to escape this world; we are to live in it fully, which is actually our best preparation for what God does with it and us later. We are to develop it with God and our neighbor, toward God and our neighbor. John Stackhouse writes, "God made us to bless the earth by exercising dominion. God did not want us to leave as few footprints as possible, leaving the earth alone as much as we can. He commanded us instead to spread out, over the whole globe, and bring it all under our influence, to subdue it for its own good, to make it even more fruitful, beautiful, and sustainable, under God's guidance and by the power he invested in it."[47] Under human care, flower blooms grow in size and variety of shapes and color. Maize seed becomes abundant corn. Bacteria is genetically programmed to make human insulin. Seeds become fruitful with minimum fertilizer or pesticides.[48] In all three of the stories in Matthew 25, errors of omission (not bringing enough oil, not multiplying talents, not caring for those in need) are treated as seriously as acts of commission. We are to do our best here. That includes our best effort to multiply and apply our service of others and our world. We have the capacity and calling to do so, but not by any means to do so alone.

Relationship

Stephen Vantassel writes that "the reason why Scripture provides so few principles to guide us in our environmental stewardship is because God desires to grant us freedom to develop our own expression of the cultural mandate."[49] That freedom is in the context of our relationship with God, each other, and the rest of creation. Creation *ex nihilo*, out of nothing, reminds us that God creates not out of need, but as a free expression of God's love. In God's own being of the coeternal Trinity, there are a generosity, openness, welcome, direction of attention, and heart to serve, of each to the other. The Father listens to the Son, and

---

46. Paul Santmire, *The Travail of Nature* (Maryknoll, N.Y.: Orbis, 1996), p. 73.

47. Stackhouse, *Making the Best*, p. 209.

48. Celia Deane-Drummond cites the example of using cystatin genes to protect banana and potato plants from nematode infestation, instead of spraying the plants and environment with heavy applications of toxic nematocides. *Genetics and Christian Ethics* (Cambridge: Cambridge University Press, 2006), p. 244.

49. Stephen M. Vantassel, *Dominion over Wildlife? An Environmental Theology of Human-Wildlife Relations* (Eugene, Oreg.: Resource Publications, 2009), p. 162.

the Son tells us what the Father tells him. The Son tells us to listen to the Holy Spirit, and yet the Holy Spirit directs our attention to the Son. This way of relating is to be echoed in how human beings relate to each other and embody their relationship with God and each other as the body of Christ, the church. This self-giving to find life is to be echoed in how human beings treat each other and the rest of creation as well. The correspondence is not identical. One cannot prune or bend God the way one would a vine, but the attitude of being caught up in something greater than oneself, of delighting in others flourishing, can be carried over to the rest of creation. God so loves the cosmos (John 3:16). All things will be united in him (Col. 1:19-20).

One corner of this God-centered creation is a garden specifically entrusted to human beings. What are we to do in it? The proffered answers are myriad, from Buddhist ceasing to desire to frenetically hedonistic attempts at fulfilling every desire. What the classic Christian tradition most highly values for us in this place is to become people who know and love God and neighbor. God is at the center of the classic Christian tradition. While this description would be obvious throughout most of church history, it has become more contested since the challenge of Ludwig Feuerbach (1804-72). He claimed that God is a human creation that we project for our own use. For Feuerbach, human beings are the center. "God" is a concept that some human beings find useful. Many theologians have accepted that critique. They then write of God as a flexible concept limited only by our imagination. Among other possibilities, the idea of God can be used to encourage moral development, give psychological comfort, or rally community. God language is used to pursue these ends without any claim that God actually exists apart from human instigation.

The ongoing classic Christian tradition finds the projection theory of God fundamentally mistaken. The apostle Paul wrote that an awareness of God is present in all human beings who are honest with themselves. Blaise Pascal, who was the first to describe the phenomenon of a vacuum, described each human being as having a "God-shaped vacuum" that can be filled only if God is welcomed. Both Paul and Pascal are referring to the need to know the actual Creator, not a human projection. Thoughtful scholars have responded to Feuerbach convincingly.[50] Our

50. Paul Vitz, *Faith of the Fatherless: The Psychology of Atheism* (Dallas: Spence Publishing, 2009).

task at this point is to continue to think through the shaping of nature in the light of the classic Christian perspective. That begins by recognizing God as the source of all that is, the reason we and the universe continue, and the only worthy point to which life can lead.

For those who are open to God's presence, it is a relationship with God that gives life the consistent joy and confidence for which humanity was designed. The highest, most fulfilling goal for human beings is a right and complete relationship with God. The Westminster Confession says it this way. The purpose of human beings is to "glorify and enjoy God always." To "glorify God" is to live the adventure of all that God would have one to be and do to God's honor. "Enjoying God" is to welcome, appreciate, and find completion in God's presence. By God's grace both are to start now and continue without end. This relationship is founded on what Jesus called the first and greatest command. Human beings are to "love the Lord your God with all your heart, and with all your soul, and with all your strength, and with all your mind" (Luke 10:27). In other words, they are to love God with everything they are and have. This love begins with, and continues to be grounded in, a conscious choice of commitment to seek the best for the one loved. The New Testament term for it is the Greek word *agape*. One is consciously to choose to welcome God's love and learn to respond in kind. The relationship with God is also described by *phileo*, which is often translated from Greek to English as "love" as well. It is sometimes argued that in Koine Greek, the language of the New Testament, *phileo* and *agape* are indistinguishable synonyms. I see different connotations continuing from their classic forms. *Agape* frequently refers more to an act of will and commitment to care for the other. It can be a one-sided decision. This is why Jesus could call his people to *agape*-love their enemies. They are not expected to generate feelings of affection toward their enemies, but rather to choose to seek what is best for others, even their enemies. In contrast, *phileo* more often emphasizes the sense of mutual enjoyment of the other's presence. In this friendship, human beings can genuinely communicate with God, which leads to communion and, increasingly, union.[51] Human beings always remain creatures

---

51. Dallas Willard, *In Search of Guidance: Developing a Conversational Relationship with God* (Eugene, Oreg.: Wipf and Stock, 1997), p. 164; recently rereleased under the new title, *Hearing God: Developing a Conversational Relationship with God* (Downers Grove, Ill. InterVarsity, 1999).

and God remains the Creator, yet human beings have received a unique potential to enter into an intimate enjoyment of God that is not possible for any other earthly creature.

Communion with God is to be extended to fellow human beings. Coupled with the goal of joyful relationship and active life with God is the goal of fellowship with God's people (John 17:20-26). Jesus said the second greatest commandment is to love your neighbor as yourself. As with God, this begins with a commitment to seek the best for the other. That choice, as an act of will, can be extended even to one's enemies, as Jesus said it should be. Yet love is best fulfilled when it is reciprocated in mutual care and enjoyment of each other. As God is one, yet three persons, human beings are invited to fulfill their individual potential by becoming part of a community of fellowship with God and one another. It is as if each note is sounded most fully when uniquely contributing to a greater harmony. The christological hymn found in Colossians praises Jesus Christ in this way: "All things have been created through him and for him. He himself is before all things, and in him all things hold together. . . . For in him all the fullness of God was pleased to dwell, and through him God was pleased to reconcile to himself all things" (Col. 1:16-20).

It is in Jesus that we see this relationship modeled. Jesus not only achieved reconciliation for those who receive it, he also lived out the kind of life God intends for us. Jesus is a model for our behavior in at least three ways. First, he is described repeatedly as God among us. When one encounters Jesus Christ, one is encountering God. What God values, Jesus valued. What Jesus did was rightly reflecting what God does. If we are to reflect God's image, Jesus is the clearest presence of God that we have. Second, Jesus is described as the perfect human being. He is what human beings look like when fully reflecting God's image. In Jesus we can see what humanity is meant to be. Part of his work as the second Adam was to live a human life rightly within human constraints. If he had acted by his own divine power, he would not have been a human being who could fittingly die in our place or model how we should live. It is often stated in the Gospels that Jesus did miracles not by the power of his innate divinity, but by the power of the Holy Spirit working through him (Matt. 12:28; Luke 4:14). That is the same Holy Spirit at work in his people. Third, the New Testament states often that the church is now the body of Christ (1 Cor. 12:12-27). God sovereignly chooses to work through human beings to carry out God's will. The work of Jesus Christ on earth continues under his leadership through his church.

Part of that task is a priestly one "to save the natural order through remedial and integrative activity."[52] Christopher Southgate, Arthur Peacocke, Vladimer Lossky, Wendell Berry, and others have described human beings as priests of creation, being that part of creation that renders praise and thanks to God, and from God sacramentally graces the rest of the creation.[53] Fulfilling their right relationship with God and the rest of creation, human beings bring awareness of God and thankfulness, offering creation's praise back to God.[54] We gradually become the kind of people that can more fully love and be loved. Since part of God's purpose is to restore human community, this process occurs both within individuals and cooperatively in the church. The goal is to become the kind of people who can and do understand, serve, and enjoy God and one another. That purpose is exemplified and encouraged in how the growth comes about.

The physical is not our ultimate concern, but if we are in a right relationship with God we should care about it because it is part of our God-given place and form. What we do with our bodies matters. The physical world generally, and our bodies in particular, are all the sphere of influence that we have. Small as it is, we can make genuine choices in matter, that matter. It gives us a place to learn attitudes, skills, and commitments, and to practice actually carrying them out. It is where we have the opportunity to become more of who we are meant to be. Our first assigned task *with* God and one another is to care for the creation in which we have been placed.

This service of God, one another, and God's creation takes place in God's presence. God, who is utterly transcendent in being, is quite capable of being infinitely immanent as well to what God has created. God is fully present and knows not only the farthest reaches beyond billions of galaxies, but also every detail of each individual's molecular

52. T. F. Torrance, *Divine and Contingent Order* (Oxford: Oxford University Press, 1981), p. 130.

53. Christopher Southgate, "Creation as Very Good and Groaning in Travail," in *The Evolution of Evil*, ed. Gaymon Bennett et al. (Göttingen: Vandenhoeck & Ruprecht, 2008), pp. 82-83.

54. Arthur Peacocke, *Creation and the World of Science: The Brampton Lectures, 1978* (Oxford: Clarendon, 1979), pp. 295-97, and Torrance, *Divine and Contingent Order*, pp. 128-30.

composition and neural net. Thankfully, rather than casting aside what has developed so far, God keeps opening ways of reconciliation and growth.[55] Wolfhart Pannenberg, Jürgen Moltmann, and Ted Peters are examples of considered and compelling theologians who each in his own way sees creation as we know it open to a higher fulfillment.[56] God brings transforming power to an ordered but not complete creation.[57] God's character and purpose are constant as nature grows in God's hands and those of his creatures. An important part of fulfilling the image of God is to be creative in becoming all that God intends human beings to be and do. Growth is part of God-given life.

God is creatively active. God has created, is creating, and will create. With regard to each of his children there is a life-giving creative pattern, which begins first with the gift of physical life. Second, reconciliation brings a new quality of life. "If anyone is in Christ, there is a new creation: everything old has passed away; see, everything has become new!" (2 Cor. 5:17). Third, living out this new life requires a daily empowerment often called "sanctification." Some traditions speak of a sudden start of sanctification, others of a long process, but whatever the terminology, all agree that there is a process of learning to live up to one's new status in Christ (Eph. 4:1). One becomes a member of God's family by accepting this new status as a gift, as freely as a child receives. Having begun as a child, one is then expected to grow up.

This takes time as one is set free from the old ways of thinking and led to new ones (Gal. 5:1; Rom. 6:18; 8:9). Intellectual assent is not enough. Nicodemus, a highly educated Pharisee and member of their ruling council, said he knew Jesus was "a teacher sent from God." Jesus still called him to experience new birth (John 3:3). This new birth is the first step of straightening out old, ingrained patterns

---

55. Robert Song, *Human Genetics: Fabricating the Future* (Cleveland: Pilgrim Press, 2002), p. 67.

56. Wolfhart Pannenberg, *Historicity of Nature: Essays on Science and Theology* (West Conshohocken, Pa.: Templeton Press, 2008); *Toward a Theology of Nature* (Louisville: Westminster John Knox, 1993); Jürgen Moltmann, *God in Creation: The Gifford Lectures, 1984-1985* (Minneapolis: Fortress, 1993); Ted Peters, *Anticipating Omega* (Göttingen: Vandenhoeck & Ruprecht, 2006).

57. Cathriona Russell sees this as an important tension between given order and incompleteness in the thought of Pannenberg. See *Autonomy and Food Biotechnology in Theological Ethics* (Bern: Peter Lang, 2009), p. 256.

(Rom. 8:1-2). Growth is needed to become someone who can know and enjoy God. The point is not only obedience. It is essential for a child's survival that the child be obedient, but the goal is not a rote following of precise instructions for every detail of the day. Most parents want their children to become the kind of people who will choose rightly and beautifully, and in some ways uniquely, without a constant drone of commands. In parallel, the end goal for God's people is to thrive in and enjoy a freely cooperative relationship with God and each other.

The transformation develops as a marathon, not a sprint (Eph. 4:15). To run a marathon one must train. It is precisely the metaphor of disciplined athletic training over time that is used in both letters to Timothy and in the first letter to the Corinthians (1 Tim. 4:7-8; 2 Tim. 3:16; 1 Cor. 9:24-27). This rigorous discipline is graciously initiated and enabled by God's Holy Spirit (Heb. 12:5-11). Each day, in each choice, one takes a step further in spiritual growth or decay. Choices become habits. Habits become virtues or vices. The sum total of one's virtues and vices is one's character. This pattern is basic to human life. To be successful in one particular moment requires a consistent life of wise and thorough preparation. A famous concert violinist was once praised by a listener who said, "I would give my life to play like you." He replied, "I have." Following Christ, being transformed to be like him, is at least as demanding as learning to play the cello or to speak a foreign language. Dallas Willard says, "some people would genuinely like to pay their bills and be financially responsible, but they are unwilling to lead the total life that would make that possible. . . . We cannot behave 'on the spot' as he [Jesus] did and taught if in the rest of our time we live as everybody else does."[58] To become what we are meant to be takes sustained commitment and effort. That is the fulfillment of grace, not its contrary. The apostle Paul writes in his letter to the Ephesians, "For by grace you have been saved through faith, and this is not your own doing; it is the gift of God — not the result of works, so that no one may boast. For we are what he has made us, created in Christ Jesus for good works" (Eph.

58. Dallas Willard, *The Spirit of the Disciplines: Understanding How God Changes Lives* (San Francisco: HarperSanFrancisco, 1990), pp. 6-7. See also the other two books of Willard's insightful and wise trilogy: *Hearing God* and *The Divine Conspiracy: Rediscovering Our Hidden Life in God* (San Francisco: HarperSanFrancisco, 1998).

2:8-10). This new way of life is not contrary to being welcomed into God's family by grace, it is the expected result of being part of God's family by grace.

The second letter of Peter states, "He has given us, through these things, his precious and very great promises, so that through them you may escape from the corruption that is in the world because of lust, and may become participants of the divine nature" (2 Pet. 1:4). As mentioned, the Eastern Orthodox tradition writes of this partaking of the divine nature as *theosis*.[59] It is often summarized as "God became human so that we may become divine." The language sounds close to the collapse of difference between the Creator and the created, but actually, the Eastern Orthodox tradition is in no danger of confusing God and his creation. This important distinction is safeguarded by its long tradition of apophatic theology, which emphasizes God as qualitatively beyond even our comprehension. "Divinization" refers to fulfilling God's image, being like God, never actually being God. God's children are to learn to love the way that God does. Jesus Christ is described as the perfect image of God (2 Cor. 4:4; Col. 1:15), and his disciples are to be conformed to his likeness (Rom. 8:29). In being like him they are in God's image as well. Living up to Christ's example and call, leaving behind the old way of life for a new one like his, is how we become renewed in God's image (Col. 3:9-10).

This does not mean that children of God become less unique as individuals. God's people come in all shapes and sizes. Most of them would not be believable in a work of fiction. The point is growth, not replacement. Gregory of Nazianzus writes, "If the spirit takes possession of a fisherman, he makes him catch the whole world in the nets of Christ. Look at James and John, the sons of thunder, thundering the things of the spirit." It is the gracious Spirit of God that sees Saul aggressively persuading, pursuing, cajoling, to stamp out the church, and then calls Saul to be the apostle Paul using the same energy to spread its presence. God's love is too much to leave human beings well enough alone. It is God's grace to give life and then transform his people to really live it.

---

59. Robert Prevost has pointed out to me that there is also an allusion to this theme in the *Western* writer Boethius, *The Consolation of Philosophy*, trans. Richard Green (New York: Macmillan, 1962), p. 63.

The cost of transforming discipleship is high, but not as great as the cost of nondiscipleship. T. S. Eliot writes,

> The dove descending breaks the air
> With flame of incandescent terror
> Of which the tongues declare
> The one discharge from sin and error.
> The only hope, or else despair
> Lies in the choice of pyre or pyre —
> To be redeemed from fire by fire.
> Who then devised the torment? Love.
> Love is the unfamiliar Name
> Behind the hands that wove
> The intolerable shirt of flame
> Which human power cannot remove.
> We only live, only suspire
> Consumed by either fire or fire.[60]

God's people are God's creation, God's workmanship. What used to be feared requirements of the law become a promise of what is to come. Yet human beings do play a part. There is a sense of cooperation with what God is doing. "Work out your own salvation with fear and trembling; for it is God who is at work in you, enabling you both to will and to work for his good pleasure" (Phil. 2:12-13). One enters the family by God's grace and then learns to live as a member of God's family by grace (Rom. 8:1-2). One learns to reflect God's image, to choose and care wisely as God does (Col. 3:7-10; Eph. 4:22-24). The result is that his people "are being transformed into the same image from one degree of glory to another; for this comes from the Lord, the Spirit" (2 Cor. 3:18).

Part of this process is for human beings to learn of God and one another in the joint task of tending the entrusted garden. Creation is out of chaos, and God bids us in God's image to continue to set the creation free. God grants the stone and the stone carver and bids her to set the statue free.[61] As we play our part in reconciling all things in him (2 Cor. 5:18-19),

---

60. T. S. Eliot, *Little Gidding, IV,* in *Four Quartets* (New York: Mariner Books, 1968).

61. Colin E. Gunton applies this Michelangelo metaphor to creation in *The Triune Creator,* p. 197.

some are concerned that attempting to heal or improve God's creation is "playing God." Paul Ramsey wrote memorably that "Human beings should not play God before they have learned to be human beings and when they are human beings they will not want to play God."[62] Ramsey does not explain the term "playing God," and in fact in a different case addressed in an earlier work uses it positively as an appropriate standard for human imitation of God's gracious impartiality.[63] The concern that human intervention in nature is in some sense playing God might find part of its resonant power in its ambiguity. One reading is that playing God is an attempt to do what only God should do. Traditional theists in Islam and Christianity emphasize their responsibility to live up to God's call, while vigorously rejecting any attempt to take God's place or role. The word "Islam" literally means submission. God is almighty Creator and Lord. Any manipulation of human beings, as any other part of life, must be at God's direction or at least allowance. To claim the authority or ability to intervene contrary to God would be a claim to equality with God that is the most heinous of sins, in Islam called "shirk," in the Christian tradition, "pride." Trying to presume God's capability or place is often considered the center of sinful debasement. From the first creation account human beings are created in God's image, in some sense like God, yet not God, always rightfully in submission to God's Lordship. When they tried to assume God's place for themselves, they fell from what they were created to be. Created in God's image, they were to reflect God in their behavior, not try to take God's place by doing what only God should do.

Any limitation to human choice is anathema to many modern movements that have placed human beings at the center of meaning. In such systems human beings set their own standards as they see fit. That is directly contrary to the Christian tradition expressed by theologians such as Augustine, Aquinas, and Emil Brunner.[64] Each one states explicitly a divine command theory with nuances between them, that God's character and will are the ultimate standard of what is good. Brunner, for example, states it explicitly that "the Good consists in always doing what God wills at any particular moment."[65] There are many subtleties

62. Ramsey, *Fabricated Man*, p. 151.

63. Paul Ramsey, *The Patient as Person: Explorations in Medical Ethics* (New Haven: Yale University Press, 1970), p. 256.

64. Thomas Aquinas, *Summa Contra Gentiles* Q19, A5; see also chapter 17. Emil Brunner, *The Divine Imperative* (Philadelphia: Westminster, 1937), p. 83.

65. Brunner, *The Divine Imperative*, p. 83.

in how God's will is perceived and carried out in these traditions, yet the central theme remains that human beings are fulfilled and just only when they are in harmony with their Creator.[66]

A related charge against changing our physical world or form is that such alteration is presumptuous. It is playing God by assuming an authority to intervene and an ability to choose wisely that only God possesses. C. Keith Boone tries to distinguish this sense of "playing God" as an abhorred attitude against faith, not a rejection of power and creativity.[67] For Boone the charge of "playing God" is a religious objection to an attitude, the attitude of blasphemy, rather than a moral objection to certain actions. While his point is well taken that few traditions reject all power or creativity, his other point that only the attitude is at fault is not as well substantiated. Those who reject "playing God" would probably agree to the abhorrence of blasphemy, as Boone suggests, but would also probably object to the actions that result from "blasphemy." While power and creativity can be put to needed and excellent use, when power and creativity are motivated by pride, harmful actions are likely to follow. Pride would be seen both as a blameworthy attitude and as leading to wrong actions. The presence of pride would be a concern in its own right, as well as seen as a motivation that leads astray.

In the above warnings against the prideful taking of God's place in shaping the world, there is an assumption that God has forbidden intervention or reserved it for God alone. I am arguing that shaping the world is part of the God-given mandate for human beings to share in the redemption and development of creation. The danger is not only in an attitude of pride. Just as dangerous is sloth. Not fulfilling the responsibility to shape the world reflects disobedient apathy. Even if we just want things to stay as they are, we are going to have to make changes, to correct the often downward track. Allen Verhey has written an insightful and wise article on the use of this phrase "playing God."[68] He describes

---

66. For a current defense of divine command ethics (in this case in the Calvinist tradition), see Richard J. Mouw, *The God Who Commands: A Study in Divine Command Ethics* (Notre Dame, Ind.: University of Notre Dame Press, 1990).

67. C. Keith Boone, "Bad Axioms in Genetic Engineering," *Hastings Center Report* 18 (August/September 1988): 10.

68. Allen Verhey, "'Playing God' and Invoking a Perspective," in *On Moral Medicine: Theological Perspectives in Medical Ethics*, ed. Stephen E. Lammers and Allen Verhey, 2nd ed. (Grand Rapids: Eerdmans, 1998), pp. 287-96.

the many ways it has been intended. The President's Commission, in its 1982 *Splicing Life Report*, reduced the phrase in effect to "new technology is powerful, we should be careful with it." That is appropriate counsel, but grants little direction. Another use emphasizes not interfering with nature, but that would rule out surgery and antibiotics. We regularly and appropriately intervene. That is basic to human survival. Verhey welcomes playing God if it means imitating God's priorities. We are called to follow God's initiative in a godly way. God is the Creator, one who heals, and one who cares for the vulnerable. In the fellowship and service of God, we should creatively heal and care too.

Philip Hefner has described human beings as "created co-creators" with God.[69] This emphasis on the creative role that God has given us is welcome, yet even paired with "created," the noun "co-creator" might be misunderstood as claiming human beings as relative equals with God in the ongoing process. In creation God seems to delegate genuine choice to human beings as to how creation develops, but any contribution human beings make is always that of a creature, not the one and only Creator. We are first and remain mere creatures compared to the One who was and is and always shall be. Yet God has sovereignly chosen to make us in such a way that we can reflect God's image. That seems to include a capacity and vocation to create within our small sphere, in a way somehow akin to how God creates. We are designed to be creative creatures. God is not threatened by our pale imitations. Even if scientists someday assemble a form of life, they will be drawing from given realities.[70] In the eleventh chapter of Genesis, the irony is clear when God says to the heavenly court something like, let us go way down there to see if we can make out in the distance below what those people in Babel are doing. The people thought they were building a tower into the highest heavens. No matter how by God's grace we develop on into the future, we will always be creatures and God will always be the Creator. There is no risk of catching up a merely chronological or quantitative gap. It is amazing that we are designed with a capacity for relationship with the God who is so far beyond us. Maybe the description "creative creatures" better captures human be-

69. Philip Hefner, *The Human Factor: Evolution, Culture, and Religion* (Minneapolis: Fortress, 1993). Gregory Peterson has furthered discussion of this telling phrase in "The Created Co-Creator: What It Is and What It Is Not," *Zygon* 39, no. 4 (2004).

70. Gunton, *The Triune Creator*, p. 89.

ings and our mandate as creatures to create as part of God's calling for us. There can be no suggestion of ever being at God's level. God is the creator; however creative we may be called to be, we will always be creatures.

The kingdom of God is not primarily a raiding party to capture people and bring them back to the safety of the Christian community. It is a mission to transform the world into the kingdom fit for its king. "The hope for the liberation of creation that Paul expresses in Romans 8 clearly implies that the destiny of the natural world is not destruction but transformation."[71] 2 Peter 3:8-13 states that the elements will be kindled and dissolved, then there will be a new heaven and earth. That sounds more like starting completely anew than reform, but Richard Bauckham argues that what the text says is that the refiner's fire will reveal the new earth, not dissolve it.[72] This was John Wesley's reading as well. In his sermon "The New Creation" in 1785, he taught that the elements of our current universe will be improved and survive into the next.[73] The firstborn resurrection, that of Jesus Christ, offers a precedent that God's plan is to transform the physical, not to destroy and replace it.[74] The resurrected Jesus Christ was clearly different in passing through doors yet the same in recognizable appearance and even eating. Colin Gunton calls this new form "transformation within continuity."[75] Human beings shall receive new eternal bodies to live in a new city on a new earth (1 Cor. 15). Death will be no more. All creation will be united in Christ (Col. 1:20; Eph. 1:10). God's plan is eventually to make all things new, not all new things (Rev. 21–22). God's plan is not to destroy creation, but rather to transform it.[76]

We are created with a purpose and ordained to be free. We can work against that designed intent or fulfill it. We and the rest of cre-

71. Douglas J. Moo, "Nature in the New Creation: New Testament Eschatology and the Environment," *Journal of the Evangelical Theological Society* 49 (2006): 463.

72. Richard Bauckham, *Jude and 2 Peter*, Word Biblical Commentary 50 (Waco, Tex.: Word, 1983), pp. 303-22.

73. Randy Maddox, "John Wesley's Precedent for Theological Engagement," in *Divine Grace and Emerging Creation*, ed. Thomas Jay Oord (Eugene, Oreg.: Pickwick, 2009), p. 28.

74. Samuel M. Powell, *Participating in God: Creation and Trinity* (Minneapolis: Fortress, 2003), p. 209.

75. Colin Gunton, *Christ and Creation* (Eugene, Oreg.: Wipf and Stock, 2005), p. 31.

76. Santmire, *The Travail of Nature*, p. 217.

ation are to be restored and developed. Salvation is not escape from the material world but rather its fulfillment. The material world is not just a temporary stage. It is part of what God is continually creating, redeeming, shaping. The womb was deeply shaping for a time and leaves its mark from the belly button on. Jesus' resurrection body showed nail holes and a side wound. What is now present is the seed for transformation. Jesus' conception, birth, life, death, and transformation in resurrection can serve as a model for human beings and for the linear development of creation: creation, redemption, sanctification, and glorification. While we cannot begin to imagine all that God is leading us to become and to do, it involves a fulfillment of the physical world that in some sense transcends current nature, both now and in the future.

Resulting Priorities between Human Beings and the Rest of Creation

All of creation matters to God and has a role to play, yet Jesus affirmed that the two greatest commandments that summarized all the law and the prophets were to love God and to love one's neighbor as oneself. On this shortest of lists, Jesus did not include a third commandment to care for the rest of creation. But it is appropriate, out of love for God and neighbor, to care for the creation loved by God and shared with our neighbors. When love for God and neighbor seem to conflict with the rest of creation in some way, humanitarian relief takes precedence over preserving wetlands, but both are redemptive activities that participate in the kingdom of God. They can be synergistic, as seen in the case of New Orleans and Hurricane Katrina.[77] Protecting the wetlands along the river and city could have prevented much of the devastating flooding.

God models caring for and serving human beings. In God's image and at God's call, human beings should care for and serve the rest of creation.[78] Jesus taught that the greatest among his people are those who serve. That disposition of service carries over to all in one's charge.

---

77. Steven M. Studebaker, "The Spirit in Creation: A Unified Theology of Grace and Creation Care," *Zygon* 43, no. 4 (December 2008): 948.

78. Andrew Linzey, *Animal Rights: A Christian Assessment of Man's Treatment of Animals* (London: SCM, 1976).

Jesus told his listeners that they were each more valuable than a sparrow (Matt. 10:29), yet Proverbs 12:10 reads that a righteous man has regard for his animals. It is the wicked who are cruel. While it may be with some intended irony, at the end of the book of Jonah God declares God's care for the people of Nineveh *and their cattle too.* Proper care of animals comes up repeatedly in the Gospels (Matt. 12:11; Luke 13:15; 14:5). Animal and human destinies are intertwined (see, e.g., Exod. 9:10; Jer. 7:20). Human beings are central to God's plan, but the rest of creation has a place as well.[79] John Calvin extends this theme when he expects that animals will be restored in the next life even though they will not be needed by humankind.[80] Yet when the needs of individual animals and humans are irreconcilable, human beings take precedence. For example, control of rats and mice is often needed to protect food for people, especially the poor.[81]

Some have advocated a Christian vegetarianism.[82] However, while the first human beings in God's garden were directed to refrain from meat, meat was later explicitly offered (compare Gen. 1:29-30 and 9:3). God directed the people of Israel to eat lamb at Passover and provided quail when they were tired of manna (Num. 11). Vantassel argues that Isaiah 11 and 65, which refer to the lion someday resting with the lamb, do not prohibit eating lamb. They describe a peaceable kingdom when human beings are delivered from predation on their livestock.[83] Further, even if Isaiah is read as hoping for the end of predation in heaven, that would not forbid it during this life. Jesus said there will be no marriage in heaven. That does not preclude marriage now.[84] Jesus helped to catch fish and allowed the drowning of pigs (Luke 5:6; Mark 5:13). He cooked

79. Lukas Vischer, "Listening to Creation Groaning: A Survey of Main Themes of Creation Theology," in *Listening to Creation Groaning: Report and Papers from a Consultation on Creation Theology Organized by the European Christian Environmental Network at the John Knox International Reformed Center from March 28 to April 1st 2004* (Geneva: Centre International Reforme John Knox, 2004), pp. 21-22.

80. John Calvin, *Institutes* 3.25.11.

81. Vantassel, *Dominion over Wildlife?* p. 166. See also how the eminent liberation theologian Leonardo Boff has integrated ecological concerns with liberation theology in *Cry of the Earth, Cry of the Poor,* trans. Philip Berryman (Maryknoll, N.Y.: Orbis, 1997).

82. Stephen R. Kaufman and Nathan Braun, *Vegetarianism as Christian Stewardship* (Cleveland: Vegetarian Advocates Press, 2002).

83. Vantassel, *Dominion over Wildlife?* p. 176.

84. Vantassel, *Dominion over Wildlife?* p. 177.

a fish for his disciples' breakfast and ate some himself (John 21:9; Luke 24:42-43). Vegetarianism could be a strategy to extend limited resources to more people, though there are places where vegetarianism would lead to starvation, such as among the Inuit, or it would disrupt good relations between people, the land, and their animals.[85]

In his influential article "Is There an Ecological Ethics?" Holmes Rolston argues that our human obligation is to protect the natural order, especially biodiversity, not individuals.[86] Evolution reinforces adaptation for species development and survival, but depends on a devastating process for many individuals. Following evolutionary history, Rolston focuses not on individual animal welfare, but rather on animal species welfare. He equates survival skill with being valuable and having an interest to be honored. Species that have managed to survive have an intrinsic value. Rolston accepts the elimination of smallpox as a good,[87] but the end of most species is like defacing a great painting. The world is a little less without each unique presence. Aesthetic value is lost. Ninety-eight percent of the species that appear in the fossil record are not alive now, but one might argue that their time was still of value, even if only as the richness of flowers that bloom for a time. There are biblical examples of protecting species more than individuals. In the story of Noah and the ark it is species that survive, not most individuals. There also seems to be a concern with maintaining species in texts such as Deuteronomy 22:6-7 and Exodus 23:11. Individual animals, however, can be sacrificed for the sake of the species, or for that matter human, welfare.[88] As argued by Thomas Aquinas, animal predation has always been part of animal life.[89]

Both human beings and the rest of creation receive life from the Spirit and are to be redeemed by the Spirit. Steven Studebaker has put it this way: "Pine trees will not participate in the eschaton in the same way that human beings will; nonetheless, in some way God promises to redeem creation, and it will share in the eschaton in a way appropriate to its life form. . . . The Spirit's work does not have two orders, creation

85. Christopher Southgate, *The Groaning of Creation: God, Evolution, and the Problem of Evil* (Louisville: Westminster John Knox, 2008), pp. 116-32.

86. Holmes Rolston III, "Is There an Ecological Ethics?" *Ethics* 85 (1975).

87. In conversation at Wycliffe Hall, Oxford University, August 2000.

88. Arlen W. Todd, "Ecological Arguments for Fur Trapping in Boreal Wilderness Regions," *Wildlife Society Bulletin* 9, no. 2 (1981): 116-24.

89. Thomas Aquinas, *Summa Theologica* 96:2.

and redemption, but one order, the redemption of creation. . . . Creation care is pneumatological participation in the eschaton."[90] God is the center and source of all of creation. There is a plan for it all to be fulfilled. We should play our part.

> So why care for the earth? For many reasons — many good reasons. Because our own existence is imperiled. Because we owe it to our children. Because an earth-friendly way of life is more joyful. Because various forms of oppression are of a piece. Because certain nonhuman creatures are entitled to our care. Because earth is valuable for its own sake. Because it is in the best interests of the entire earth community. Because God says so. Because we are God's image-bearers. Because grace begets gratitude, and gratitude care. Because, in sum, care for the earth is integral to what it means to be a Christian — it is an important part of our piety, our spirituality, our collective way of being authentically Christian. Care for the earth is an expression of our devotion to the God whom we love and serve.[91]

When by God's initiative we freely yield to God, God nurtures our relationship with God, one another, and the rest of creation that all might flourish. While we cannot now begin to imagine all that God is leading us to become and to do, human beings are invited to both fulfill and extend this creation, now and in the future.

---

90. Studebaker, "The Spirit in Creation," pp. 953-54.

91. Stephen Bouma-Prediger, *For the Beauty of the Earth*, 2nd ed. (Grand Rapids: Baker, 2010), p. 173.

2 Using Tools

Jesus spent most of his earthly life using tools to shape the natural world to serve God and people. The Gospel of Mark (6:3) tells us that he was the town builder/carpenter, as was his father. In that work probably he would have shaped trees into plows and set clay or stone into walls for homes. This was his service until his public ministry began at age thirty. In Exodus 31 God anointed Bezalel with knowledge and craftsmanship to work gold, silver, and bronze for the tabernacle. A discussion in the Talmud notes that God created wheat, not bread, and milk, not cheese.[1] Human creativity is endowed by God. Technology can be an expression of our God-given nature to shape nature.

The question for any technology is: How can we develop this best to love God, our neighbors, and the earth entrusted to us? Asking that question is not trying to be God; rather it is following God's direction, fulfilling a God-given call to maximize our service while we are here. "The Spirit himself is drawing nature beyond what it is now. This suggests that human intervention in nature by the means of various technologies might be permitted. This is in fact to be encouraged and affirmed where such activities are found to be consistent with the lifegiving work of the Spirit, whom we might even expect to be gifting people throughout his creation for these tasks."[2] Improving what is at hand

1. Ronald M. Green, *Babies by Design: The Ethics of Genetic Choice* (New Haven: Yale University Press, 2007), p. 177.

2. Andrew Gabriel, "Pneumatological Perspectives for a Theology of Nature: The Holy Spirit in Relation to Ecology and Technology," *Journal of Pentecostal Theology* 15, no. 2 (2007): 212.

obeys God's direction to develop what God has made. Our current situation could be better. We are responsible to do the best we can with what we have. As God's people we, as the rest of creation, are being developed by God. Part of our calling is to participate in that process by sustaining and improving what has been entrusted to us.

Such development takes many forms. To give an example, one night not that long ago, about ten thousand people stood together in the dark. They were crowded around the Wabash, Indiana, courthouse, waiting expectantly. The courthouse bell began to ring. Suddenly the town square was as light as day. The gathered throng had expected it. Many had traveled miles to see it happen. But when it did, there was no roar of appreciation, no applause, just stunned silence. In the blinding light some people gasped, others fell on their knees. It was overwhelming to take it in. All their lives, if there was any outdoor light at night it was the slight illumination of the moon and stars. Indoors there might be the faint flame of a candle, fire, or gas lamp. Man-made light flickered, smoked, and went out, consumed. Here suddenly was intense light everywhere, as if the sun had been turned on at will. All was color and detail, steady, unblinking. At the throw of a switch, the town fathers had lit four three-thousand-candle arc lights on top of the courthouse, and the Wabash of 1880 would never again be seen in quite the same way, at least at night.[3]

The dramatic lighting of the town square held the media's attention, but the transformation came elsewhere. Downtown lighting was spectacular, but that was not where electric lighting made the greatest difference. What most changed the way people lived was the rapid but incremental extension of electricity to one house at a time. Wiring a house was not the stuff of headlines, but it was a transforming moment for each household electricity reached. Electric light was so valued that by 1934, 18 percent of the households in Muncie, Indiana, were still using outdoor privies, 34 percent had no running hot water, and more than half had no central heating, but 96 percent had electric lighting. By 1945, half of Muncie's households were still without a telephone, but almost all used electric light.[4] Electric lighting had many valuable uses,

---

3. David E. Nye, *Electrifying America: Social Meanings of a New Technology, 1880-1940* (Cambridge: MIT Press, 1991), pp. 2-3. Firsthand accounts: *Wabash Plain Dealer*, February 7, 14, 21, 28, 1880.

4. Nye, *Electrifying America*, p. 22.

but it was in one home at a time that it most changed the way people lived, not merely in bringing light, but in opening the way for all the other electric machines that so shape our time, from television to the iPod.

Technology shapes us far more than most people realize. We often fear it when it arrives but come to take it for granted as necessary to our lives. What can technology actually achieve, and just as important, what can it not do? If we can guide it toward particular ends, which ones should we prefer? The goal of this chapter is to avoid both a mindless boosterism of every new thing and — just as much — a paralyzing fear of technological advancement that leaves us stunned into inaction like a deer caught in the glare of headlights. We need to start by gaining a better understanding of the momentum of the tools that we use to shape our world and that also end up so deeply shaping us. It is our God-given nature to shape nature. We use tools to survive and thrive. While some technologies, such as cruel instruments of torture, have no appropriate use, most technology can be used for good or ill. Of the two greatest technological feats in the book of Genesis, Noah's ark and the Tower of Babel, one artifact is praised and the other rebuked.

Technology as Necessary

Science is a method of careful observation of the physical world to understand material causation. In contrast, technology is the sum of the tools that we use not just to understand our physical world, but to shape it. Our tools can be as simple and solid as a hammer or as intricate and conceptual as a hospital system.[5] In some ways the distinction between science and technology is quite artificial. The two drive each other. Copernicus's solar system theory intrigued Galileo to study the planets with his new tool, the telescope. The telescope enabled him to make observations of Jupiter's moons. Those observations were then substantial evidence for the solar system theory of Copernicus. While

---

5. Ian Barbour refines the definition this way: technology is "the application of organized knowledge to practical tasks by ordered systems of people and machines." *Ethics in an Age of Technology: The Gifford Lectures*, vol. 2 (San Francisco: HarperSanFrancisco, 1993), p. 3.

science and technology are intertwined, it may be that "science is concerned more with what is, not what ought to be."[6] In contrast, technology is about changing the physical world.

Changing the physical world is necessary for most of us to survive. That includes not only those depending on respirators, kidney dialysis, or daily doses of insulin. Very few of us live where it is always near 20 degrees centigrade (68 degrees Fahrenheit), with ample food available that can be caught with bare hands and eaten raw. The simple fishhook is a tool, as are fire and a pan for cooking, as are the clothes on our backs. Even the Amish, especially famous for maintaining older ways, depend on technology. Horse-pulled reapers, hand water pumps, and barn architecture are all technologies. They are just the continued technologies of an earlier era. Making and using tools are characteristic of human beings who otherwise would be hard pressed to live out the week. According to the Christian tradition, this needed capacity to shape the world is not contrary to God's provision. It is God's provision. As created, we need technology to survive. This does not detract from God as Creator. Sir Isaac Newton wrote concerning farming, "If any think it possible that God may produce some intellectual creature so perfect that he could, by divine accord, in turn produce creatures of a lower order, this so far from detracting from the divine power enhances it; for that power which can bring forth creatures not only directly but through mediation of other creatures is exceedingly, not to say infinitely greater."[7]

Technological Change Is Accelerating

While technology is necessary to our survival, it has developed far beyond that minimum and its development continues to accelerate. Certain inventions have increased the pace of technological development. The printing press made information about what others had discovered more widely available. Telecommunications have dramatically quickened the spread of information, and the Internet has compounded that.

6. R. J. Berry, *God and the Biologist: Faith at the Frontiers of Science* (Leicester: Apollo, 1996), p. 27.

7. As quoted by John Hedley Brooke, "Visions of Perfectibility," *Journal of Evolution and Technology* 14, no. 2 (August 2005): 7.

From one country to another, different people receive credit for inventing the telephone. That is not just national chauvinism. Different people did invent the telephone independently of each other within a period of a few years. Without rapid communications they did not know what the others were doing. With modern communications new discoveries are quickly heralded so that people are working on advancing the next step, rather than reduplicating what has already been worked out elsewhere. The pace of invention quickens.

Not only are the people who do research more efficient, but there are more of them. It has been suggested that most of the full-time scientists who have ever lived are working today. New information is discovered and quickly applied to discover more. Product cycles are short and becoming shorter. Proceeding from invention to widespread use takes less time. The television was invented in the 1930s and took thirty years to become ubiquitous in our homes. Personal computers took less than fifteen years from inception to widespread home use. The commercial Internet took four years to be adopted in fifty million homes. The iPod took three years to sell its first fifty million units. Facebook was adopted by fifty million users within two years.

Technology Is Becoming More Intricate

Robert Pool describes how a Turkish Airlines DC-10 crashed shortly after takeoff from the Paris airport. A cargo door blew open when the plane reached 12,000 feet. The sudden loss of pressure collapsed the passenger compartment floor, which severed the control lines to the tail control surfaces and brought the plane down. No one person designs the more than five million individual parts in a commercial airliner. Different teams of engineers had made design choices, some of which interacted in a lethal way. The doors opened out rather than in. That made it easier to load the plane, but also meant that air pressure at flying altitudes would be pushing the doors open rather than pushing them securely in place. The team that designed the door handles allowed the handles to close without fully engaging the pins that were to keep the door secure. The group that routed the control cables under the passenger floor had chosen a path that was well protected from outside injury but vulnerable to passenger floor movement. The builders of the passenger floor chose lightweight materials that were more than adequate to carry foot traffic and airline seats, but could not sustain a loss of cabin pressure below the deck. It was the interaction of all these choices that was lethal.[8]

The science of ecology has helped us to realize how interrelated the natural world is. Lose one species at one location and the effects can be drastic at quite a distance. The ecology of modern technical systems is also vulnerable to seemingly irrelevant changes. When a hurricane knocks out power in a city, cars start to run out of gas. Gasoline can be abundant, but it is stored in tanks accessed only by electric pumps. Disabling one part has ripple effects far afield. It is like pulling on one thread in a tapestry and discovering that it is connected to many other threads. Such intricacy means that it is increasingly difficult both to foresee the results of new technology introduction and to withdraw damaging technology that has already been integrated. The complexity of modern technology means that we are more dependent on experts to maintain it and that whole systems depend on single parts. The experts are dependent on other experts to manage the subsystems fundamental to their own systems. This makes it difficult to predict all eventual implications when introducing or removing a technology. Effects and the expertise needed to predict and manage them are dispersed. The discipline of technology assessment has been developed with particular emphasis on this problem of expecting the "unintended, indirect, and delayed" effects of present and new technology.[9] Daniel Bricklin and Robert Frankston designed computer spreadsheet software as a convenient editor for accounting past expenditure. As it turns out, their program VisiCalc became enormously popular as a simulation tool for business planning. An unintended use came to be its most significant contribution.[10] Of course, surprises can be negative too.

8. Robert Pool, *Beyond Engineering: How Society Shapes Technology* (New York: Oxford University Press, 1997), pp. 133-34.

9. Joseph Coates, "The Identification and Selection of Candidates and Priorities for Technology Assessment," in *Technology Assessment*, vol. 2 (London: Gordon and Breach Science Publishers, 1974), p. 77.

10. Alan Kay, "Computer Software," *Scientific American* 251 (September 1984): 52.

Technology Is Formative

Technology affects how we live and who we are. It has been suggested that if one has a hammer in hand, everything looks like a nail. Our tools do influence our perception and choices. Think of how deeply shaped we have been by the introduction of electricity, as described earlier. It does not just make certain tasks easier such as household chores with dishwashers and vacuum cleaners, it also changes our environment with air-conditioning, entertains us with music and images, even extends the hours of "the day" available to us for work and play. It makes possible whole new tool systems such as the computer. It is so ubiquitous that it is its absence during a power outage that we notice, not its presence.

There is an old joke about a drunk looking for his lost keys under the streetlight. He thought he lost his keys farther down the block, but he is searching under the lamppost because that is where the light is. Our activitiy is drawn to the place a tool is at hand, whether it is the best place for action or not. Available technology can draw our interest and shape our perception of what is doable and desirable. Gerald McKenny argues that the availability of Viagra may move endurance in sexual intimacy from an attendant desire for some to their central pursuit.[11]

Think of the invention of the automobile. Compare life for those living on farms or in small towns before the automobile, with their lives today. The comparison would hold for most major North American cities and suburbs as well, since they too are dependent on the automobile. For example, contrast living in a rural town before and after the advent of the automobile system. Previously, friends would be drawn from the few family groups within walking distance. With the automobile, one's closest friends may live tens of miles away. People are able to spend more time with others who share special interests. While there might be only one family with twins in town, one could drive a short distance to a city and join the "Mothers of Twins Club" with hundreds of members. One can also associate with a particular religious group. Before the automobile, one's choice for worship within walking distance was one of two churches. Now, within a half hour's drive are several hundred congregations and tens of different religions. Since the ad-

11. Gerald P. McKenny, "Technologies of Desire: Theology, Ethics, and the Enhancement of Human Traits," *Theology Today* 59 (2002): 102.

vent of the automobile one can associate with more specialized groups that are similar in some way, yet one is regularly exposed to more people with whom one might not have as much in common. To reach a particular place of worship one may drive past tens of places gathering people with quite different commitments. Meeting a stranger used to be a noteworthy event. It was strange. Yet now one is exposed to countless strangers. On a trip to the grocery store, one sees hundreds of fellow drivers, shoppers, clerks, and cashiers. One might be surprised to know any of them personally. Exposure to more people can enrich one's life, but it also makes it easier to enrich one's life at the expense of another. Not only can one flee a crime scene in the getaway car, one can also use the stolen goods in relative anonymity only a few minutes away by car from their original owner.

Even the flavors of our food and when we eat have been affected by the automobile. It makes possible in suburban or rural housing the Arcadian dream of living in a quiet garden setting far from industry. That means that family members are often dispersed during the workday and gather again at its end. The main meal of the day used to be at noon, but now for most it is in the evening when family members have returned from workplaces that can be quite distant from where they live. The food at dinner has probably come from a giant supermarket accessible only by car or a restaurant drive-up window.

A major portion of the workforce is involved in making possible the system of high personal mobility offered by the automobile. There are jobs involved in making basic materials such as glass and steel for cars, as well as other jobs for design, transport, parts, assembly, sales, and finance to buy the machine. To operate it, there are insurers, appraisers, traffic police, courts, driving instructors, maintenance and repair mechanics. Further, the automobile depends on an intricate and pervasive system of road construction and maintenance; parking lots; garages; parking decks; petroleum discovery, refining, and transport; service stations; toll booths; mapmaking . . . The automobile system absorbs a substantial part of the personal and national economy.

Time is affected as well. The average North American drives about 12,000 miles a year. If one includes stoplights, drive-up windows, parking hassles, traffic tie-ups, and other limitations on speed, an average of thirty miles an hour for these 12,000 miles would be generous. That places most Americans in their steel boxes for at least four hundred hours a year. That is the equivalent of a full-time job from January

1 to mid-March. The automobile is just *one* technology system that affects people's friends, religion, food, education, land use, personal and social economy, place of work, and for many their very livelihood. Technology shapes our lives.

When the automobile was first introduced, it was available only to the wealthy. With mass production and the government's commitment to build roads, it became an option to more people. Today much of North America is structured so that one cannot work, obtain food, or worship in a community without it. Residential neighborhoods are deliberately zoned away from industrial areas. Grocery stores have abundant variety in centralized locations. What begins as optional, if widely adopted, tends to become necessary. In some parts of the world a shiny new car would be useless, except to polish the finish and listen to the radio until the first tank of gas ran out and the battery died. Technology often comes in complex and integrated systems that need and then enforce widespread adoption.

This integrated nature means that it is difficult to remove one part of the system without affecting others. Technology becomes entrenched over time and often builds its own momentum. The existence of the technology is often pushed forward to use by multiple societal dynamics. One of these dynamics is the widespread assumption that new is better. Products can receive a noticeable bump up in sales simply by adding to the packaging that it is new in some way. There is optimism that technology will always produce a better way, as if human beings could resolve any question with enough technological insight and application.[12] Further, innovation is craved. Last year's product or method is not good enough. Surely there are more power, more space, more speed, more something to add to the experience. People who lived quite well a few years ago without any Internet access at all feel the need for ever greater download speed, myself included. Ironically, while innovation is desired, the media has become so adept at projecting future developments in order to sell magazines, newspapers, and science fiction films that when new technologies become available people often feel that the capability has already been around for some time. Expectations are high (and often fulfilled) that new capabilities and the refinement of already present ones occur frequently.

12. Craig M. Gay, "The Technological Ethos and the Spirit of (Post)Modern Nihilism," *Christian Scholar's Review* 28, no. 1 (1998): 90-110.

There is some resistance to this trend of constant innovation. England was traumatized by the "mad cow disease" disaster.[13] English beef producers fed ground-up-beef by-products such as cow brain to their cattle to speed growth. This practice made possible the spread of a brain disease lethal to cattle and apparently lethal to some humans who ate their meat. This understandably sensitized people to possible danger from the agricultural industry that provides their food. With the advent of genetically modified (GM) crops, the reaction has been horror that changes are again being made in the food system. Further concerns have been raised about limiting seed access through patents and lost choice through contamination.[14] But virtually all our food is genetically modified, and has been for centuries. Standard plant crossbreeding that has produced our seed for millennia is a clumsy and slow type of genetic modification, but it is GM nonetheless. Domestic sheep have been intentionally bred, genetically modified, to grow high-quality wool and docilely accept human handling to shave it off regularly. For the most part GM is just a more precise and quick way of crossbreeding, granted that genes can be introduced that have not been in plants before. The main impetus for concern may be that after the mad cow disease fiasco, people have reason not to trust the food industry. In practice the public debates have been more over whether civil disobedience or private property should prevail when a group masses to trample a farmer's crop, than concerning the actual effects of the technology.

We have transitioned from external risks being the most prominent in life to manufactured risk being the greatest concern.[15] Can we thoughtfully resist or direct the new technologies that so deeply shape us, or are they unstoppable juggernauts? Are we so quickly dependent on their accelerating and interlocked development that there really is no time or leverage for choice? Is technology like the *Star Trek* aliens the Borg, who always announce their presence with "We will assimilate you. Resistance is futile"?

13. Bovine spongiform encephalopathy.

14. For an accessible narrative, see Lisa H. Weasel, *Food Fray: Inside the Controversy over Genetically Modified Food* (New York: AMACOM Books, 2009).

15. Anthony Giddens, *Runaway World: How Globalization Is Reshaping Our Lives* (New York: Routledge, 2003), p. 26.

Technology Can Be Shaped

Refrigerators are ubiquitous, and almost every one of them hums. The hum is the sound of the electric compressor. In contrast, gas refrigerators are utterly silent. With no moving parts they do not wear out. They are also more energy efficient and no more expensive to mass-produce. Why do we not all have gas refrigerators? It is the more efficient technology and was invented first. The commercial triumph of the electric refrigerator is an example that the most efficient technology is not always the one that is adopted. In this case the key reason electricity prevailed was the timely and concerted effort of a relatively small group, the leaders of electric-power-generating corporations.[16] What could be more beneficial to the sale of their product, in this case electricity, than an appliance in each person's home that uses their product twenty-four hours a day and could be turned off only at substantial financial loss to the owner? The corporation was willing to invest great sums of financial resources to mass-produce the electric refrigerator so that they could drive the per unit cost down to competitive levels with gas ones. They then opened stores across the land to make their refrigerators more accessible and sustained a massive marketing campaign to introduce people to their product. The resulting economics of scale and development of widely available electric power gave electric refrigerators not only the lead over gas units but also the structural supports for their dominance to become complete. Electric power lines became more accessible than gas ones. Gas refrigerators still exist, but usually in commercial buildings that have the size and independence to have a custom system. Electric refrigerators own the domestic market. This history does not reveal that economics determines all. That is not the case.[17] It is an example that the most efficient technology is not always the one widely adopted. Another example that already seems a technological aeon old was when VHS videotape triumphed over another type of videotape called Beta. Generally, "Americans have traded away the neighborhood, local businesses, the walking city, and mass transit, for the detached

16. Ruth Schwartz Cowan, "How the Refrigerator Got Its Hum," in *The Social Shaping of Technology*, ed. Donald MacKenzie and Judy Wajcman (Philadelphia: Open University Press, 1985), pp. 202-18.

17. Arnold Pacey nicely contravenes that conclusion in his book *The Maze of Ingenuity: Ideas and Idealism in the Development of Technology*, 2nd ed. (Cambridge: MIT Press, 1992).

suburban house, the shopping mall, and the freeway." Most American cities are "designed less to be lived in than to be moved through."[18] Granted that there is currently a movement toward denser housing that can support services within walking distance as the pendulum swings the other way. Conscious, conscientious, or not, individuals and communities make formative choices about what technology to use and then have to live with. It is difficult to change the integrated systems once they are in place.

Jacques Ellul suggests that such technology has taken on an independent life of its own. "It is artificial, autonomous, self determining, and independent of all human intervention."[19] Langdon Winner sees much the same momentum, but has more hope that technology can be shaped to human needs. "Human 'somnambulism,' rather than any inherent technological imperative, has allowed large technical systems to legislate the conditions of human existence."[20] We have the capability to destroy human life on the planet with nuclear missiles, but have so far resisted carrying out that capability. What can be done has not always been done. Possibility is not necessity. We do have a choice.

That choice is usually greater when a new technology is just beginning. Once a technology is formed and adopted, it tends to preclude other options. A choice for one system is often a choice against another. That is not always a negative. Offering a choice socially legitimizes the offered options. On the one hand, we no longer allow the choice of dueling. Prohibiting dueling eliminates a method of conflict resolution, but also frees people from being challenged to a duel.[21] On the other hand, commitments to particular technologies can shape us in ways we later regret. Such problems are often hard to detect or predict at the beginning when they are still relatively easy to change. By the time adverse results are evident to all, the technology is often entrenched and difficult to disentangle. In the late 1990s billions of dollars were spent

18. David E. Nye, *Consuming Power: A Social History of American Energies* (Cambridge: MIT Press, 1998), pp. 256-57.

19. Jacques Ellul, "The Technological Order," *Technology and Culture* 3 (Fall 1962): 10.

20. Merritt Roe Smith, *Does Technology Drive History? The Dilemma of Technological Determinism* (Cambridge: MIT Press, 1994), p. 32.

21. Allen Verhey, "Luther's 'Freedom' and a Patient's Autonomy," in *Bioethics and the Future of Medicine: A Christian Appraisal*, ed. John F. Kilner, Nigel M. de S. Cameron, and David L. Schiedermayer (Grand Rapids: Eerdmans, 1995), pp. 89-90.

to rewrite computer software that was not designed to accommodate dates in the 2000s. The original shortfall in design came from an economy measure to save a computer's expensive memory space. Few considered the future confusion and expense that were being embedded in the system.

It is difficult to control the development of new capabilities, but one can try to guide applications thoughtfully. Technology shapes all of us. Its already pervasive presence and influence are increasing at an accelerating pace. We need to, can, and should choose where it takes us. So where should we go? Who should we be? These are fundamental questions for technology. Technology shapes us but we can shape it. The technology of tower building was used to destruction at Babel. The technology of ark building saved Noah and his fellow creatures. Most technology can be directed to help or harm. We are both part of nature and responsible for it, tools and all.[22]

22. Michael S. Hogue, *The Tangled Bank: Toward an Ecotheological Ethics of Responsible Participation* (Eugene, Oreg.: Pickwick, 2008).

3 Body and Soul

Changing

Human beings live where the physical and spiritual worlds meet. Material nature includes the human body. The human body includes the human brain. The human brain includes the human mind. The human mind can be open to spiritual life. The body is where we human beings live and interact with God and each other. The body is the God-given nexus for so much of what God is doing in raising up individuals and a people to forever know and enjoy God, one another, and all else that God has made.

Jesus was fully committed to this bodily life even as he was the one who has completely shown God's image. He cared for and sustained his body with food for over thirty years. He provided food for his disciples, even the best drink for a wedding feast. The central events in his life were substantially body events. The incarnation, birth, crucifixion, resurrection, and ascension are all physical landmarks. Matter *matters*. Gnostic ideas that the body does not really exist can lead to either license — since the body is not real, it does not matter what is done with it — or neglect — since the body is not real, there is no need to take care of it. On the contrary, the body is real and does matter. It is at least an essential school for whole people. The physical creation is the stage in location and process where human beings have the opportunity to learn to live. C. S. Lewis wrote,

> Healing for the sick and provision for the poor should be less important than . . . the salvation of souls; and yet very important. Because

God created the Natural — invented it out of His love and artistry — it demands our reverence; because it is only a creature and not He, it is, from another point of view, of little account. And still more, because Nature, and especially human nature, is fallen it must be corrected and the evil within it must be mortified. But its essence is good; correction is something quite different from Manichaean repudiation or Stoic superiority.[1]

When Paul speaks of "subduing the flesh," he is not trying to escape the body. Adam and Eve are described as having bodies before the brokenness of their rebellion. God's children will have imperishable bodies in heaven (1 Cor. 15). When "the flesh" is named negatively, it is in reference to embedded patterns of sinful perspective and choice (Rom. 7–8). These are associated with body-flesh because that is where human beings live, where human beings have most of their small sphere of influence. Our bodies are hardwired to recognize our own needs first and to feel them most acutely. It is easier to recognize one's own hunger than someone else's. That natural self-centeredness is reinforced and compounded by the habits we build up in our life choices, habits that come to be embodied in the neural circuitry of our brains. The physical world in general and our bodies in particular are where human beings can make choices. The flesh is to be consciously, consistently yielded to God. The body is a place to learn commitments, attitudes, and skills. Here one can practice actually carrying them out, not only once, but over time. Here one can become more of who one is meant to be. One can reflect God's image in creatively sustaining, healing, and developing the physical world. Here one can learn to reflect Christ, who reveals humanity as God intended it to be. Yielded, the body can be filled with God's Holy Spirit and shaped to God's service as part of the body of Christ. The prophet Joel gives a promise from God that "I will pour out my spirit on all flesh" (Joel 2:28; cf. Acts 2:17).

As argued thus far, what God has created is to be sustained by God's stewards, who act as God guides them. As God has redeemed one, one is to redeem and heal the world. As God transforms one over time, one is to transform the world for the better. The theme for the 1974 Lausanne Movement Congress was "the whole gospel for the whole per-

---

1. C. S. Lewis, "Some Thoughts," in *God in the Dock: Essays on Theology and Ethics*, ed. Walter Hooper (Grand Rapids: Eerdmans, 1970), pp. 148-49.

son for the whole world." That should include the larger environment and our bodies. We are to sustain our physical bodies. We should restore our bodies when they are damaged, and we should improve them as best we can to serve God and our neighbors. But some have argued that calling is to be exercised over the rest of physical creation, but not our own human form. The human body is off-limits. Some say this prohibition stems from a feeling of repugnance at the idea of altering the human form.[2] It is respectful and wise to consider the feelings of others and oneself.[3] But the feeling of repugnance is an alert, not an argument. Like anger, it demands that something needs attention. The issue at hand does need attention, but not necessarily rebuke. Feelings can intensify or dissipate upon reflection. If a gut reaction encourages us to think carefully about the motivation and ramifications of human intervention, that is most welcome, but not as a dictator by itself.

Consider what sign was required of Abraham to show that he and his descendants were people of God. God directed them to cut off a normal part of the male body to confirm and show that they were God's people. This was the surgery of circumcision. As Laurie Zoloth-Dorfman points out, "Judaism is not a nature-based religion; the very assertion of circumcision rests on the notion that the body is neither sacred nor immutable."[4] There is no biblical injunction that the body should never change. Jesus' resurrection body was recognizable but quite different from his original form. That transformation was not a travesty of the created order but rather a foretaste of its intended fulfillment. Recognizing that the body can change as seen in circumcision by the command of God, and that human bodies will be transformed in the resurrection, we ask: Are genes in particular an exception, parts of the human body that are not to change? Genes are not more intimate or progeny-related than circumcision. We have always made decisions with genetic impact, such as whom we marry. Population genetics are already affected by our individual treatment decisions, such as to avoid mental retardation from PKU. Genes provide only part of our physical

2. Leon Kass has articulated this concern with pugnacious elegance.

3. In a lively narrative, Jonah Lehrer describes some of the constructive roles and limitations of feelings in decision making. *How We Decide* (Boston: Houghton Mifflin Harcourt, 2009).

4. Laurie Zoloth-Dorfman, "Mapping the Normal Human Self: The Jew and the Mark of Otherness," in *Genetics: Issues of Social Justice*, ed. Ted Peters (Cleveland: Pilgrim Press, 1998), p. 190.

heritage. They do not set who future people will be. Changing genes is one factor among many, not the sole determinant of future people. Human life is more about cultural evolution than genetic evolution. Cultural evolution is much more immediately responsive. Day care workers have more impact on future generations than geneticists. Genetics is a substrate to the physical, and the physical is a substrate to where the most important action is. When the National Science Foundation sponsored a study entitled *Converging Technologies for Improving Human Performance*, genetics was only one avenue of intervention studied.[5] However, genetic change does have the potential to be deeply formative, and we are now developing attitudes and standards for its use.

Ronald Green has written that

> the disagreements about intervening at the genetic level will grow in intensity in the years ahead. During the twenty-first century, human gene modification is likely to move to the center of religious debates, possibly eclipsing the controversies about abortion, embryonic stem cell research, and cloning. Beginning with more widespread prenatal gene selection and moving on to germline therapies and enhancements, each new manipulation will precipitate a skirmish in the war between differing worldviews. . . . If we implement it well, gene modification will become a routine and accepted part of our lives, joining anesthesia during childbirth, birth control, and in vitro fertilization on the list of reproductive technologies that religions once opposed.[6]

In what ways Green's prediction should be implemented or resisted is the task before us in this work.

Genes and the Human Body

The human eye is marvelously complex. Could you design one in all its intricacy? One would have to know the exact chemical formula for the

5. Mihail C. Roco and William Sims Bainbridge, eds., *Converging Technologies for Improving Human Performance* (Washington, D.C.: National Science Foundation, 2002).

6. Ronald M. Green, *Babies by Design: The Ethics of Genetic Choice* (New Haven: Yale University Press, 2007), p. 196.

translucent cornea and how to vary its thickness to focus the light on the retina. Rod and cone light receptors would need exquisite array and connections to the optic nerve. Then brain tissue would have to be in place to interpret optic nerve impulses into understandable pictures. It would be a task of vast intricacy. Since you are reading this book, it is likely that you have successfully assembled precisely this design already, probably twice. How did you do that?

All the necessary information for design, assembly, and basic operating of your eye and the rest of you is contained in your DNA. DNA is an abbreviation for deoxyribonucleic acid. It consists of a varied sequential pattern of just four chemicals: adenosine (A), cytosine (C), guanine (G), and thymine (T). They are set in a double helix that looks something like a spiraling ladder and is organized into two sets of twenty-three chromosomes in human beings. Each rung of the ladder is a pair of A-T, T-A, G-C, or C-G. Each sequence of three rungs codes for a particular amino acid. It is the assembly of these amino acids into proteins that builds the incredibly intricate and interactive system called the human body. By their sequence the four constituent parts of DNA encode a vast amount of varied information, just as the twenty-six letters of the English alphabet, by varying their order, can record the plays of Shakespeare, love letters, or a Blu-ray Disk player manual. Another parallel is found in computers that run word processing, spreadsheets, and vivid simulations from at root a simple binary on/off code.

Except for a few viruses that use RNA, it appears that DNA is the chemical code for the structure of all the rest of earthly life. Yeast, daisies, mice, and human beings all record and duplicate their instructions in the same system. At the cellular level, human and other mammalian cells are almost interchangeable in many respects. That is why medical research for human medicine can be advanced by studies with mice and other animals. One of the first steps in understanding and combating most human diseases is to find an animal with virtually the same disease to serve as a model of how the disease progresses and whether particular treatments are effective. That avoids the sacrifice of human beings. A parallel use of animals is when a pig is well treated through life and then is sacrificed to provide a heart valve for a human patient whose own valve has failed. What makes human beings unique is our capability to know God, not that we are of different "dust" than the material world or different DNA than other living things. We share many of our cellular-level genes with bacteria! There has always been much cross-species genetic interchange. Chimeras, creatures with genetic overlap, occur naturally throughout the biosphere.

DNA also has a strong community dimension within humanity. Most people are genetically unique.[7] Yet the individual's genes have come from just two other people. Except for an infinitesimal percentage of random mutations, an individual has no genes that were not present in one of her two parents, each of whom received genes from just two people as well. On the one hand one is closely tied genetically to just a few people, yet on the other hand one's genes have been passed on for untold generations from people who lived before, and future people may carry on those genes present now. Our genes combine uniquely and intimately in individuals, yet are held in common by families, ancestors, and descendants. The system of human genetics is one of diversity, but also unity; it is one of variation and continuity. Genes tie together individuals, humanity, and life.

Associations and the rest of the environment are as influential to the individual's form as genetic heritage. "Genotype" is the individual's genetic instructions. "Phenotype" is how those genetic instructions are expressed in the individual. Genotype is not phenotype. There are myriad steps in between. In human beings, genes often encode multiple proteins. That is why a mustard weed can have 25,706 genes and the immensely more complex human being has only about 20,000. In a human, each gene is part of a network of internal environments that trigger multiple uses, typically three to ten proteins rather than just one. These proteins are then assembled in patterns that further complexify. Some eventual physical characteristics are shaped more by genetics and others more by environmental factors external to the body. No amount of nutrition, stretching, or other environmental influences is able to add substantially to one's height beyond a certain range of genetic predisposition, yet lack of optimum nutrition can severely limit height. Winston Churchill was overweight, smoked an ever present cigar, drank copious amounts of alcohol, and died at ninety years of age. Sergei Grinkov was a nonsmoker, a light drinker, an Olympic athlete, and died at twenty-eight. Genes can predispose one to build muscle mass, but only exercise, diet, and hormonal activity will accomplish muscle mass. Our physical form and health are the result of an intricate interaction between genes

---

7. Unless, through twinning, there might be one or two other persons having the same genetic combination.

and their surroundings within and outside the body. Even in the most limited variations of water crystallizing to form a snowflake, when multiplied countless times in reaction to a changing environment the snowflake that results may not be precisely like any other. Small variations multiplied in an interactive environment can result in large differences. If one of two genetically identical twins has diabetes type 1, the other twin has about a one-in-two chance of eventually developing the disease. That is a much higher rate of diabetes than we observe in the general population, yet half of the identical twins never develop the type 1 diabetes that affects their twin with identical genes. Genes are important, but not by themselves destiny. Epigenetics turn on or off certain genes. The environment, including the choices of the organism, affects which genes are turned on or off. Genes and environment interact.[8]

Genes and Human Behavior

Within the animal kingdom it is clear that genes guide not only structure but also certain behaviors. Seeking water, hiding by day, and fleeing the unusual are examples of such behaviors. Genes provide both structure and operating instructions. In a computer such would be called hardware and software. These genetically encoded behaviors are multiplied in a population because they increase the number of the carrier's young that survive or the survival of relatives who carry many of the same genes. For example, cockroaches have a strong genetically encoded tendency to flee light. If a cockroach developed a tendency to seek light, it would probably not live long enough to propagate that genetic tendency. On the other hand, any gene combination that enhances its carrier's survival is more likely to spread through a population. Survival selection could even account for some tendency toward altruism. The proposals that there could be genes for altruistic tendency and that they could give an adaptive advantage that would spread them in a given population were among the most noteworthy and influential postulates of Edward O. Wilson's book *Sociobiology*.[9]

8. John B. Cobb Jr., ed., *Back to Darwin: A Richer Account of Evolution* (Grand Rapids: Eerdmans, 2008), particularly part II.
9. Edward O. Wilson, *Sociobiology: The New Synthesis* (Cambridge: Harvard University Press, 1975).

71

Wilson argues that such genetic tendencies might well apply at the human level too.[10] The argument is from analogy or statistical correlation. There are no experimental protocols changing one gene in a human being and then observing over a lifetime to see how that affects behavior. Human beings and human culture are too complex and long-lived for that kind of study, not to mention the trouble such a study would have passing a standard ethics review board. Now we can observe that half of our twenty thousand genes seem to be associated with the development of our central nervous system. For instance, an inherited aversion to certain smells may protect people from eating rotten foods that might well be poisonous. It needs to be noted that such hypotheses can explain too much. John Avise points out that if one measured that babies cry mostly at night, such could be explained as an adaptive attempt to contravene competing conceptions. On the other hand, if one measured that babies cry less at night, one could argue that such is a genetic advantage to hide better the babies from predators.[11] Conjecture in this regard can be quite flexible. However, statistical evidence is beginning to confirm some genetic influence on behavior.[12] A team led by R. P. Epstein has found genetic variation associated with novelty seeking, correlating forms of a particular gene with personality test scores.[13] The K. P. Lesch team has found a correlation between a particular polymorphism and anxiety reactions.[14] Other studies have shown that infants with no experience of falling or training to avoid falling, resist moving onto a transparent surface that appears to be a drop-off. They seem to have an inherent antipathy to unsupported heights. Mary Midgley asks in response to those who argue that all human be-

10. Edward O. Wilson, *On Human Nature* (Toronto: Bantam Books, 1982). Charles J. Lumsden and E. O. Wilson, *Genes, Mind, and Culture: The Coevolutionary Process* (Cambridge: Harvard University Press, 1981). On this theme applied directly to ethics and theology, see Arthur Peacocke, ed., "The Challenge of Sociobiology to Ethics and Theology," *Zygon* 19, no. 2 (June 1984): 115-232.

11. John C. Avise, *The Genetic Gods: Evolution and Belief in Human Affairs* (Cambridge: Harvard University Press, 1998), pp. 155-56.

12. Terry E. Goldberg and Daniel R. Weinberger, eds., *The Genetics of Cognitive Neuroscience* (Cambridge: MIT Press, 2009).

13. R. P. Epstein et al., "Dopamine D4 Receptor (D4DR) Exon III Polymorphism Associated with the Human Personality Trait of Novelty Seeking," *Nature* 12 (1996): 78-80.

14. K. P. Lesch et al., "Association of Anxiety-Related Traits with a Polymorphism in the Serotonin Transporter Gene Regulatory Region," *Science* 274 (1996): 1527-31.

havior is learned from the environment: "How do all the children of eighteen months pass the word along the grapevine that now is the time to join the subculture, to start climbing furniture, toddling out of the house, playing with fire, breaking windows, taking things to pieces, messing with mud, and chasing the ducks? For these are perfectly specific things which all healthy children can be depended on to do, not only unconditioned, but in the face of all deterrents."[15] Of course, not all behavior is genetically determined. At the human level of complexity, genes determine that we will be free.[16] Reductionist descriptions ignore the documented influence of environment and our choices.[17] Not only do experiences shape our ongoing choices as persons, but they can also sometimes affect the activity level of the genes that we have. It appears for example that seizures can turn on the expression of certain genes involved in the brain's response to injury that would have otherwise remained quiescent.[18] As with physical characteristics, genotype is not phenotype. Having a gene that has an influence on behavior does not tell to what degree it will be expressed, nor is it usually determinative even if expressed to the maximum possible influence. Human beings develop in a complex interaction that includes far more than just genes. Over the years behavioral geneticists have fairly consistently concluded inheritability rates ranging typically from roughly 40 to 60 percent for a number of behaviors.[19] Identical twins raised apart have more similarities in personality traits and social attitudes than fraternal twins raised together.[20] But while genetic heritage is influential, it is not determinative. Inheritance seems to have as much, not more, influence as environment for a number of personality differences.[21]

15. Mary Midgley, *Beast and Man: The Roots of Human Nature* (New York: Meridian Books, 1978), p. 56.

16. Nicely put by Ted Peters in his chapter "The Evolution of Evil," in *The Evolution of Evil*, ed. Gaymon Bennett et al. (Göttingen: Vandenhoeck & Ruprecht, 2008), p. 40.

17. Holmes Rolston III, *Genes, Genesis, and God: Values and Their Origins in Natural and Human History* (Cambridge: Cambridge University Press, 1999).

18. Bruce R. Reichenbach and V. Elving Anderson, *On Behalf of God: A Christian Ethic for Biology* (Grand Rapids: Eerdmans, 1995), p. 253.

19. For example, Thomas J. Bouchard Jr., "Genes, Environment, and Personality," *Science* 264 (June 17, 1994): 1700-1701.

20. Auke Tellegen et al., "Personality Similarity in Twins Reared Apart and Together," *Journal of Personality and Social Psychology* 54 (1988): 1031-35.

21. Reichenbach and Anderson, *On Behalf of God*, p. 268.

This is why it is not possible to clone an individual's personality. Only a person's genes can be cloned. The resulting baby would be a younger genetic twin. The child would have much in common with the older sibling, but would develop as a unique person. Duplicating someone's genes would lead to another human being much younger than the first, with strong physical resemblance. The genetic twin would experience the womb, infancy, and childhood in a markedly different environment and make his or her own choices. A different person results. If you have ever met identical twins, you have met naturally occurring clones, two people who have the same genetic code, who despite sharing a womb and identical genes are still unique individuals, each a different person. That uniqueness remains despite sharing the same genes. Our genes are formative for our physical structure and some temperamental inclinations, but are not finally determinative of the complete person.[22]

For a worker ant, genes are destiny. The ant is born with instinct embedded in genetic instructions to behave one certain way. The behaviors may be intricate but they are rote and unchangeable. A more complex animal such as a Labrador retriever may still have strong genetic instructions. Present a Labrador retriever puppy with a tub of water and the dog will be more likely to jump into it than drink from it. Yet at this level of genetic complexity instinct is not destiny. The puppy can be trained to avoid water or only to jump in on command. Environment is beginning to play a more formative role. By the time we reach human beings, we find genetic drives, such as to protect our young, but we also have the ability to choose to channel or resist them. Our drives are not destiny; rather, they are different degrees of tendency. For example, the same temperament could be channeled to be constructively steadfast or harmfully stubborn, another to be either energetic or impulsive. Granted, some genetic conditions can be so powerfully destructive that they are difficult to channel positively.

Glenn McGee gives a mirthful caricature of the idea of genetic tendency controlling us. According to the view of genetic determinism,

22. V. Elving Anderson ably explains the links between genes and behavior in "Genes, Behavior, and Responsibility: Research Perspectives," in *The Genetic Frontier: Ethics, Law, and Policy,* ed. Mark S. Frankel and Albert H. Teich (Washington, D.C.: AAAS, 1994), pp. 105-30. See also Theodosius Dobzhansky, "The Myth of Genetic Predestination and of Tabula Rasa," *Perspectives in Biology and Medicine* 19 (1976): 156-70.

not his own, "we think that we choose, while we are really determined, pushed, or persuaded by the genetic call of our innards. It is as if the overeater hears a voice from the pantry, which is really projected from within the genome: 'eat more guacamole.'"[23] Of course, one's genes have no voice box or telepathic skills. However, they can "communicate." What actually may be happening at the refrigerator door is the appearance of a genetic tendency that has been helpful for most of human history. Fat is a high-energy food of particular value when food is scarce. Since for most human beings food has been in short supply, physical pleasure in eating fat would encourage one to seek it out, a successful strategy. When food is in short supply, the usual genetic tendency to enjoy the taste and texture of fat such as found in a juicy steak, poutine, or premium ice cream is a good first choice. One tends to reach for the Häagen-Dazs before the celery. The natural desire for that taste can be overridden by one's awareness and conscious choice that under conditions of plenty, the celery would be better for health after all. Genes can encode rewards such as physical pleasure for valued behaviors, but what they reward does not have to be pursued.

An apt metaphor might be the sailboat. The size, shape, and condition of the hull and sails represent the genetic endowment. The strength and direction of the wind and water currents are the environment, and the way one sets the sails and rudder correspond to one's will. Some people hit the genetic lottery jackpot. They are born with countless genetic advantages of strong hull and sails. The wind of environment is at their back, and yet they just sail in circles. Other people have poor initial resources and a contrary wind, yet manage to achieve great things. Genetics reminds us that everyone starts with a different set of givens. Genes and environment deal varied hands. Our will plays a decisive role in what we do with them and hence what we become.

It appears that some family lines have a propensity toward alcoholism. That does not mean that their descendants are obligated to be alcoholics or are most fulfilled as such. The strongest genetic correlation with criminal violence is the Y chromosome, held only by men.[24] That does not mean that everyone with a Y chromosome must or

23. Glenn McGee, *The Perfect Baby: A Pragmatic Approach to Genetics* (Lanham, Md.: Rowman and Littlefield, 1997), p. 61.

24. David Wasserman and Robert Wachbroit, eds., *Genetics and Criminal Behavior* (Cambridge: Cambridge University Press, 2001).

should be criminally violent. Nor should everyone with a Y chromosome be assumed to be violent. Nor should those who have the Y chromosome be punished simply for having it. Family history, genetic or social, gives insight into given tendencies but does not direct us to what we should be nor fully form what we are.

We are born with a propensity to ally ourselves with others, but also to put ourselves first, even to the harm of others. That is in striking contrast with what God intends and promises for the future. Whether that compulsion is a result of evolutionary history or a decisive fall or some combination thereof, the point is that it is not now the way it should be or the way it will be. One example is that human beings consistently distinguish between insiders and outsiders. It seems to be rooted in our genes that "outsiders are subject to demonization and decimation," even to the point of genocide.[25] Could our genetic propensities be what has come to be called inheritable original sin (Rom. 5)? Some have argued that "the origins of sinfulness, it would seem, are rooted not in the act of an original, historical couple, but in the complicated evolutionary process itself."[26] If so, did God make a good creation? This might not be a contrary. Before relationship with God, actions destructive of self or others would be harmful, but not sinful. Sin is rebellion against God. There could be pain and suffering before sin. Once God introduces Godself to human beings, the vast opportunities for which they were made become a possibility, and so does the tragic rejection of that offer.

Body and soul are so interrelated that it is a false expectation to change only one or the other. Drinking caffeine to stimulate the body can help one stay alert to pray. Body affects soul. When change in character is achieved through repeated mental choice, a pattern of behavior has changed the pathways of the brain's neural net. Soul affects body. The brain has changed structure so that one actually comes to react and think differently.[27] Soul affects body and body affects soul. We operate on all levels interactively. Change at one level alone will have integrated ramifications or wither away. Chemical and genetic interventions are

25. Peters, "The Evolution of Evil," p. 41.
26. Gregory R. Peterson, "Falling Up: Evolution and Original Sin," in *Evolution and Ethics*, ed. Philip Clayton and Jeffrey Schloss (Grand Rapids: Eerdmans, 2004), p. 283.
27. Paul N. Markham, *Rewired: Exploring Religious Conversion* (Eugene, Oreg.: Pickwick, 2007).

blunt tools. In regard to behavior, they influence temperament but do not decide what one does with the inclination. Again, our genes destine us to be free.

Genetics Are an Important *Part* of Human Life

So much of being human is physical. We are almost always conscious of our experiences of hunger, thirst, sleep, posture, pleasure, heat, and cold. Søren Kierkegaard wrote that the curse of the philosopher is always having to turn aside from the sublime world of thought in order to sneeze. In the words of Genesis, we are dust and to dust we shall return. In the meantime we are physical beings. As stewards of our bodies we should brush our teeth regularly. This is valuing and sustaining them as given. After all, if we ignore our teeth they will go away. When cavities occur we should fill them. This is healing, a necessary part of sustenance in a damaged and damaging world. Even better would be to place a sealant on our teeth. This is a technology that renders them relatively impervious to cavities. We thereby improve their resistance beyond what they would have had on their own. It is wise for us to eat nutritiously and to sleep adequately. That is sustaining our God-given bodies. When we have difficulty fighting off a bacterial infection, the healing of targeted antibiotics is welcome. Even better is a vaccine that quickly and cheaply improves part of our bodies' immune system so that we do not fall sick to a particular disease in the first place.

Our task of growing and improving is progressively more complicated as we age. Sustaining and restoring our physical form require more attention. Our physical life inevitably, eventually, falls apart. Aging is not for sissies. How fitting that the task of living through our bodies becomes more difficult as we are hopefully developing the needed discipline and skills to handle it. It is who we are, not just our current physical form, that has the potential by God's grace to go on beyond this life, dwarfing its fragile and limited starting point. God is creatively sustaining, restoring, and improving the people of God as individuals and as a community. Part of that process is for us to do the same — bearing God's image as individuals and community. That goal is achieved in part by how we sustain, restore, and improve our physical world in general and our bodies in particular. Whether from sin or a good creation that can grow or both, there are aspects of the physical world entrusted to us that could be better. We are called to care for and develop ourselves and our world. How we fulfill that mandate is as crucial as what is developed.

Genetics plays an important role in our physical suffering and relief, our physical capacities and infirmities. Genetic intervention can increasingly address that aspect of our physical life. Genetic tests that trigger effective treatment for hemochromatosis or warn one in time to plan for dementia can be a boon. Genetic pharmaceuticals such as Humulin that sustain a body afflicted with diabetes and genetic surgery that may someday increase capacity to fight disease or to remember are examples of the genuine service genetic intervention can offer. We are physical beings who can be deeply affected and greatly helped by genetic intervention. Human genetics is part of that small temporary dominion where we learn and grow and become more of all we are meant to be.

Even if genetic intervention is widely implemented, there will be limits to what it can physically accomplish. It can be a boon to curing diseases and increasing physical capacity and all the opportunities that may produce. Most of its eventual benefits are probably not yet even envisioned. However, there will still be handicaps, accidents, and disease unresponsive to genetic intervention. Correcting the genetic code cannot cure all physical ills, and a maximum of successful genetic intervention would not meet all genuine physical needs. Physical suffering would not be eliminated. There would still be a need to treat nongenetic diseases, to protect human genes from environmental damage, and to provide people with opportunities to develop the capabilities they have.[28] Further, it appears that daily self-care is far more important for health than any medical intervention. Genetic endowment cannot free persons from personal discipline and responsibility. Genetic intervention can never guarantee physical health, nor can mere physical health guarantee a worthwhile life.

Genes are not all there is to physical life, and the physical is not all there is to life as a whole. Our God-given bodies should be appreciated in their own right, but whether they last for 70, 100, or someday 200 years, they are wonders dwarfed by what lasts. What goes on past this physical life is our person. That is our will, priorities, loves, character, discipline, joys, not our physique. Our physical form is essential

28. World Council of Churches, Church and Society, *Manipulating Life: Ethical Issues in Genetic Engineering* (Geneva: World Council of Churches, 1982), p. 9.

here, intimately instrumental for while we are here. This is where we temporarily live and choose as we become all we can be or less. Part of that process is learning to give our lives in care for others. The physical world is a temporary stage, a place to choose and learn. It is also a stage in the process of what God has in store for his children. Human destiny is beyond the physical world that we know now and that has temporary written all over it.[29] Even our sun will burn out eventually, probably exploding to engulf our planet in flame before leaving anything left of it alone in the dark. Our own lives flicker with no guarantee from day to day and with a maximum length that looks shorter as we approach it.

It is difficult for most of us to remember life in the womb, although all readers of this work have spent considerable time in one. It was dark and warm. All the food and oxygen that one needed were provided, although one had no awareness of the source of that sustaining cord that conveyed them. It was a puzzling place. One was growing legs that only made the close quarters more cramped. Eyes had nothing to see. Lungs were ill suited for the fluid environment. A voice was available but had no one to talk to. Then things took a nasty turn. One was flipped upside down and squeezed hard between the walls. The following hours were probably painful for everybody involved. Then suddenly there were colors for the eyes and the freedom to swing one's legs and arms. One's voice was heard for the first time and welcomed. And then, one met face-to-face the one who had been sustaining one all along.

The classic Christian tradition sees this life compared to the next much as life in the womb was to this one. There is continuity such as the belly button, but also growth to the point of transformation. The brief transition of death leads to a life more colorful and free than this one. God's children will meet face-to-face the One who has sustained them all along and feel more at home than ever before. But one should not be born prematurely. There are things in the womb and in this life that are best done in each. There is growth and development that take place uniquely in each. For a time human beings are this material, but only for a time. The womb matters. The physical world matters. Both deserve appreciation for their maker and how they are used to make us. Neither is the final point. To the degree they go on, they will be transformed. They are places that give opportunities for becoming. Learning

29. Charles E. Curran, "Theology and Genetics: A Multi-faceted Dialogue," *Journal of Ecumenical Studies* 7 (Winter 1970): 75-76.

to rightly sustain, restore, and improve our physical world, including our bodies, is part of that process.

Saint Basil wrote almost two millennia ago that "whatever requires an undue amount of thought or trouble or involves a large expenditure of effort and causes our whole life to revolve, as it were, around solicitude for the flesh must be avoided by Christians."[30] Richard McCormick concurs that "excessive concern for the temporal is at some point neglect of the eternal."[31] Since human beings are physical beings, our physical nature and condition cannot be well ignored,[32] yet the body is not the purpose of human life. Augustine writes that people are to use *(uti)* the world as we enjoy *(frui)* God.[33] Too often people reverse the designed order and try to use God to enjoy the world. As essential as the physical is, it is not all-encompassing. The physical world and health in it are a good, not God. We are all at best only temporarily able-bodied. Life goes on for most without physical perfection. Jesus' own priorities were that he forgave sin first, healing the inner human being, and only then healed the outside body. When Jesus declared that his followers should be perfect-complete, he said nothing of their physical bodies (Matt. 5:48). The physical is important to sustaining our current existence. It is worth sustaining, restoring, and improving, but it is only a part of who we are.

Should We Then Shape Our Genes?

The articulate Robert Song is concerned about the motivation for genetic intervention. "Is this an effort to show what God is like, or an effort to be like God?"[34] As presented, the question is a false dichotomy. Created in

---

30. From "The Long Rules," as quoted by H. Tristram Engelhardt Jr., "Genetic Enhancement and Theosis: Two Models of Therapy," *Christian Bioethics* 5, no. 2 (1999): 198.

31. Richard A. McCormick, "Theology and Bioethics," *Hastings Center Report* 19 (March/April 1989): 10.

32. Midgley, *Beast and Man*, p. 310; C. S. Lewis, *Screwtape Letters* (Grand Rapids: Baker, 1943), pp. 24-25.

33. George Forell, *History of Christian Ethics* (Minneapolis: Augsburg, 1982), p. 169.

34. Robert Song, *Human Genetics: Fabricating the Future* (Cleveland: Pilgrim Press, 2002), p. 77.

God's image, we are called to show what God is like by patterning ourselves after God's character, priorities, and creativity. No degree of
change compounded for a billion years would approach being God. God
is the Creator. We are creatures. Yet by God's grace reflecting God's
presence and care, in that way being *like* God, can show what God is like.
Now Song is right to raise the question of intention. Although intention is
often complex and difficult to discern, it does matter. God knows. With
careful reflection, guidance from the Holy Spirit, and accountability, we
can seek to recognize motivations too. Genetic intervention to try to sup-
plant God would be perverse and doomed to failure. Genetic intervention to reflect God's image in creatively developing what God has entrusted for that purpose could be a fruitful part of our calling.

Would genetic differences make us automatically less human? Or
might certain genetic changes make us *more human* as humans are intended to be? It has been suggested that "no development in the scientific age has challenged our understanding of the nature of man more
than the rapid emergence of the field of clinical genetics."[35] The possibility of altering to some degree human physical attributes through genetic intervention tests our understanding of the nature of human beings. "The question of what constitutes the normatively human is the
most important issue that lurks in all the more specific and concrete
problems we face when ethical issues are raised about developments in
the field of genetics."[36]

The physical nature of human beings is part of what it is to be human. We spend much of our time providing for physical needs, such as
food and shelter, and would quickly cease to exist if such concerns were
not actively pursued. Even if one thinks of human beings as primarily
mind or soul or only temporarily physical while preparing for a transformed eternal life, the current nature of human life is mediated
through and dependent upon the physical body. How one perceives the
purpose and capacity of that physical nature is crucial to whatever
change is appropriate. "Our fundamental decisions will be made, per-

35. Robert M. Veatch, "Ethical Issues in Genetics," in *Progress in Medical Genetics Volume Ten*, ed. Arthur Steinberg and Alexander Bearn (New York: Grune and
Stratton, 1974), p. 224.

36. James M. Gustafson, *Theology and Christian Ethics* (Philadelphia: Pilgrim
Press, 1974), p. 274. This important point is raised as well by others, such as more re-
cently Mark J. Hanson, "Indulging Anxiety: Human Enhancement from a Protestant
Perspective," *Christian Bioethics* 5, no. 2 (1999): 121-22.

haps they have already been made, at the point where we accept a particular understanding of man."[37]

Does being human include remaining as we are physically or changing physically? Human beings have studied what it is to be human for centuries, and have thought about conscious choices that would affect physical heritage. Already 2,500 years ago Plato made a program to encourage good physical inheritance as part of his republic. But for the first time we are now facing the ability to directly and precisely change physical endowment. H. Tristram Engelhardt Jr. has suggested that "human nature, as we know it today, will inevitably — for good secular moral reasons — be technologically reshaped."[38] I will first critique arguments from the nature of humanity for not doing so, and then reasons why we should.

Evaluating Arguments That Physical Attributes Should Remain as They Are Now

Anything Different Would Not Be Human

Appeals to the static nature of human nature take five forms. One is that anything other than our current form would not be us. Leon Kass is concerned that changing the current physical nature of human beings would make us less human. If alteration occurs, "the nonhuman life that may take our place will in some sense be superior — though I personally think it most unlikely, and certainly not demonstrable. In either case, we are ourselves human beings; therefore, it is proper for us to have a proprietary interest in our survival, and in our survival as human beings."[39] For Kass, *current* human physical form is essential to what it is to be human. Paul Ramsey made the same affirmation in *Fabricated Man* when he stated that to transform human beings physically is to re-

37. Paul Ramsey, "Genetic Therapy: A Theologian's Response," in *The New Genetics and the Future of Man*, ed. Michael P. Hamilton (Grand Rapids: Eerdmans, 1972), pp. 171-72.

38. H. Tristram Engelhardt Jr., "Human Nature Technologically Revisited," in *Ethics, Politics, and Human Nature*, ed. Ellen Frankel Paul, Fred D. Miller Jr., and Jeffrey Paul (Oxford: Basil Blackwell, 1991), p. 183.

39. Leon R. Kass, "Making Babies — the New Biology and the Old Morality," *Public Interest* 26 (Winter 1972): 54.

place the current species with a life mistakenly thought to be superior. Ramsey called such an action "species suicide." Our present condition should be the final standard. Human beings are the particular bodies that they are now as much as they are souls and minds. To change this flesh is as much a violation of what is human as violating human will or freedom. The human body is not a tool for a given human being. Human beings *are* bodies. The current human body is part of what it is for a person to be human. To change the current physical form of humans would make us less human or even less than human.

In response, the Christian tradition promises that someday God's people will be transformed as Jesus Christ was. Jesus' resurrection body was recognizable down to the scars in his wrists and side, yet he was also able to pass through doors and to live forever. "What is sown is perishable, what is raised is imperishable. It is sown in dishonor, it is raised in glory" (1 Cor. 15:42-43). That is quite different from our current bodies. God's people will still be the same individuals, but in a strikingly new form. There is still embodiment, but in a new way. Our current physical form is not required to be human. Our current bodies are not necessary to who we will eventually become.

As for the present physical condition of humanity, it is common for many newborns to have major genetic disabilities. Most people do not feel an allegiance to Tay-Sachs disease or inherited diabetes, yet that is part of the human condition currently. Society invests substantially to change, if possible, nature in this regard. Why not in others? Here one might advocate change of current nature to a nature that is disease-free, in which cure of disease would be acceptable, but not further enhancement. However, the goal of maintaining the current form of human beings does not by itself clarify whether it is acceptable to include elimination of common diseases or handicaps, in that current life for human beings includes such maladies. If it does include correcting those conditions, why not include preventative or strengthening interventions? If preventative or strengthening interventions are included, at what point is such intervention straying from loyalty to our present form?

Part of the essence of civilization is to modify our environment and ourselves. Our society has considered it particularly beneficial to change what naturally occurs when the natural is deemed detrimental. Smallpox was a naturally occurring disease until it was eradicated by protracted intentional immunization. In fact, if one is arguing from what seems to be natural, the natural pattern seems to be one of development and change. We have dachshunds and Great Danes within a few centuries. In just the last generation the average height of a Japanese male has increased almost six inches. It is incontrovertible that we have seen change. Is our generation less human because it is taller than past generations? Will our descendants be less human to the degree that they change? Only if "human" is tied to our current physical form.[40] Francis Fukuyama worries that "the most significant threat posed by contemporary biotechnology is the possibility that it will alter human nature and thereby move us into a 'posthuman' stage of history."[41] But are current well-nourished generations, generally healthier than those of the past, more human, less human, or unchanged in humanness due to that evident physical change? Is "human" a static concept that has already been quintessentially achieved or qualities that can be positively developed? That human beings are physical beings does not of itself require that their physical nature remain unchanged. Future descendants, in some ways physically different from our current state or development, may be more human in what we value as human.

Grounding Ethics

Paul Ramsey adds the further concern that modifying our physical form separates us from the ethics of medical practice and our civilization.[42] Apparently for Ramsey the ethics of medical practice and our civilization are based on the current physical state of human beings. To change our physical state would cut us loose from our ethical moorings. Actually this concern leads not to being adrift, but to shifting anchorage. If the point of ethics is to live out appropriately one's physical endowment as the argument assumes, a new physical endowment would

40. David DeGrazia alters the essentialist question from maintaining our identity as *Homo sapiens* to maintaining our identity as hominids. Within the identity of hominid there has been and can continue to be substantial change before and beyond *Homo sapiens*. "Enhancement Technologies and Human Identity," *Journal of Medicine and Philosophy* 30 (2005): 278.

41. Francis Fukuyama, *Our Posthuman Future* (New York: Picador, 2002), p. 7.

42. Paul Ramsey, *Fabricated Man: The Ethics of Genetic Control* (New Haven: Yale University Press, 1978), p. 105.

lead to a new ethic, not a state of being ethics-free. Granted, such an ethic could eventually be quite different from the old one. Genetic change would shift the stated foundation, not eliminate ethical systems being built upon it.

Wisdom of Evolution

A third argument for static human nature is that the current human genome is the pinnacle of billions of years of perfecting trial. It is wise to assume that present approaches have a purpose. There are probably reasons why things are as they are now. But that does not mean that such is already the best that it can be. To reach this point, there has always been room for improvement. If the wisdom of evolution is the standard, would not that indicate that we should keep changing? Why assume that now is the time to stop the lauded process?

By Divine Command

Paul Ramsey argues that God-given dominion reaches over the entire animal world but not to human beings themselves.[43] To intervene in human genetics is to make oneself lord and creator of future generations. Human beings are to serve life, not to change it.[44] Human beings are in no position to claim the ability to improve on what God has made. To even attempt such would be a hubristic attempt to be what we are not. Ramsey adds the further concern that even as human beings gain in knowledge, they will never have sufficient wisdom to use that knowledge properly for any physical change. "The boundless freedom of genetic self determination leads to boundless destruction since no human being or collection of human beings will ever have the wisdom to do it rightly."[45] Only God possesses such wisdom.[46] At this point Ramsey appears to be evaluating human will and discernment more than human knowledge and predicting it to be permanently wanting. Henry Stob

43. Ramsey, *Fabricated Man*, pp. 88, 132.
44. Ramsey, *Fabricated Man*, pp. 95, 138.
45. Ramsey, *Fabricated Man*, p. 96.
46. Ramsey, *Fabricated Man*, p. 149.

concurs that "To tamper with the genes seems to me to 'outrun' God into an unknown future and to exercise an 'elective' discrimination mere men do not possess," nor ever will.[47] In short, for these authors such an attempt would claim the wisdom and right that belong to God alone. Only God has both the authority and ability to form and change us. Altering human physical form is taking on a role that human beings do not possess and should not usurp. Human beings are to enjoy and work within the God-given design of the world as we have received it. Since the body is human, it is not part of the nonhuman world given to human beings for dominion of stewardship and potential modification. Such a position might allow some genetic intervention for the cure of disease to better maintain the God-given design, as Ramsey himself advocates. Further change would be unacceptable. Carl Henry speaks in a similar vein about genetic intervention when he writes, "it is the tragic irony of human existence, however, that when fallen man seeks to elevate himself to super humanity, as if he were himself God and the creator of his cosmic destiny, he soon succeeds only in transforming himself into an iniquitous monster who grandiosely rationalizes the aberrations he elevates as sacred and moral."[48]

A key assumption in these statements is that God's will is known, and it is to maintain the present physical attributes of human beings just as they are. That such is God's will may not be immediately clear.[49] Traditions such as Islam, traditional Roman Catholicism, and evangelical Christianity are convinced that God is all-powerful and purposeful, the source and active sustainer of the world, indeed the founding and ultimate standard of all that is. The key issue for these traditions is delineating precisely what God wants human beings to do and what God retains as God's sole initiative.[50] Different understandings of God and

47. Henry Stob, "Christian Ethics and Scientific Control," in *The Scientist and Ethical Decision,* ed. Charles Hatfield (Downers Grove, Ill.: InterVarsity, 1973), p. 20.

48. Carl Henry, "The New Image of Man," in *The Scientist and Ethical Decision,* ed. Charles Hatfield (Downers Grove, Ill.: InterVarsity, 1973), p. 170.

49. Richard McCormick, in a testimony during United States Congress Committee Hearing on Human Genetic Engineering, Committee Print #170 (1983), p. 334; Curran, "Theology and Genetics," p. 78; Ronald S. Cole-Turner, "Is Genetic Engineering Co-Creation?" *Theology Today* 44 (October 1987): 340.

50. For an apologetic on behalf of divine command ethics (in this case in the Calvinist tradition), see Richard J. Mouw, *The God Who Commands: A Study in Di-*

God's will lead to different conclusions concerning appropriate genetic intervention. Is current human nature already the perfect and final creation of God? Answering yes neglects the effects of sin or the possibility that the first humans were the starting point, not the grand finale of God's intent.

Jesus as the Perfect and Final Form of Humanity

Nigel Cameron and Amy DeBaets argue that the humanness that Jesus Christ bore in the incarnation "sets the standard of all excellences in time and space."[51] Any attempts at enhancement would depart from this standard. The argument has a powerful emotional pull for those in the classic Christian tradition. The tradition looks to Jesus Christ as the perfect image of God who is to be emulated and followed. Cameron and DeBaets's application here of the doctrine of the incarnation, however, is odd at several points.

1. For Jesus' bodily attributes to be a model for us, we would have to know what they were. We do not. Was he tall or short? More active or contemplative? The Gospels do not think this important enough to record.

2. From his time and place, he probably had brown eyes and a Middle Eastern complexion. Is that thereby a standard for all of his followers? Will those with green eyes or freckled skin never reflect the image of Christ or God? Almost every cell of Jesus' body bore a Y chromosome. Will human beings who do not have Y chromosomes never fully reflect his and God's image? Why would some bodily attributes be "the standard of all excellences" and others not?

3. Cameron and DeBaets emphasize that Jesus retains his humanity forever. We do have some descriptions of Jesus' body after the resurrection. He could eat fish and pass through locked doors. If their point is that he is still and forever human even with that resurrected body, then there is a great deal of room for our improvement to ap-

---

vine Command Ethics (Notre Dame, Ind.: University of Notre Dame Press, 1990). Mouw addresses criticism from moral development theories to feminist critiques of inherent patriarchy.

51. Nigel Cameron and Amy DeBaets, in *Design and Destiny: Jewish and Christian Perspectives on Human Germline Modification*, ed. Ronald Cole-Turner (Cambridge: MIT Press, 2008), p. 105.

proach his model of human. Tristram Engelhardt Jr. is also concerned that human beings continue to have the biological humanity that was taken on by Christ.[52] On the same page he cites Methuselah as an early human being who lived for 969 years. If perfected humanity is the standard, there may be quite a bit of room for current human beings to catch up.

Evaluating Arguments That Physical Attributes Should Change

Dynamic Nature

This perspective is not that human beings should abandon their nature. The argument is that human nature is to change. In contrast to Ramsey's understanding of human beings as already in the peak form they are meant to be, James Gustafson for example sees human form developing. Human beings are not yet what we should be, and indeed, we find our purpose in development. When considering obligations to future generations, the current physical form of human beings is not a given. In physical form and the rest of what it is to be human, there is a central place for change. It is primarily in our experience and scientific observation of the human that we gain a sense of what values preserve and enhance the qualities of life that give a sense of fulfillment.[53] That sense of fulfillment is found in having a vocation to surpass what we are now, to move toward a telos we have not yet obtained.[54] The telos is not a set image of what human beings already are or should be, but rather one to be discovered, one that changes and develops as human beings change and develop.[55] The self-creativity of human initiative and freedom is central to humanity itself.[56] For Ramsey human beings are static, for Gustafson dynamic. For Ramsey it is pridefully and foolishly step-

52. H. Tristram Engelhardt Jr., in *Design and Destiny*, p. 86.
53. James M. Gustafson, "Basic Ethical Issues in the Bio-Medical Fields," *Soundings* 52 (1970): 178.
54. James M. Gustafson, "What Is the Normatively Human?" *American Ecclesiastical Review* 165 (1971): 207.
55. Gustafson, "What Is the Normatively Human?" p. 207, and "Basic Ethical Issues," p. 178.
56. Gustafson, *Theology and Christian Ethics*, p. 285.

ping outside of the God-given role for human beings to modify their God-given selves. For Gustafson, self-creation is part of the essence of being human. Genetic enhancement could be a welcome part of that self-creation.

Gustafson argues at length that ethics should be theocentric, but means something quite different from Ramsey's and this author's appeals to God's person and authority. By theocentric Gustafson does not suggest that God has an intention for the future of humanity. For Gustafson God has no intention at all.[57] Rather, Gustafson describes God as the limiting order closely akin to if not synonymous with the current natural order.[58] In any choices, including ethical ones, if human beings hope to survive, they must not choose actions that will destroy their physical existence. God, as the natural order, while not offering positive direction of what is desirable, does make demands as to what must be taken into account if human beings are to survive. Concern for maintaining the physical is then a necessary factor to take into account as human beings modify themselves, if they value the continuance of their lives and that of their descendants.[59] Genetic intervention could be pursued within those survival limitations.

By Divine Command

Authors such as scientist Donald MacKay and theologian Bernard Häring agree with Gustafson that human beings would do well to change, but carry on the Irenaean tradition that God intentionally created this world and is not finished with it yet. It is not now all that the Creator intends it to be. Human beings are called to be part of God's ongoing creation. MacKay does not argue that human dominion may act out its every whim; rather it is to be exercised in a spirit of stewardship responsible to God. Such intervention maintains the world, mitigates some of the effects of human rebellion against God, and develops the world toward a better form. Hans Schwartz and Ronald Cole-Turner have also empha-

---

57. James M. Gustafson, *Ethics from a Theocentric Perspective*, vol. 1, *Theology and Ethics* (Chicago: University of Chicago Press, 1981), p. 272.

58. See the discussion in "Part One: Focus on the Ethics of James M. Gustafson," ed. James F. Childress and Stanley Hauerwas, *Journal of Religious Ethics* 13, no. 1 (1985): 1-112.

59. Gustafson, "Basic Ethical Issues," p. 173.

sized this latter theme of redemption.[60] Current fallen nature is not identical with God-given creation.[61] Without hesitation we often try to repair disabilities that come from genetic heritage. When a child is born with a harelip, we immediately do surgery so that the child can eat and speak with greater ease. When a child is born with the genes for retinoblastoma, we heighten vigilance and treatment so that the child will not lose her eyes or die of cancer. The common warning against the prideful taking of God's place in genetic intervention assumes that God has forbidden intervention or reserved it for God alone. Those who argue that genetic intervention is part of the God-given mandate for human beings to share in creation would see danger not just in pride, but also in fear and sloth. Not fulfilling the responsibility to turn genetic intervention to service would reflect a dangerous and destructive attitude of disobedient apathy. James Walter says that for Roman Catholicism, genes have the same honored status as the rest of the human body, not a unique status.[62] If one can do surgery on other parts of the body, one can do surgery on one's genes.

Human beings are able to change themselves, but in their finitude are always at risk of endangering themselves in those choices. MacKay specifically warns of the potential havoc of even one well-intentioned error. MacKay's response, however, is that such risk does not of itself necessarily abrogate the responsibility to proceed. The implication for MacKay is not inaction, but rather that human beings need divine guidance.[63] Illustrating the problem, he says that navigating by a landmark tied to your own ship's head is pointless.[64] MacKay's response is that a proper heading can be set by seeking God's revealed will such as is found in Christian Scriptures. MacKay writes as one convinced that God has purposefully created the world and human beings and that

60. Hans Schwartz, "Theological Implications of Modern Biogenetics," *Zygon* 5 (September 1970): 263; Cole-Turner, "Is Genetic Engineering Co-Creation?" pp. 338-49, and *The New Genesis: Theology and the Genetic Revolution* (Louisville: Westminster John Knox, 1993).

61. Max L. Stackhouse, *Public Theology and Political Economy: Christian Stewardship in Modern Society* (Lanham, Md.: University Press of America, 1991), p. 144.

62. James J. Walter, "Theological Perspectives on Cancer Genetics and Gene Therapy" (Memphis: St. Jude Children's Research Hospital, May 28, 1999).

63. Donald MacKay, "Biblical Perspectives in Human Engineering," in *Modifying Man: Implications and Ethics*, ed. Craig Ellison (Washington, D.C.: University Press of America, 1978), p. 72.

64. Donald M. MacKay, in *Man and His Future*, ed. G. E. W. Wolstenholme (Boston: Little, Brown, 1963), p. 286, as quoted by Ramsey, *Fabricated Man*, p. 124.

God sets standards for their best development. If one is open to listen and obey, God will guide one to the best service of God and others. MacKay is hopeful on the basis of biblical texts such as James 1:5 that God will graciously give wisdom to those who ask for it. Sufficient guidance will not come from the current order of nature. The Christian apostle Paul wrote that the whole creation groans in travail waiting for redemption (Rom. 8:19-23). It is not currently all that it was meant to be. The standard for intervention is prayerful submission to God and then acting as seems best to express love of God and neighbor. "All human exploitation of natural laws and resources must be an expression of this love, and of nothing else, if it is to be acceptable."[65] MacKay is not sanguine that people will consistently listen to God or listen well. Granting the presence of sin that obscures judgment and twists motives, MacKay calls for "answerability" to God and others in all such decisions. Any intervention must be incremental and reversible so that adjustments can be made in the face of tremendous complexity.[66]

One's understanding of being human, as physically fixed or changing, will determine whether physical change of itself has the potential to lead toward the positive development of human beings or, in choosing to change, the destruction of humanity. If the description of human beings as physically static beings is most compelling, no genetic improvement is appropriate. If human beings are called to develop themselves, then purposeful and direct enhancement of capacity could be appropriate, even sometimes required.

Is Procreation a Special Off-Limits Case?

If it is natural and our mandate as human beings to intervene in nature, including our genes, does procreation remain a special off-limits case? Procreation is the place where we welcome into the world new human beings, people with potential to know God and live with God forever. Nurturing these new lives is one of the most important things we can do. Is it essential that we not intervene in any part of the life-giving process? Human beings were created to naturally change nature. We al-

---

65. MacKay, "Biblical Perspectives," p. 69.

66. Donald MacKay, *Human Science and Human Dignity* (London: Hodder and Stoughton, 1979), p. 61.

91

ready without hesitation intervene in the natural process of procreation by giving painkillers to mothers during the often arduous process of birth and resorting to the surgery of a Cesarean section if needed to save the life of the mother or baby. Neither intervention detracts from God's purpose in human procreation. Would gamete selection detract from what God is doing? If one's view of providence includes God choosing the genetic start for each human being, God can work through the intentional acts of human beings as well as through apparently random acts of nature. God can write straight even if our lines are crooked.

For Paul Ramsey, altering human biological development would be making human beings less human.[67] Unless natural human parentage is kept inviolate, technological civilization will fragment the personal and biological dimensions of human procreation.[68] To separate in any way procreation from the act of love is to be reduced to reproduction, not procreation, a manufacturing process rather than embodied personhood.[69] In contrast Joseph Fletcher argues that it is artificial reproduction that is particularly personal and human in that "it is rationally willed, chosen, purposed and controlled."[70] For Fletcher the very definition of "civilized" is to intervene artificially.[71] More in parallel with Ramsey, the magisterium of the Roman Catholic Church instructs that each conjugal act should always be open to procreation as its natural course.[72] Since sexual intimacy is where procreation naturally begins, the unitive and procreative aspects are God-designed and inseparable. One cannot for example use a barrier method of birth control. Now it is fascinating that the Roman Catholic Church does encourage the

67. Ramsey, *Fabricated Man*, p. 137. Also see Leon Kass, *Toward a More Natural Science: Biology and Human Affairs* (New York: Free Press, 1985), p. 109, and more recently Leon Kass, "The Moral Meaning of Genetic Technology," *Commentary*, September 1999, p. 36, and Dennis P. Hollinger, "Sexual Ethics and Reproductive Technologies," in *The Reproductive Revolution*, ed. John F. Kilner, Paige C. Cunningham, and W. David Hager (Grand Rapids: Eerdmans, 2000), pp. 79-91.

68. Ramsey, *Fabricated Man*, p. 136.

69. Ramsey, *Fabricated Man*, p. 89.

70. Joseph Fletcher, "New Beginnings in Life: A Theologian's Response," in *The New Genetics and the Future of Man*, p. 87.

71. Joseph Fletcher, *The Ethics of Genetic Control* (Garden City, N.J.: Doubleday, 1974), p. 15.

72. *The Gift of Life (Donum Vitae): Instruction on Respect for Human Life in Its Origin and on the Dignity of Procreation* was published by the Congregation for the Doctrine of the Faith of the Roman Catholic Church.

rhythm method of birth control. One may intentionally time inter-course to avoid conception. This is understood as working with God-given nature, not contrary to it. Even for the Roman Catholic tradition one can consciously shape the overall process, but to what degree?

It makes sense that rightly lived sexual intimacy is an ideal place to welcome new life. Sexual intimacy in the Christian tradition is a gift of God to celebrate a lifelong commitment between a woman and a man.[73] The husband and wife choose to love and share intimately at every level. Their marriage is to be a place of acceptance and enjoyment, a place where they develop habits of self-giving and forgiveness needed to enjoy any long-term commitment. Their relationship skills grow and mature over time. Where that is done well is an ideal place to start a new human life. The newborn enters a family where care and enjoyment of one another are modeled and consistent. In contrast, when sex is merely sport between temporary sequential playmates, it is no longer associated with the welcoming place for new life, hence one of the reasons for the high demand for abortion in cultures that have demeaned the role of sexual intimacy. Sexual intimacy can be a committed, unitive, celebration of lifelong commitment without bearing children, and a couple who cannot conceive children on their own can still provide the intended welcome and place for new life while receiving physical help in conception or pregnancy.

Psychological studies have shown that "children conceived by ART [artificial reproduction techniques] did not differ from naturally conceived children in emotions, behavior, or quality of family relations."[74] For that matter, the model of becoming part of God's family is one of adoption. In what is often called the holy family of Joseph, Mary, and Jesus, the family into which God chose to be incarnate, the son was not genetically related to his father nor was he conceived by sexual intimacy. While this is a special situation, it would not seem that God would use an inherently destructive method to enter the world. The unitive and procreative aspects of sexual intercourse fit well together, but they are

73. Dennis Hollinger describes this gift as ideally one of consummation, procreation, love, and pleasure. "Sexual Ethics," pp. 80-86.

74. Susan Golombok et al., "Families Created by the New Reproductive Technologies: Quality of Parenting and Social and Emotional Development of the Children," *Child Development* 66 (1995): 285, 295; Frank van Balen, "Child-Rearing Following In Vitro Fertilization," *Journal of Child Psychology and Psychiatry and Allied Disciplines* 37 (1996): 687, 692.

93

not in every case inseparable. Sexual union can be a celebration of life intimacy and commitment even if one does not bear children. A wife and husband can provide a welcoming home for children even if their sexual union by itself does not achieve procreation. Intervening in the biological course of procreation is not automatically harmful to the child or the parents. What is central is how the child is welcomed and raised by her mother and father, not her point of origin. A further question of whether intervention to enable or shape procreation encourages harmful attitudes toward children will be addressed in chapter 5.

So What Place for Human Genetic Intervention?

Money does not have to be the point of life for us to seek to improve our economic system. Economic success is an instrumental good. For most places and times raising enough food to survive has been all-consuming. When there is material abundance, people can be freed from the all-encompassing pursuit of basic needs to pursue what matters most. Material abundance makes possible reading this book, rather than weeding a bare subsistence vegetable patch. Improving medical care does not require that health is all that matters. Rather, it is worth bettering medical care to support physical health so that society and individuals are that much freer from disabilities that distract from what most matters. Genetic improvement would be a poor end in itself, but it can free one from certain constraints and enable one in some ways to pursue what does matter most. Genetic change can aid in survival, relief of suffering, and increased abilities to communicate, enjoy, and serve one another and the rest of God's creation. The point is to be content, but never complacent. We are to seek what is better, not to expect to achieve perfection. While some translations of Matthew have Jesus calling his people to be "perfect as your heavenly Father is perfect," a better translation would be that we are to be complete, whole. By God's grace we are to fulfill our calling. At the center of that calling is rest in God and nothing less. Rest does not have to mean frozen in place. Rest in God should live and breathe and move and grow.

George Herbert (1593-1633) writes in "The Pulley":

When God at first made man,
Having a glass of blessings standing by,

"Let us," said he, "pour on him all we can:
Let the world's riches, which dispersed lie,
Contract into a span."
So strength first made a way;
Then beauty flowed, then wisdom, honour, pleasure;
When almost all out, God made a stay,
Perceiving that, alone of all his treasure,
Rest in the bottom lay.
"For if I should," said he,
Bestow this jewel also on my creature,
He would adore my gifts instead of me,
And rest in nature, not the God of Nature:
So both should losers be,
"Yet let him keep the rest,
But keep them with repining restlessness;
Let him be rich and weary, that at least,
If goodness lead him not, yet weariness
May toss him to my breast."

While genetic intervention could offer substantial changes for the better in individual or community lives, the most significant choices of life will not be enhanced or set right by any kind or degree of physical intervention.[75] The most important choices in life are not primarily physical ones. Some have hoped that the use of genetic intervention over time and enhanced by culture will eventually lead to earthly utopia.[76] Others have observed that in human experience solutions consistently lead to further problems and questions.[77] This expectation has been reflected in most modern utopian literature, which describes worlds of indeterminate process, hopefully progressing rather than making claims of an achieved final standard.[78] Yet many religious and

75. Hessel Bouma III et al., *Christian Faith, Health, and Medical Practice* (Grand Rapids: Eerdmans, 1989), p. 267.

76. Robert Sinsheimer, as quoted by Leon Kass, "New Beginnings in Life," in *The New Genetics and the Future of Man*, p. 59.

77. Roger L. Shinn, "The Ethics of Genetic Engineering," in *The Implications of the Chemical-Biological Revolution* (North Dakota State University, 1967), p. 22; Curran, "Theology and Genetics," p. 81.

78. Elizabeth Hansot, *Perfection and Progress: Two Modes of Utopian Thought* (Cambridge: MIT Press, 1974), p. 13. An example of the former might include Plato's

nonreligious traditions are quite hopeful that despite severe setbacks, good can and will increase. Whatever one's eschatology, it is not genetic intervention that will bring heaven or a utopia.[79] Published hopes that genetic intervention might deliver us from homelessness, alcoholism, criminality, divorce, and more are expecting more than change in our bodies can provide.[80]

Genetic intervention, however, could make a portion of life better for people. Some increases in one kind of capability would be mutually exclusive with other enhancements. The physique of a weight lifter is not suitable for a long-distance runner. Yet probably all could benefit from greater resistance to cancer or a better ability to remember what one wants to remember. Christians are responsible to God as faithful stewards to use well the capabilities they have. Allen Verhey has suggested a balance of vision and realism, hope and prudence, that knows both the common grace of God and the intransigence of human pride and sloth.[81] Genetic intervention in human beings may at best change the physical capacity of human beings. What human beings would choose to do with that increased capability remains an open question. We do well to keep in mind not only the boon of the proposed changes, but also the limitations of what genetic change can do for physical health and capacity, as well as what physical change can achieve for life in general.

Our bodies do not have to be perfect to serve God well. Yet, more capable bodies are more capable. Having a body genetically freed from consuming pain frees us to focus on more important things. Having a body genetically enabled to a greater capacity may give us more ability to pursue what matters most. If genetic intervention could someday increase our powers of perception and understanding of human emotion,

---

Republic, while of the latter Marge Piercy's *Woman on the Edge of Time* (New York: Fawcett Crest, 1976) or B. F. Skinner's *Walden II* (New York: Macmillan, 1948).

79. John Passmore, *The Perfectibility of Man* (New York: Scribner, 1970).

80. Neil A. Holtzman, "Policy Implications of Genetic Technologies," *International Journal of Technology Assessment* 10, no. 4 (1994): 570-71; Robert N. Proctor, "Genomics and Eugenics: How Fair Is the Comparison?" in *Gene Mapping: Using Law and Ethics as Guides*, ed. George J. Annas and Sherman Elias (New York: Oxford University Press, 1992), pp. 76-93.

81. Allen Verhey, "The Morality of Genetic Engineering," *Christian Scholar's Review* 14, no. 2 (1985): 133. John Stott has described such a course as refusing to be deceived by utopian dreams but also refusing to give up in hopelessness, in *The Year 2000* (Downers Grove, Ill.: InterVarsity, 1983).

we could provide more effective counseling. Of course, we would also be equipped better to run a more lucrative con game.[82] Increasing our ability does not automatically direct those newfound possibilities to good ends.

Genetic technology, as with other technologies, at least makes nature less demanding. Our responsibility is for what we do with our newfound freedom. Central heating guided by a thermostat frees us from devoting a major portion of the day to monitoring room temperature and then chopping and hauling wood. Central heating is a gift of time that can be used to watch television, listen to Scripture, enjoy a friend, repair a leaky faucet, teach a child, nurse a sick parent, or create a work of art. With the modification of ourselves and our environment, there are fewer external requirements for conscious choice and self-discipline. It used to be that if one lazed away the day, one was cold that night. Now one can be just as comfortable anyway. The newfound freedom from meeting natural needs gives greater responsibility for what one chooses to do. With more choices there is more responsibility. Jesus said, "To whom much has been given, much will be required" (Luke 12:48). We are responsible for what we do with what we have. The freedom that used to be available only to the wealthy, who could use servants to insulate themselves from daily tasks, is now available to most of us in technologically rich countries. We can go on to new challenges or not challenge ourselves at all.

Genetics does not automatically make us better. It can make us more capable. Genetic intervention, like many technologies, frees us from some constraints and increases our abilities and choices. Pursued as an end in itself, it is at best a distraction, and when all-consuming, idolatry. If all we manage to do is relieve physical suffering and control our physical world in the finest degree, our potential will be wasted.[83] Such an effort is worthwhile as a means, but is not the ultimate point. The gain is not substantial if the newly available time and energy are squandered. Genetics can free and empower us in some ways, but for what? Staying in retirement resorts frittering away years of hard-won

82. Allen Buchanan et al., *From Chance to Choice: Genetics and Justice* (Cambridge: Cambridge University Press, 2000), pp. 179-81.

83. Gerald P. McKenney calls the single-minded effort to relieve suffering and expand human choice "the Baconian Project." He critiques it in *To Relieve the Human Condition: Bioethics, Technology, and the Body* (Albany: State University of New York Press, 1997).

growth and insight on self-entertainment? Having a genetically honed body is potentially helpful to more worthy goals; it is an instrumental good, not an intrinsic one. It can even be harmful if the pursuit or use of its extended life and capacities either distracts us from what most matters or so insulates us from challenges for a time that we fail to realize our most important needs in time.

Genetically healing or increasing our physical capacity gives one more opportunity to do the things that matter. As in the parable of the talents, we are to multiply what we have in order to serve better (Matt. 25:14-30). Having great memory is just a parlor trick by itself. Using an expanded ease in memory to learn a new language so that one can encounter, enjoy, and serve firsthand people with whom one could not communicate before, is a worthy use. An improved immune system that frees one from cancer or the common cold so that one can more comfortably play cards or hit the slot machines misses the point. Freedom from disease and increase of capacity so that one can better worship, care, serve — so that one can better *live* — is the point. The womb was essential to our presence and development, but it would not be a fully satisfying human life if our lives stopped there. The physical world, including our genes, is the place where we choose, learn, and grow now. It does not have to be our end. It can by God's grace be our beginning. Even as we are part of the world, part of our calling is to transcend what it would be without us, to add to it uniquely, to become more than what we started with. The service of genetic intervention need not pursue perfection, just improvement. As human genetics offers us increasingly formative interventions, how do we discern their best use? That is the endeavor of the following chapters.

II Three Helpful Cautions, but Inadequate Guides for Shaping Human Nature

4 Cure versus Enhancement

Human nature is constantly changing and, consciously or not, we play a role in what we become. We should be conscious of our part and act conscientiously. How do we discern what is appropriate direction for that change? I will describe and evaluate three often proffered lines of demarcation that are helpful cautions, but misleading as standards. Each one extends due warning but, if applied woodenly, also rules out things we should do. I will point out how we can gain by their counsel without grinding to a halt where we should proceed.

The first caution is cure versus enhancement. Mechanical enhancements are routine. We are happy if eyeglasses give us sharp 20/15 vision or impact-resilient running shoes extend the distance our legs can run. It is commonly argued, however, that genetic interventions in particular should be used only to cure or avoid ailments, not to improve our bodies.[1] It is welcome that genetically manufactured human insulin helps millions of diabetics to sustain their bodies. But genetic intervention should not be used to increase resistance to diabetes first occurring. The prohibition is further complicated in that genetic pharmaceuticals that are accepted to improve function toward typical levels will often be capable of improving function beyond typical levels. A gene product to increase muscle mass of a patient with degenerative muscle disease might be able to increase muscle mass desired by a competitive weight lifter.[2] A child with attention

---

1. For example, Jürgen Habermas, *The Future of Human Nature* (Cambridge: Polity Press, 2003), p. 52.
2. Example from Erik Parens, "Is Better Always Good? The Enhancement Pro-

deficit disorder can use Ritalin to focus better, while others can use it to concentrate at work or enjoy a contemplative experience. Pharmaceuticals developed for one purpose are sometimes quite effective for another. Once a substance is available, it is difficult to control off-label uses.

Yet there are thoughtful people who argue passionately that any human genetic intervention should be used only to cure disease or maintain health.[3] Sustaining and restoring the body are welcome, but not attempts at improvement.[4] In 1985 W. French Anderson, a leading scholar in molecular hematology then at the National Institutes of Health, may have been the first to use the now standard term "enhancement" for genetic attempts at improvement.[5] He stated that "on medical and ethical grounds we should draw a line excluding any form of enhancement engineering. We should not step over the line that delineates treatment from enhancement."[6] The Medical Ethics Code of the American Medical Association affirmed as well that genetic intervention should "be utilized only for therapeutic purposes in the treatment of human disorders — not for the enhancement or eugenic development of patients or their offspring."[7] European medical research

---

ject," in *Enhancing Human Traits: Ethical and Social Implications,* ed. Erik Parens (Washington, D.C.: Georgetown University Press, 1998), p. 2.

3. For example, Sondra Wheeler, "A Theological Appraisal of Parental Power," and Cynthia B. Cohen, "Oversight of Germ-Line Intervention," in *Designing Our Descendants* (Baltimore: Johns Hopkins University Press, 2003), pp. 238-51 and 296-310, respectively.

4. Michael J. Sandel, *The Case against Perfection: Ethics in an Age of Genetic Engineering* (Cambridge: Harvard University Press, 2007); Leon Kass, "Ageless Bodies, Happy Souls: Biotechnology and the Pursuit of Perfection," *New Atlantis,* Spring 2003, pp. 9-28.

5. In congressional hearings and "Human Gene Therapy: Scientific and Ethical Considerations," *Journal of Medicine and Philosophy* 10 (1985): 275-91. Also in regard to human genetics, but with quite a different process in mind, Hermann J. Muller called for "*enhancing* genetic selection" (Muller's italics) in a 1963 article advocating voluntary artificial insemination by selected donors: "Genetic Progress by Voluntarily Conducted Germinal Choice," in *Man and His Future,* ed. Gordon Wolstenholme (Boston: Little, Brown, 1963), pp. 247-62.

6. W. French Anderson, "Genetics and Human Malleability," *Hastings Center Report* 20 (January/February 1990): 24; "Human Gene Therapy: Why Draw a Line?" *Journal of Medicine and Philosophy* 14 (1989): 681-93.

7. As quoted by Arash Kimyai-Asadi and Peter B. Terry, "Ethical Considerations in Pulmonary Genetic Testing and Gene Therapy," *American Journal of Respiratory and Critical Care Medicine* 155, no. 1 (January 1997): 7.

councils have affirmed correcting specific genetic defects while stating that attempts at enhancement should not even be contemplated.[8] At the Council for International Organizations of Medical Sciences XXIVth Round Table Conference in Inuyama, Japan, Working Group B: Genetic Screening and Testing concurred that "the paramount guiding principle in the proper use of genetic services must be the concern about an actual or possible health problem."[9] In contrast, at the same conference, Working Group C: Human Gene Therapy acknowledged the distinction between cure and enhancement as important, but called for more discussion, not a ban, on whether enhancing normal capacities might be appropriate.[10] Paulina Taboada writes that drawing "a distinction between the use of gene transfer techniques to enhance traits in relation to the treatment of health problems and their use to enhance or improve human traits *per se* seems to be of the utmost importance."[11]

This has been a common conclusion as well for many scholars approaching the issue from specifically the varied Christian tradition.[12] Robert Song states that the distinction is important theologically:

> There is, in other words, a proper role for therapeutic intervention against disease and bodily disorder, as a sign of the Kingdom which is the restoration and fulfillment of creation. But if this is so, somehow a distinction needs to be made between those activities which are genuinely therapeutic, and those which, in a more Gnostic spirit, amount to efforts to transcend the created order. Despite the difficulties we have already seen, and although the distinction still needs to be properly located, some kind of distinction between therapy and enhancement is at the heart of Chris-

8. H. Danielson, "Gene Therapy in Man: Recommendation of European Medical Research Councils," *Lancet* 1 (1988): 1271.

9. Council for International Organizations of Medical Sciences, "The Declaration of Inuyama and Reports of the Working Groups," *Human Gene Therapy* 2 (1991): 126-27.

10. "Declaration of Inuyama and Reports," pp. 128-29.

11. Paulina Taboada, "Human Genetic Enhancement: Is It Really a Matter of Perfection?" *Christian Bioethics* 5, no. 2 (1999): 192.

12. Andrew Lustig, "Enhancement Technologies and the Person: Christian Perspectives," *Journal of Law, Medicine and Ethics* (Spring 2008): 41-50; D. P. O'Mathuna, "Genetic Technology, Enhancement, and Christian Values," *National Catholic Bioethics Quarterly* 2 (2002): 227-95.

tian claims about the nature of human beings and the meaning of salvation.[13]

I have already argued against the idea that the created order is static, as well as misplaced hopes for genetic salvation. What I want to note here is again the prominence of drawing a line between therapy/cure and enhancement. Distinguishing between intervention to cure disease and enhancement is so commonly cited as the line between right and wrong use that I will devote the rest of this chapter to thinking through what the differences are between cure and enhancement. The distinction depends on how one defines disease and health, so that will be my focus. Three definitions of disease and six definitions of health will be described. It will be clear that the divide between cure and enhancement is often difficult to distinguish. Most important to this discussion will be that all but one of the definitions welcome physical improvement over time and the definition that rejects change is not persuasive. Since the more compelling definitions accommodate physical improvement over time, there is actually little difference between the ultimate goals of cure and enhancement. More clear and relevant criteria are needed to guide the use of genetic intervention. Two other distinctions that are helpful cautions but poor guidelines are addressed in chapters 5 and 6. A workable set of standards will be offered in part III.

Intervention Only to Cure Disease

Some ethical systems emphasize choice guides other than lines of demarcation. For example, virtues can take central place. Virtues are "a kind of second nature that dispose us not only to do the right thing rightly but also to gain pleasure from what we do."[14] Even from this perspective emphasizing character, descriptive lines may be used to help recognize what is indeed virtuous.[15] Another possible focal point

13. Robert Song, *Human Genetics: Fabricating the Future* (Cleveland: Pilgrim Press, 2002), pp. 68-69.

14. Stanley Hauerwas, "Virtue," in *The Westminster Dictionary of Christian Ethics*, ed. James F. Childress and John Macquarrie (Philadelphia: Westminster, 1986), p. 648.

15. Edmund D. Pellegrino makes this case in *The Christian Virtues in Medical Practice* (Washington, D.C.: Georgetown University Press, 1996).

for ethical evaluation is the situation itself met by responsive flexibility, yet here one still typically uses some sort of standard to judge the particular situation. Joseph Fletcher, famous for his "situation ethics," was actually more of a rule-monist than a total situationist.[16] While emphasizing flexibility in context, he still appealed consistently to one rule, namely, to always do the loving thing. Some sort of line-drawing is typical of moral reflection. It is also characteristic of law or other public policy-making where consistent expectations and results are highly valued. "Line-drawing is the ordinary business of moralists and lawmakers. It says that up to a certain point such-and-such a value will be preserved, but after that point another value will have play."[17]

Some scholars accept the possibility of conceptual distinctions but despair of lines actually functioning in society, yet historically there have been some ethical lines effectively drawn and honored. What can be done is not necessarily what is done. Our society's ban on using prisoners for medical research is a case in point.[18] While the utility of a controlled population with a debt to society invited experimentation in the past, a line has been drawn not to use prisoners as research subjects. The coercive environment in prison makes freedom of choice too problematic. That line is currently honored in North American society and elsewhere.

Is there a line that should be honored between ethically acceptable and unacceptable genetic intervention?[19] LeRoy Walters has created an influential diagram to classify genetic intervention into four types.[20]

	Cure of Disease	*Enhancement of Capacity*
somatic cells	1	3
germ-line cells	2	4

16. Joseph Fletcher, *Situation Ethics: The New Morality* (Philadelphia: Westminster, 1966).

17. John T. Noonan Jr., "An Almost Absolute Value in History," in *The Morality of Abortion: Legal and Historical Perspectives*, ed. John T. Noonan Jr. (Cambridge: Harvard University Press, 1970), p. 50.

18. John Fletcher, "Evolution of Ethical Debate about Human Gene Therapy," *Human Gene Therapy* 1 (Spring 1990): 65.

19. Paul J. M. Van Tongeren, "Ethical Manipulations: An Ethical Evaluation of the Debate Surrounding Genetic Engineering," *Human Gene Therapy* 2 (1991): 73.

20. LeRoy Walters, "Genetics and Reproductive Technologies," in *Medical Ethics*, ed. Robert M. Veatch (Boston: Jones and Bartlett Publishers, 1989), pp. 220-21.

The classification depends on two lines of distinction.[21] One is the difference between somatic and germ-line therapy, which will be discussed in chapter 6. The other is a distinction between interventions to cure disease and those to enhance capacity. We will test that latter line here.

The difficulty of setting an exact line between cure of disease and enhancement of capacity has been freely admitted since first proposed by those who advocate the distinction.[22] Yet advocates persist.[23] Others reject the distinction due to its lack of clarity, for when a disease is cured the capacity of the recipient *has been enhanced*. Cure of disease includes increase in functional capability. Someone cured of blindness has gained the capacity to see. People cured of a fever have gained the capacity to regulate their body temperature and energy to pursue tasks of their choice. The words "cure" and "enhance" both refer to development from a person's present state to one that is preferred. Almost any desired change can be described as relief from a negative, hence a cure, or attainment of a positive, hence an enhancement. "Cured" and "enhanced" do not of themselves differentiate one end state from the other. Distinguishing between them rests on stipulation of their end goals. Some authors stipulate that what they mean by enhancement is improvement beyond cure. Juan Torres offers a variation on this view,

21. Others have developed four-part typologies, although as in the case of W. French Anderson, the distinguishing terms are not always the same. In 1985, Anderson termed his four divisions "somatic-cell therapy, germline cell therapy, enhancement genetic engineering, and eugenic genetic engineering." See his "Human Gene Therapy: Scientific and Ethical Considerations," pp. 275-91. Richard A. McCormick uses the same description in *The Critical Calling: Reflections on Moral Dilemmas Since Vatican II* (Washington, D.C.: Georgetown University Press, 1989), p. 265.

22. Clifford Grobstein and Michael Flower, "Gene Therapy: Proceed with Caution," *Hastings Center Report* 14, no. 2 (April 1984): 15; Thomas H. Murray, "Ethical Issues in Genetic Engineering," *Social Research* 52, no. 3 (Autumn 1985): 488-89; Gregory Fowler, Eric T. Juengst, and Burke K. Zimmerman, "Germ-Line Gene Therapy and the Clinical Ethos of Medical Genetics," *Theoretical Medicine* 10 (June 1989): prepublication copy pp. 2 and 18; John Lantos, Mark Siegler, and Leona Cuttler, "Ethical Issues in Growth Hormone Therapy," *JAMA* 261, no. 7 (February 17, 1989): 1020-24; Martin Benjamin, James L. Muyskens, and Paul Saenger, "Short Children, Anxious Parents: Is Growth Hormone the Answer?" *Hastings Center Report* 14, no. 2 (April 1984): 5-9.

23. For a recent example see Paul Jersila, *The Nature of Our Humanity: A Christian Response to Evolution and Biotechnology* (Minneapolis: Fortress, 2009), p. 112.

arguing that what is important is not whether there is an actual enhancement, but rather what the goal of the enhancement is.[24] An enhancement of the body's immune system in general or in its ability to survive a disease treatment is an enhancement beyond the cure of a single disease, yet it is appropriate since the intent is related to the cure of disease.[25] Enhancement of traits other than those related to avoiding or curing disease would not be acceptable. Torres' distinction, like all other attempts to distinguish between cure and enhancement, depends on effectively defining disease. Enhancement works toward a point where improvement is no longer possible in that the optimum state has been reached, while cure of disease works toward being disease-free as an optimal state. What is this "disease" that cure seeks to eliminate?

It will not help to focus on specifically *genetic* disease. Defining a genetic subcategory of disease raises complicating questions, such as whether to include recessive heterozygotes or only phenotypes.[26] It is enough here to define the more general term "disease." The distinction between cure of disease and enhancement of capacity for genetic intervention depends simply on the cure of disease through genetic means. Any disease that could be treated through genetic intervention would be included without needing to define the disease as exclusively or primarily a *genetic* disease. For example, cardiovascular disease is not generally categorized as a genetic disease, yet genetic drugs have been projected as a way to prevent or ameliorate it.[27]

Definitions of disease are many.[28] Some have despaired in print over

24. Juan Manuel Torres, "On the Limits of Enhancement in Human Gene Transfer: Drawing the Line," *Journal of Medicine and Philosophy* 22, no. 1 (1997): 43-53; or, more recently, E. Parens, "Authenticity and Ambivalence: Towards Understanding the Enhancement Debate," *Hastings Center Report* 35 (2005): 34-41.

25. Eric T. Juengst argues a similar tack specifically for the profession of medicine in "Can Enhancement Be Distinguished from Prevention in Genetic Medicine?" *Journal of Medicine and Philosophy* 22 (1997): 125-42.

26. For a detailed analysis of the concept of genetic disease in particular, see Eric Thomas Juengst, *The Concept of Genetic Disease and Theories of Medical Progress*, vols. 1 and 2 (Ann Arbor: University Microfilms International, Dissertation Service, 1985).

27. William B. Schwartz, *Life without Disease: The Pursuit of Medical Utopia* (Berkeley: University of California Press, 1998), p. 129.

28. Whether disease is in some sense an entity in itself as in the medieval realism of the Platonic tradition or descriptive of a recurring pattern with no ontological reality outside its particular manifestation, as in nominalism, does not have to be re-

trying to define disease as carefully as the rest of evidence-based medicine.[29] Yet since definitions of disease often set general expectations of health-care givers and others, they have continued to receive a great deal of attention.[30] This is said with full recognition that individual treatment choices are often influenced more in practice by highly specific guidelines for particular situations than by broad general theories of disease.[31] Theories of disease broad enough to account for treatment programs for everything from emergency surgery to counseling for clinical depression are generally not specific enough to guide direct treatment decisions. A physician faced with a child's bulging eardrum and pain is more likely to think in terms of ampicillin dosage than whether "disease" is present. On the other hand, clinical judgments do not occur in a vacuum. The concepts of disease brought to bear by the physician, patient, and society in a clinical encounter will set perspective and expectations that influence the considerable latitude of negotiated treatment choices.

I am particularly interested for this study in whether definitions of disease lead to a steady state of maintaining function as we now know it or to gradual improvement in physical capacity. If the latter, cure of disease and enhancement might differ more in speed of change than in goal. Granting the complexity of offered definitions, most can be grouped roughly into two sets.[32] These two sets receive various titles, including complaint/functionalist,[33] normativist/neutralist,[34] and

---

solved here. If one wishes to pursue the venerable discussion of the metaphysics of disease, a good place to become oriented would be with Lester S. King, "What Is Disease?" in *Concepts of Health and Disease: Interdisciplinary Perspectives,* ed. Arthur L. Caplan, H. Tristram Engelhardt Jr., and James J. McCartney (Reading, Mass.: Addison-Wesley, 1981), pp. 114-18.

29. Andreas Gerber, Frieder Hentzelt, and Karl W. Lauterbach, "Can Evidence-Based Medicine Implicitly Rely on Current Concepts of Disease or Does It Have to Develop Its Own Definition?" *Journal of Medical Ethics* 33 (2007): 394-99.

30. Mervyn Susser, "Ethical Components in the Definition of Health," in *Concepts of Health and Disease,* p. 94. See also H. Tristram Engelhardt Jr. and Stuart F. Spicker, eds., *Evaluation and Explanation in the Biomedical Sciences* (Dordrecht: D. Reidel, 1975).

31. Mark Siegler, "The Doctor-Patient Encounter and Its Relationship to Theories of Health and Disease," in *Concepts of Health and Disease,* p. 631.

32. Bjorn Hofmann, "Complexity of the Concept of Disease as Shown through Rival Theoretical Frameworks," *Theoretical Medicine* 22 (2001): 211-36.

33. Siegler, "The Doctor-Patient Encounter," p. 629.

34. H. Tristram Engelhardt Jr., "Health and Disease, Values in Defining," in *The Westminster Dictionary of Christian Ethics,* pp. 261-62.

evaluatory/explanatory.[35] The labels carry different connotations and emphases, but in each pair the first term refers to disease as rooted in the preferences of the evaluator and the second to disease as a particular measurable standard of human biology. In other words, disease is usually characterized as either a matter of human preference as to what is undesirable or a matter of human biology in failing to meet a physical standard.

If disease is defined by human preference, eliminating it calls for improvement toward a physical form that best meets human goals. In contrast, definitions of disease based on human biology attempt to be value-free. However, the biology-based definitions face a new situation with the development of genetic intervention. Human biology can be genetically changed. Definitions of disease based on human biology are built on potentially moving ground. Only one influential definition of disease and health has an unchanging application over time. Its standard is not in human preference or biology. We will address that one last. The other definitions offer standards that welcome improvement over time.

Disease as a Value-Free Description

If patients presented that they regularly fall into periods of muscle paralysis and hallucination, we might be alarmed until we realize that they were sleeping. Jordan W. Smoller suggests that childhood could be described as a disease that includes congenital onset, dwarfism, and legume anorexia. Context and expectation seem to play a prominent role in what we perceive as disease. To alleviate this confusion, Christopher Boorse defines disease in terms of the value-free observation of human biology. For Boorse "diseases are internal states that depress a functional ability below species-typical levels."[36] The attempt is to make disease judgments value-neutral. Disease can be recognized as a matter of the natural sciences without evaluation of whether the observed state is desirable or not. In "Health as a Theoretical Concept," Boorse critiques several alternative definitions of disease.[37] To be disease-free

35. H. Tristram Engelhardt Jr., "The Concepts of Health and Disease," in *Concepts of Health and Disease*, p. 31.

36. Christopher Boorse, "Health as a Theoretical Concept," *Philosophy of Science* 44 (1977): 542.

37. Boorse, "Health," pp. 544-50.

is desirable, but many undesirable shortcomings such as clumsiness are not necessarily diseases and some diseases are in fact desirable, such as cowpox before an outbreak of smallpox, so value judgments are not definitive. He rejects the definition of medical positivism that maintains that disease is whatever undesirable condition physicians treat, since doctors often recognize diseases that they are not able to treat and do other procedures such as circumcision or cosmetic surgery that are not considered disease treatment. Statistical abnormality alone is neither a necessary nor a sufficient criterion for disease, since red hair and type AB blood are unusual conditions but not diseases. Pain and suffering are not sufficient in that teething and childbirth are both extremely painful yet not generally considered diseases. Disability is more favorably received by Boorse as a possible definition, but requires careful qualification so as not to include for example the inability to swim. Adaptation is rejected as too dependent on a given environment, and homeostasis is too narrow to account for deafness or limb paralysis.

As an alternative to this, Boorse advocates beginning with a reference class consisting of an age group of one gender of a species. Disease is then a type of internal state that reduces one or more functional abilities below the usual efficiency of one's class. By function he means "contributions to individual survival and reproduction."[38] "Normal efficiency" includes everything within or above typical functioning. Diseases then are inferences from empirically discoverable species design, requiring no value judgment about what forms of life are desirable. Boorse wants to keep an empirical, value-neutral recognition of physical freedom from disease distinct from "the most controversial of all prescriptions — the recipe for an ideal human being."[39] Note, however, that if all individuals are cured to the "usual efficiency of one's class," some individuals will naturally be better off than average and the average will consequently rise. Human abilities fall in ranges. If everyone at the lower end of the typical range is brought up to the midpoint in the range, the midpoint of the range will rise. Only in the fictional Lake Wobegon can all the children be above average. Over time, what was once considered enhancement beyond species-typical functioning would become cure to reach the raised typical level.

---

38. Boorse, "Health," p. 556.
39. Boorse, "Health," p. 572.

Disease as a Rejected Physical State

Is aging a pathology or a desirable natural course? If a pathology, then extending life span would be a therapy. Caroline Whitbeck emphasizes the role of values for such a determination: "Diseases are, first of all, psychophysiological processes; second, they compromise the ability to do what people commonly want and expect to be able to do; third, they are not necessary in order to do what people commonly want to be able to do; fourth, they are either statistically abnormal in those at risk or there is some other basis for a reasonable hope of finding means to effectively treat or prevent them."[40] Here the emphasis is on desired capability with no firm tie to statistical norms or current form. Disease is a normative concept that designates certain states as unwanted.[41] While a particular disease often refers to a set of physical phenomena, the judgment that a particular set of phenomena constitutes a disease is value-laden, hence flexible according to the values of the definers. For example, in an 1851 edition of the *New Orleans Medical and Surgical Journal*, the desire of a slave to run away was labeled a disease, "Drapetomania."[42] Nearsightedness could be deemed a disease, as well as could a lack of resistance to heart failure. Thus, the terms "*disease* and *health* appear to involve evaluation as well as description."[43]

The thesis is not that disease is in every case a net loss, but that every disease involves something unwanted. "Either medicine is blindly bent on curing disease, oblivious to other consequences, or medicine serves the best interests of its patients, but not both."[44] The individual patient defines the relevant values and the physician technically meets them.[45] "What defines diseases are true benefits and

40. Caroline Whitbeck, "A Theory of Health," in *Concepts of Health and Disease*, p. 615.

41. William K. Goosens, "Values, Health, and Medicine," *Philosophy of Science* 47 (1979): 102.

42. Samuel A. Cartwright, "Report on the Diseases and Physical Peculiarities of the Negro Race," *New Orleans Medical and Surgical Journal* 7 (May 1851): 707-9. This article was first brought to my attention by F. C. Redlich, "The Concept of Health in Psychiatry," in *Concepts of Health and Disease*, p. 381.

43. Hessel Bouma III et al., *Christian Faith, Health, and Medical Practice* (Grand Rapids: Eerdmans, 1989), p. 266.

44. Bouma et al., *Christian Faith*, p. 104.

45. L. Nordenfelt, *On the Nature of Health: An Action-Theoretic Approach* (Dordrecht: Klewer Academic, 1995); *Health Science and Ordinary Language* (Am-

harms."[46] "There is then no theoretical difference between beneficial abilities never had by a species and those lost by individuals. . . . The moment a newly created beneficial ability became available, persons without the 'treatment' would be considered as lacking something."[47] "Disease increasingly means whatever we have a reimbursable treatment for."[48] By this view, medical care should be guided by whatever serves as a benefit, not by a concept of proper functioning. Disease is that harm, inherently functioning or not, that persons believe they would benefit from being without.[49]

One response to the terms changing is to further stipulate that by cure of disease one means relief of "suffering, morbidity, and mortality."[50] Actually, "suffering" is still an evaluative bracket that changes in definition as much as the concept of disease that it is meant to specify. "Morbidity" is usually defined as that which is related to disease, and so does not help us to define disease. Even relief from "mortality," as the most clear of the three qualifiers, might shift over time with changing expectations of appropriate forestalling. Human evaluation remains central even with these three descriptors.

Lester King brings statistical norms back into the formulation of what constitutes disease, but qualifies that requirement to an almost entirely value-determined definition. "Disease is the aggregate of those conditions which, judged by the prevailing culture, are deemed painful, or disabling, and which, at the same time, deviate from either the statistical norm or from some idealized status."[51] When labeling a particular pattern a "disease" depends on the judgment of the prevailing culture and includes the option of appeal to ideals as well as statistical norms, values again predominate. Cure of disease and enhancement could be indistinguishable by this definition.

---

sterdam: Rodopi, 2001); and "The Concepts of Health and Illness Revisited," *Medicine, Health Care and Philosophy* 10 (2007).

46. Nordenfelt, *Nature of Health*, p. 108.

47. Nordenfelt, *Nature of Health*, p. 109.

48. David Healy, "Good Science or Good Business?" *Hastings Center Report* 30, no. 2 (March-April 2000): 19.

49. George Khushf, "An Agenda for Future Debate on Concepts of Health and Disease," *Medicine, Health Care and Philosophy* 10 (2007): 19-27.

50. John Fletcher, "Evolution of Ethical Debate," p. 64.

51. King, "What Is Disease?" p. 112.

Disease as a Hindrance

H. Tristram Engelhardt emphasizes the ambiguity of the concept of disease and traces this characteristic of the term to the presence of both explanatory and evaluative notions.[52] Descriptive and normative, disease describes factual conditions and judges them good or bad. With acknowledged indebtedness to Hegel and Kant, Engelhardt argues that the perception and portrayal of reality are a cultural product.[53] The application of medical knowledge, defining and treating disease, is as pervasively shaped by human goals as any other human activity. Even if one could define what is typical of a species, as Boorse does, why should that be of interest? Boorse may be defining typical biological function, but for Engelhardt disease has to do with how human beings evaluate that biological function. The definition of disease is not only an observation of a physical pattern; it is a judgment of how well the current level of function enables or hinders the individual's goals, leading to an individual and social construct of what will be treated medically. As a social agreement, what constitutes disease is subject to negotiation that cannot be resolved by appeal to empirical observation. Even if all could agree on the empirical observation that something is typical or atypical, whether that state is desirable or not (and the appropriate response) would not thereby be automatically resolved.

"What is considered a disease condition in one biomedical tradition may not exist at all in others, as appears to be the case with AD [Alzheimer's disease]. Other diseases only labeled as such in certain cultures include post-traumatic stress disorder (PTSD) and premenstrual syndrome (PMS) in the United States, dropped stomach and *shinkieshitsu* in Japan, neurasthenia in China, *triste tout le temps* and *crise de fois* (liver crisis) in France, and heart insufficiency in Germany."[54] There is no universally recognized definition of health, disease, or the goals of medicine. Lyme disease in North America could have been termed "erythema chronicum migrans," a disease already present and described in Europe.

52. Engelhardt, "Concepts of Health," p. 31.

53. H. Tristram Engelhardt Jr., *The Foundations of Bioethics* (Oxford: Oxford University Press, 1986), pp. 157-59, 194-95.

54. Atwood D. Gaines, "Culture and Values at the Intersection of Science and Suffering," in *Genetic Testing for Alzheimer Disease: Ethical and Clinical Issues*, ed. Stephen G. Post and Peter J. Whitehouse (Baltimore: Johns Hopkins University Press, 1998), p. 258.

Despite having a similar if not identical pathological basis, the identification of Lyme as a new disease affected both how it was investigated and which therapies were proposed.[55] The diagnosis rate of clinical depression has increased dramatically since the DSM-IV modified its criteria for clinical depression.[56] The definition had always excluded depression associated with situational pressure. If one experienced despair at the death of a significant other, one was working through grief, not pathologically depressed. Impairment was present but not diagnosed as a disease. All the way back to Aristotle the diagnosis of melancholia required that it could not be attributed to an external cause. Situational pressure such as job loss, the death of a friend, divorce, and society stress such as war or terrorism might cause temporary impairments that are understandable and indeed appropriate ways of coping and adjusting, not a disease process. Such situational impairments result from normal biological and psychological functioning needed for long-term health. Diagnosing them as a disease and masking them pharmaceutically may in some cases forestall needed growth.[57]

Considering such cases, Engelhardt writes that since the perception of disease will reflect evaluative goals, response should reflect the personal goals of the recipient and only more broadly that of the community. Such an understanding would protect individual choice, but it could allow limitless permutations of what is or is not disease. Edward Berger and Bernard Gert have attempted to avoid such idiosyncrasy by describing disease as characterized by "universal evils" that all human beings avoid.[58] Such a definition still reflects social values, but seeks some objectivity in wide consensus. However, universal consensus would be difficult to prove, and consensus may vary in degree at many points.

Joseph Margolis has made an interesting proposal that could be

55. Robert A. Aronowitz, *Making Sense of Illness: Science, Society, and Disease* (Cambridge: Cambridge University Press, 1998), pp. 16-17.

56. Ronald Kessler et al., "The Epidemiology of Major Depressive Disorder: Results from the National Comorbidity Survey Replication (NCS-R)," *Journal of the American Medical Association* 289, no. 23 (June 2003): 3095-3105.

57. James C. Peterson and Kelvin Mutter, "Discerning Pain to Guide Its Alleviation," *Journal of Spirituality and Mental Health* 12, no. 3 (2010): 182-94.

58. Edward M. Berger and Bernard M. Gert, "Genetic Disorders and the Ethical Status of Germ-Line Gene Therapy," *Journal of Medicine and Philosophy* 16 (1991): 671-72, 675.

helpful in light of all the above. Disease could be described as any disorder of the body relative to basic prudential function.[59] Basic prudential function includes those capabilities that enable basic necessities of human life. Such a definition, which recognizes a strong value component, would be more inclusive and goal oriented than a definition tied to species-typical capacity. Disease would not be merely a statistical abnormality, but that which hinders prudential function. Typical dental caries or cavities can be disease as much as an atypical enzyme deficiency. Prudential function is desired by virtually all human beings since it is basic to life. By limiting disease to lack of prudential function, a recognizable standard is possible. Would such a definition be objective? Substantially yes. A measurable standard of what was generally necessary to support basic life choices could be recognized and pursued. However, application of such a standard could change over time. It would reflect the environment that challenges and constrains survival, as well as what the society considers appropriate levels of basic life. At a time when almost everyone has eyesight genetically corrected to the best naturally occurring 20/15, signs and public events would assume such and having 20/20 vision would be perceived as in need of cure up to basic levels. What could be described at one point in time as enhancement could later be categorized as cure of disease. Each of the above definitions of disease is open to physical improvement that raises the standard expectation of physical capacity. By these definitions the goals of curing disease and enhancing capacity are not distinguishable over time.

A case where we already have substantial experience with treatment limited by the cure-of-disease rubric is the use of the genetic product human growth hormone (HGH). To affect stature, HGH is administered before a child is of legal age to give consent. The attempt is to change end physical height. Studies show that three shots a week for four years produce increased ending height of 1.5 to 4 inches compared to placebo injections. Twenty thousand children in the United States currently receive HGH. Of these, 75 percent are HGH deficient. Most of the rest are girls with Turner's syndrome (a condition that leads to average adult height of 4 feet 8 inches). HGH treatment costs about $20,000 a year for the drug and requires daily injection

59. Joseph Margolis, "The Concept of Disease," in *Concepts of Health and Disease*, p. 575.

over several years.[60] Lantos, Siegler, and Cuttler approve of such therapy only if there is a measurable disease of growth hormone deficiency or as a cosmetic intervention for shortness that is at a level of "deformity."[61] Here basic conceptions of disease and deformity are setting the parameters for medical intervention.[62] They advocate using HGH only for cure of disease, not enhancement.[63] Yet the U.S. Food and Drug Administration has now approved Humatrope (recombinant developed human growth hormone) for idiopathic short stature (short stature for no known medical reason). Children with short parents but no lack of human growth hormone can receive HGH. The question that now guides practice is not whether a disease etiology can be found to justify treatment, but whether increased height would be helpful to the patient.

Intervention Only to Health

When discussing the point of curing disease, the summary term often used is "health." In the last section we saw that over time the goal of curing disease is not easily distinguishable from the attempt to enhance capacity. Both welcome improvement. Does the definition of health offer a clearer distinction? How is health as the pursued goal of cure of disease different from an ideal pursued by enhancement of capacity? As with the definition of disease, the definition of health is varied and complex.[64] We will look at several approaches.

Three definitions of health are too ambiguous to guide us on this particular question. The World Health Organization stated in 1958 that "health is a state of complete physical, mental, and social well being and not merely the absence of disease or infirmity." This grand definition of health might call for fixed or changing application, depending on the definition of "complete physical, mental, and social well being." The

60. LeRoy Walters and Julie Gage Palmer, *The Ethics of Human Gene Therapy* (New York: Oxford University Press, 1997), p. 113.

61. Lantos, Siegler, and Cuttler, "Ethical Issues," pp. 1021-23.

62. Juengst, "Can Enhancement Be Distinguished?" pp. 125-42.

63. Lantos, Siegler, and Cuttler, "Ethical Issues," pp. 1020-24; Benjamin, Muyskens, and Saenger, "Short Children, Anxious Parents," pp. 5-9.

64. Per-Anders Tengland, "A Two-Dimensional Theory of Health," *Theoretical Medicine and Bioethics* 28 (2007): 257-84.

question has merely moved from what is "health" to what is "well being." Pope John Paul II gives a similarly expansive definition. "From a Christian perspective, then, health envisions optimal functioning of the human person to meet physiological, psychological, social, and spiritual needs in an integrated manner."[65] It is easy to picture improvements beyond current forms that would more clearly approximate "optimal functioning." A third definition, health as "intuitively self-evident," may also be unclear on this point in that whether pursuing health leads to the current status quo or change over time would depend on the individual's intuitive apprehension of that self-evidence. While appeals to self-evidence have a long and august history, including functioning as the opening warrant of the founding document of the United States,[66] it is often difficult to gain consensus by appeals to intuition, and no such consensus has yet been reached on a definition of health.

Here are three definitions of health that welcome physical improvement.

Health as a Statistical Norm

Health could be defined as a statistical norm.[67] Anything outside of a small average range would be unhealthy. This standard has the advantage of being grounded in objective data but raises at least three problems. The first is that few people advocate that health includes eight teeth cavities per person or a life expectancy of thirty-five years in Uganda, or osteoporosis that in some populations is a common condition for elderly women. These are statistical norms in their contexts.[68] Defining health as the statistical norm would affirm as health what

65. Pope John Paul II, "The Ethics of Genetic Manipulation" (October 29, 1983), in *Origins* 13, no. 23 (November 17, 1983): 385, cited by Kevin D. O'Rourke and Philip Boyle, *Medical Ethics: Sources of Catholic Teachings*, 2nd ed. (Washington, D.C.: Georgetown University Press, 1993), p. 8.

66. "We hold these truths to be self evident that all men are created equal . . ." (Thomas Jefferson, "The Declaration of Independence" [Philadelphia: Continental Congress, 1776], p. 1).

67. E. Murphy, *The Logic of Medicine* (Baltimore: Johns Hopkins University Press, 1976).

68. The noting of this ambiguity can also be found in Tristram H. Engelhardt Jr., "Persons and Humans: Refashioning Ourselves in a Better Image and Likeness," *Zygon* 19 (September 1984): 282.

many would object to as unhealthy. Second, what is "typical" changes from one society to another and from day to day.[69] Such a definition is not consistent across time or place. Third, such a standard could produce the oddity of declaring people with unusual longevity or strength unhealthy, since they would be deviating from the small average range. The definition can be qualified that health is the statistical norm plus desirable abnormality, but that qualification introduces the role of values to the definition, which is something the statistical norm approach is often cited to avoid.

Normal health could also be defined as the greatest capacity naturally occurring, without the limit of what is naturally occurring *now*. There is naturally a range of abilities. Typically some people have genetic endowments that combine or mutate in a way that offers an advantage. A standard tied to average functioning will increase over time if one brings any below-average heritage up to the average. Some people will naturally have genetic endowments that combine or mutate a little better. If positive changes are left intact while negatives are corrected, over time the statistical norm will rise. What was previously average becomes below average. Correcting to average would lead to incremental and continuing enhancement of physical capacity. Change would be relatively slow, but change would occur nonetheless. While enhancement of capacity is associated with an ideal that may be considerably different from the present state of humanity, and cure of disease is associated more closely with our present state, the two would converge over time.

Health as Whatever Evolution Produces

Christopher Boorse argues for defining health as whatever maintains the evolutionary goals of survival and reproduction.[70] Enhancement might then coincide with the pursuit of health as a powerful adaptive and sustaining strategy. In contrast, it has been argued that we should submit to the cumulative wisdom of evolution by remaining just as we are, but it is difficult to derive that commitment from the "wisdom of

69. Robert M. Veatch, "Ethical Issues in Genetics," in *Progress in Medical Genetics*, vol. 10, ed. Arthur Steinberg and Alexander Bearn (New York: Grune and Stratton, 1974), p. 257.

70. Christopher Boorse, "On the Distinction between Disease and Illness," *Philosophy and Public Affairs* 5 (1975): 49-68.

evolution." Such an argument would be for prudence, not commitment to the present. If we are convinced that evolution has adapted humanity so far, then the very nature of humanity is to continue to change and adapt to an environment quite different from that in the past. An appeal to the wisdom of evolution calls for respectful care to insure that future changes work as well as those already long proven, but does not offer commitment to present forms nor positive guidance as to what is desirable.

Health as a Means to What Is Valued

"Health" may be to maximize those physical capabilities that are valued for the goals they render attainable.[71] This would include the definition presented by Talcott Parsons: "somatic health is, sociologically defined, the state of optimum capacity for the effective performance of valued tasks."[72] Health is essentially goal oriented, hence varying with people and circumstances. For Bernard Häring, health is "the fullest possible capacity to develop relationships with God, with one's neighbor, and within the community."[73]

These explicitly value-oriented definitions of health are sometimes called "normativist."[74] Feet crippled by binding would be unhealthy in our society, while such was the epitome of health and desirability for upper-class Chinese women during part of China's history. Some forms of hallucination that would now be labeled schizophrenia have at times been honored as insight into higher realms and as such a special blessing. If health is whatever physical capacity we value, that leaves open the restriction or encouragement of enhancement of capacity according to those values. The definition of health as the maximization of the physical capabilities that we value could be limitless.[75]

71. Nordenfelt, *On the Nature of Health.*

72. Talcott Parsons, "Definition of Health and Illness in the Light of American Values and Social Structure," in *Concepts of Health and Disease*, p. 60.

73. Bernard Häring, *Manipulation: Ethical Boundaries of Medical, Behavioral, and Genetic Manipulation* (Slough, U.K.: St. Paul Publications, 1975), p. 56.

74. Arthur L. Caplan, "The Concepts of Health and Disease," in *Medical Ethics*, edited by Robert M. Veatch, p. 57.

75. Elisabeth Beck-Gernsheim, ed., *Welche Gesundheit wollen wir?* (What kind of health do we want?) (Frankfurt: Suhrkamp, 1995).

Whitbeck has argued that "the absence of an upper limit on health does not make that concept any more obscure than concepts such as wealth, which also have no upper limit."[76] Such a definition would welcome enhancement of capacity.

There has been considerable continuity geographically and temporally in what people physically value. If conceptions of health are as fluid as human values or power relations, why has there not been more variety in how health is perceived? It could be argued in response that despite the great variety of human cultures, survival needs are consistent due to the consistent physical nature of human beings. While kinds of shelters vary from igloos to palm frond huts, human beings generally require shelter. While food varies from blubber to grubs, all human beings require food. Such common survival issues remain whether living in the Arctic or tropical jungles. Strategies to meet them vary with circumstances but maintain considerable commonalities. Health could reflect the diversity of human values while still maintaining a considerable consensus, if it reflects common needs basic to human function.

Health as Tied to Our Current Condition

The Catholic Hospital Association defines health as "a functional whole, in which all necessary functions are present and acting cooperatively and harmoniously."[77] This functional focus is common to a number of definitions. Here it is left unclear what is cooperative, harmonious, and necessary. For our inquiry the crucial ambiguity is in the word "necessary." It may imply basic prudential function as discussed earlier in Margolis's work,[78] or it may intend an appeal to the *current* natural order. A theme in part of the varied Christian tradition has been that the current natural order should be supported because God designed and ordained its present form. Created by God, the natural course as we have received it bears divine authority. This is the one definition of disease and health that is permanently tied to our present state. Health is not defined here by human choice or biology, but rather by God's prerogative as Creator.

76. Whitbeck, "A Theory of Health," p. 616.
77. Catholic Hospital Association, *Health Care Ethics: A Theological Analysis* (St. Louis: Catholic Hospital Association, 1978), p. 28.
78. Margolis, "The Concept of Disease," pp. 561-78.

We discussed in chapter 1 the difficulty of discerning God's purpose merely by observing nature. How do we identify which natural patterns are the God-given ones? There have been numerous mutually exclusive interpretations. The standard that one uses to distinguish what of nature is God-given and what is not, or what is the underlying God-given intent, may then be the actual standard. The appeal to reading nature directly would be reflecting hermeneutical commitments that are the operative standards. If the natural order is perceived as ordained and set, efforts to enhance it would be contrary to the God-established pattern. If the natural order is perceived as one that God is not only restoring but also improving over time, enhancement may be part of the fulfillment of human responsibility. Earlier chapters addressed these possibilities.

Holding the Line at Cure of Disease

Some who reject the distinction between cure of disease and enhancement of capacity because they find it imprecise are concerned about attempts at the cure of disease beginning a slippery slope to attempts at enhancement.[79] By "slippery slope" I am referring to an argument also described by metaphors such as "the thin edge of the wedge." The slippery slope argument depends on two assertions. The first is that the projected end result of crossing a particular line is undesirable. The second is that once one crosses the line, one is on a slope where there is no place to stop. This is due to the lack of a conceptually clear moral distinction at which to stop along the slope or to the fear that, even if there is a clear stopping point, it would probably not be honored in practice.[80] Bernard Williams calls these two versions of the slippery slope argument the "arbitrary result" argument and the "horrible result" argument.[81]

C. Keith Boone sees no slippery slope between cure of disease and enhancement of capacity. For Boone the distinction between the two is "seismic," so that a slippery slope argument at that point would be a

79. Bouma et al., *Christian Faith*, p. 266.

80. James F. Childress, "Wedge Argument, Slippery Slope Argument, etc.," in *The Westminster Dictionary of Christian Ethics*, p. 657.

81. Bernard Williams, "Which Slopes Are Slippery?" in *Moral Dilemmas in Modern Medicine*, ed. Michael Lockwood (Oxford: Oxford University Press, 1985), pp. 126-37.

"bad axiom," unhelpful and misleading.[82] In contrast, the World Council of Churches paper on genetic engineering claims a conceptual (or arbitrary) slippery slope between cure of disease and enhancement of capacity. "There is no absolute distinction between eliminating 'defects' and 'improving' heredity. Correction of mental deficiency can move imperceptibly into enhancement of intelligence, and remedies of severe physical disabilities into enhancement of prowess."[83] Willard Gaylin observes a social pattern that he projects will create a practical slippery slope for human genetic intervention. "This technology can and will be used to reduce genetic faults and increase the opportunity for a normal, healthy child. It will also be used to effect changes whose merits are not so cut-and-dried, changes that will be seen as making a more nearly ideal or optimal child . . . we inevitably turn from the replacement of deficiencies to additions for enhancement and ennoblement."[84] This is already our pattern from dental braces to correct a bite problem, to braces for that perfect smile.

Sheldon Krimsky seems to argue *both* conceptual and practical slippery slopes at the line between cure of disease and enhancement of capacity.

> Moral rules based upon nebulous distinctions are most vulnerable to slippery-slope outcomes. . . . The distinction between enhancement and medical therapy is a socially constructed category influenced by many factors that contribute to the current taxonomy of clinical disorders. Moreover, once the right of somatic cell therapy becomes established, it is doubtful that its use can be restricted to "medical therapy." Consider all the surgical techniques that are used for cosmetic purposes. . . . No satisfactory moral rule has been advanced that sets boundaries on somatic cell human genetic engineering.[85]

82. C. Keith Boone, "Bad Axioms in Genetic Engineering," *Hastings Center Report* 18, no. 4 (August/September 1988): 11.

83. World Council of Churches, Church and Society, *Manipulating Life: Ethical Issues in Genetic Engineering* (Geneva: World Council of Churches, 1982), p. 7.

84. Willard Gaylin, *Adam and Eve and Pinocchio: On Being and Becoming Human* (New York: Viking Penguin, 1990), p. 9.

85. Sheldon Krimsky, "Human Gene Therapy: Must We Know Where to Stop Before We Start?" *Human Gene Therapy* 1 (1990): 173.

For Krimsky, there is no clear division between cure of disease and enhancement of capacity, and the distinction would probably not be honored in practice even if it was conceptually clear. Before one can hope for a distinction to be honored in practice by society, there needs to be a clear conceptual distinction. That distinction is lacking between cure of disease and enhancement of capacity. The color spectrum shades from red to orange to yellow without precise moments of transition, yet we still refer to distinct, recognizable colors. But for genetic intervention the stakes are much higher. Conceptual clarity is essential if the distinction is actually to be applied.

If disease or health is fixed to the current average and not any future average, there is a clear and permanent distinction between cure of disease and enhancement of capacity. Almost any restoration to health could be characterized as enhancing the recipient's capacity, but one could stipulate that there should be no improvement beyond *the present* average. One could cure to today's typical level of health and no further. There would then be no conceptual slippery slope. The question of relevance would remain. If curing disease is enhancing an individual's capacity to an average level typical today, why stop there? Why not use the technique to prevent diseases from occurring in the first place or to further augment desired capability? Why limit health and capacity to today's average that, as cures are achieved, will become statistically less than average?

If the definitions of health and disease that have changing application are more convincing, there may still be a rough distinction between cure of disease and enhancement of capacity *at any given time*, but its application would vary over time. The line of division would move. What would be ruled enhancement of capacity now might well fall under cure of disease later. By these definitions the applied result of the distinction would be conceptually consistent but not fixed in application for all time.

Would a changing application of cure of disease necessarily be a dangerous slippery slope? The distinction could still be serviceable as a method of prioritization if the projected end state of increased capacity is not rejected. In such a case there would be change, but it would not be uncontrolled or negative as implied by the metaphor of the slippery slope. W. French Anderson, who advocates the distinction between cure of disease and enhancement of capacity, consistently states his affirmation of genetic cure as cure of *serious* disease. He often qualifies his affirmation with words such as "initial";[86] others use the phrase "at least for the time being."[87] For Anderson the diseases chosen for therapy "should and undoubtedly will" expand to less serious diseases as the techniques improve. Early therapy, entailing more risk than when refined, would be more appropriate for those at greater risk from the severity of their disease.[88] The earliest interventions, then, should be for the most severe diseases. When techniques are proven to be safe and effective, less serious disease could be treated.

Anderson ends one of his articles with the statement, "But until we have acquired considerable experience with regard to the safety of somatic cell gene therapy for severe disease, and society has resolved at least some of the ethical dilemmas that this procedure would produce, non-therapeutic use of genetic engineering should not occur."[89] The implication from the word "until" seems to be that just as less serious disease may eventually be treated, so nontherapeutic intervention, enhancement, might begin at a future date. Since according to Anderson the main current limitation is our ignorance, as our knowledge increases, the range of appropriate interventions may increase as well.[90] The distinction between serious and less serious disease, as well as between cure of disease and enhancement of capacity, could be a way to set research priorities at any given time, even as its precise application shifts over time. Once risk and expense are incurred by intervening, it will probably not be much more difficult to enhance than to restore to a current average.

The difference between some current therapies and genetic interventions might eventually parallel the difference between polio vaccine and the iron lung. The iron lung, in an expensive and painful manner, tried to replace function after a disease had already run its course. This is

---

86. Anderson, "Human Gene Therapy: Why Draw a Line?" pp. 688, 690, and "Genetics and Human Malleability," p. 24.

87. Grobstein and Flower, "Gene Therapy," p. 15.

88. W. French Anderson and John C. Fletcher, "Gene Therapy in Human Beings: When Is It Ethical to Begin?" *New England Journal of Medicine* 303 (November 1980): 1293.

89. Anderson, "Human Gene Therapy: Why Draw a Line?" p. 691.

90. This position may be a development from his earlier statement in 1985 that interventions should not be for other than therapeutic reasons "regardless of how fast our technological abilities increase" (Anderson, "Human Gene Therapy: Scientific and Ethical Considerations," pp. 289-90).

the tactic of much of modern medicine, trying to replace lost function rather than prevent the loss from occurring. Triple bypass heart surgery and kidney dialysis do not cure heart or kidney disease, but are worthy attempts to sustain the body despite the damage already incurred. Polio vaccine, however, is an inexpensive enhancement to the human immune system that keeps the disease from developing in the first place. Genetic intervention may eventually offer many such opportunities.

One could retain the distinction between cure and enhancement for general research funding priorities. The more clearly an intervention is to cure disease, the greater the importance with which it should be pursued, but pursuing health while avoiding enhancement is problematic. The problem is both with the indistinctness of the line and with the rationale for holding it. There is no adequate conceptual distinction between cure of disease and enhancement of capacity that would allow us to make a principled argument for cure of disease that would not over time also allow genetic intervention for what might now be considered enhancement. D. Gareth Jones sees a frequent false dichotomy in rhetoric between either genetic intervention to the immortality of a transformed posthuman state or no intervention at all. He says we are already enhanced compared to earlier generations, and that is good. Jones advocates the thoughtful extension of abilities without seeking radical transformation.[91] The discerning question is not just how to cure disease. The better question is how to enable the body to yield more support for human flourishing.

91. D. Gareth Jones, *A Tangled Web: Medicine and Theology in Dialogue* (Oxford: Peter Lang, 2008), pp. 123-42.

5 Welcoming versus Making

The Attitudes of Parents, Recipients, and Providers

Parents

The desire to have children is often powerful. If it were not, far fewer people would take on the drastic loss of freedom and increase in responsibilities entailed in caring for children. In fact, in many wealthy societies the current generation of adults is not having enough children to even replace itself. So why *do* some of us have children? To share our lives? Because of mindless biological drive? To provide for someone to take care of us in our old age? To escape from current family? To prove our virility? To have someone to love? Duty? Calling? Surprise? No doubt each of these has motivated parents at some time. Whatever the original intent or lack thereof, none of us is here without a great deal of effort by our parents and others. Parental effort probably begins with eating vitamins during pregnancy and avoiding toxins that can cause harms such as fetal alcohol syndrome. Should that effort on behalf of one's child include seeking the best genetic start?

M. J. Sandel thinks not. He advocates "openness to the unbidden."[1] To the degree this resonates, what is probably being smuggled in is an expectation that the unbidden is not actually random or malevo-

---

1. M. J. Sandel, "The Case against Perfection: What's Wrong with Designer Children, Bionic Athletes, and Genetic Engineering," *Atlantic Monthly* 292, no. 3 (2004): 50-62.

lent, but a birth state intended by God. Yet we do not treat the genetic condition of retinoblastoma, resulting in cancer of the eye, as a gift from God. Upon its detection we diligently treat it to save the child's sight because we care about the child. It seems that genes do not always get it right on their own. Part of our calling is to set right what we can. Leaving alone what could be better is not a virtue, and making choices cannot be avoided. We are still choosing when we decide not to carry out what is available to us. One does not have to act, but one cannot avoid deciding whether to act, and if so in what way, and the attendant responsibility.

If parents do intervene, does that action encourage destructive attitudes? There are thoughtful authors who think that deliberately shaping genetic heritage shifts procreation from welcoming a child to making a child. Children should be begotten, not made. They are gifts to be received, not designed. Families need to be built on acceptance of people as they are, with all their imperfections.[2] This acceptance is part of what we value in our families as distinct from wider society. Michael Sandel calls this the difference between accepting love and transforming love.[3] But this might not be such an easy dichotomy to maintain. Appreciating the giftedness of life is not synonymous with declaring the gift to be static. As described earlier, Irenaeus appreciated the gift of life as our starting point. He thought the highest appreciation is to develop what has been entrusted to our care. Some cultures regard a child that seeks to gain more education or do more service than his parent as betraying the received legacy. Others see a child building upon a parent's launch as the highest endorsement of the parent's investment and hope.

Gilbert Meilaender insists that "one whom we beget shares in our being, is equal in dignity to us. One whom we make has been distanced from us, become the product of our will."[4] "We need the virtue of love. Love that can say, without qualification, to another: 'It's good that you exist.'"[5] If one fully accepts other human beings, one should not seek to change their genetic endowment. Any favoring of characteristics is bad

---

2. Thomas H. Murray, *The Worth of a Child* (Berkeley: University of California Press, 1996), pp. 5-6.

3. Sandel, "The Case against Perfection," p. 57.

4. Gilbert Meilaender, "Mastering Our Gen(i)es: When Do We Say No?" *Christian Century* 107, no. 27 (October 3, 1990): 875.

5. Meilaender, "Mastering Our Gen(i)es," p. 874.

parenting. As a parent one needs to accept whatever child one has regardless of physical characteristics.

Here Meilaender seems to be conflating accepting children as fellow human beings with being resigned to whatever happens to be their current physical state, but Meilaender himself seeks to avoid this confusion when he says, "we should turn against disease, not against those who are diseased."[6] While it is true that parents should love and accept their children as they are, part of parenting is also giving the best available support to one's child. For example, one should do the best one can to provide medical care to correct a genetic disability. While fully accepting a child born with a cleft palate, one should do one's best to provide surgery to correct that genetic condition so that the child can more freely speak and eat. It is routine to free people from disabilities if possible, rather than yield to the loss of function as a God-planned design to be embraced. If an ability cannot be restored, then one looks to see if by grace the condition can be a teacher and not just an enemy. But the first goal is to restore the function. In response to cleft palate, it would be a matter of respect and care for parents to select a genetic heritage by which the facial bones and teeth would grow normally in the first place. Such would avoid later suffering and repeated invasive intervention. It is good parenting both to accept *and to help* one's child.

That help should not be a cover for trying to predestine a child. Genetic intervention should increase the recipient's choices rather than reduce them. Chapter 9 will discuss the importance of an open future. Another concern may be that genetic intervention might come to be organized by sales order and purchase. Intervention as a contract to purchase a guaranteed product could extend into treating the child like a commodity.[7] That would subvert the all-important attitude of welcome for every child. But giving offspring the best possible genetic start is not grounds to treat them as disposable products once they have arrived, any more than financing a tonsillectomy means one can toss out Jennie the toddler if she later needs more surgery. People should not be treated as if they were mere objects. However a child comes to be and whatever her condition, she should be welcomed, loved, and nurtured.

6. Gilbert Meilaender, "Human Cloning Would Violate the Dignity of Children," in *The Human Cloning Debate*, ed. Glenn McGee (Berkeley, Calif.: Berkeley Hills Books, 1998), p. 194.

7. Murray, *Worth of a Child*, p. 33.

Recipients

Some groups have argued that intervention may impart harmful perceptions to the recipients. The Enquete Commission was established in Germany to inform the public and advise the Bundestag concerning genetic legislation. The commission concluded that "everybody must have the possibility of seeing himself or herself, his or her own essence, as the result of a fate separated from human beings — or as created by God — but not as the project and as the more or less successful experiment of other human beings."[8] For the commission, finding one's origin in chance or providence is essential to securing individual worth and independence. Jürgen Habermas articulates this perspective as concern that adolescents who have received genetic intervention will perceive themselves as something made. He thinks such a perception would deeply alienate a person from her body. One needs a sense of freedom that is rooted in not being designed by anyone else.[9] "With the realization of the noncontingency of her manufactured biological origins, the young person risks losing a mental presupposition for assuming a status necessary for her, as a legal person, to actually enjoy equal civil rights."[10] Habermas is convinced that if one's genetic heritage is not random, one will perceive oneself as an object, not a person. It is not clear why Habermas expects such a result. If this is a philosophical concern, is Habermas actually concerned that a fellow human being is less a person if some of his genes are chosen? He does not make an argument to that effect. If Habermas is making a psychological prediction, is it indeed important to self-identity to perceive oneself as unformed by others? Is it more difficult to be a whole person if one realizes that one's family and culture have been formative? Also, is lack of identity found in children who were born ostensibly to save a marriage, to balance the genders among siblings, or to care for their parents in old age? As long as we are speculating, there might be just as much risk of feeling less care and specialness in discovering that one's parents could have given one a better start genetically and did not do so.

8. Enquete Commission, "Prospects and Risks of Gene Technology: The Report of the Enquete Commission to the Bundestag of the Federal Republic of Germany," *Bioethics* 2, no. 3 (1988): 257-58.

9. Jürgen Habermas, *The Future of Human Nature* (Cambridge: Polity Press, 2003), pp. 53-58.

10. Habermas, *Future of Human Nature*, p. 78.

Providers

A further concern is what attitudes may develop in those who provide genetic intervention. Genetic intervention is "a giant step toward turning begetting into making, procreation into manufacture, making man himself simply another one of the man-made things. . . . As with any other product of our making, no matter how excellent, the artificer stands above it, not as an equal but as a superior, transcending it by his will and creative prowess . . . human children would be their artifacts."[11] Manipulation by human beings of other human beings renders the recipients "thingified."[12] It makes human beings objects rather than fellow children of God. Recipients should not be perceived or treated as manufactured objects, hence disposable or discounted from full respect. Children are our progeny, not our creations.[13] "What we beget is like ourselves. What we make is not; it is the product of our free decision, and its destiny is ours to determine . . . it is, in fact, human begetting that expresses our equal dignity, we should not lightly set it aside."[14] "Man as a manipulator is too much of a god; as object, too much of a machine."[15]

Leon Kass articulates such concerns this way:

> Finally, there may well be a dehumanizing effect on the scientist himself, and through him on all of us. On the one hand his power of mastery increases, but on the other hand his power of mastery decreases. . . . The sense of mystery and awe I am speaking of is demonstrated by most medical students on their first encounter with a cadaver in the gross anatomy laboratory. Their uncomfortable feeling is more than squeamishness. It is a deep recognition, no matter how

---

11. Leon Kass, "The Wisdom of Repugnance: Why We Should Ban the Cloning of Humans," in *The Human Cloning Debate*, pp. 169-70. See as well Conrad G. Brunk, "Religion, Risk, and the Technological Society," in *The Twenty-first Century Confronts Its Gods: Globalization, Technology, and War*, ed. David J. Hawkins (Albany: State University of New York Press, 2004), p. 52.

12. Paul Ramsey, *Fabricated Man: The Ethics of Genetic Control* (New Haven: Yale University Press, 1978), p. 151.

13. Charles Frankel, "The Specter of Eugenics," *Commentary* 57, no. 3 (March 1974): 33.

14. Meilaender, "Human Cloning," p. 194.

15. Ramsey, *Fabricated Man*, p. 103.

inarticulate, that it is the mortal remains of a human being in which they are to be digging, ultimately a recognition of the mystery of life and death. The loss of this sense of awe occurs in a matter of days or weeks; mastery drives out mystery in all but a very few.[16]

Kass is concerned that the scientist and others might eventually view human beings who have received intervention as less mysterious, hence less worthy of awe. Without that sense of awe toward human beings, respect for human freedom and dignity may be lost.[17]

However, Kass does acknowledge in the next paragraph that the increase of knowledge can increase one's sense of awe. What may have appeared to be a simple phenomenon may turn out to be wondrous in its intricacy. Our language has two meanings for "wonder." It may be to be puzzled as to how something is, or it may be to be amazed at what we do understand. Increasing knowledge has the potential to add to that sense of wonder, not always lessen it. In his reference to the "practice" of "most ordinary men of science," Kass's concern may be rooted more in the familiarity of routine exposure than in lack of understanding. Sheer repetition of involvement and responsibility does tend to dull people to their power in shaping others, whether they are genetic scientists or day care workers. If one regularly shapes developing human beings, one might start to see those persons more as objects than as fellow human beings.

Genetic intervention could be done in such a way that it treats the other as merely an object, but that is not a unique problem. The often decried tendency in modern specialized medicine is to think of patients as cases rather than human beings. "Have you seen the liver yet in room 203?" That is not surprising when a physician must briefly advise tens of patients a day. It may be difficult to show that clinical cure of disease through genetic means is more potentially dehumanizing in this regard than other treatments now widely practiced and accepted.[18] Mass inoculations against flu can look like assembly lines, yet they are not necessarily dehumanizing. One could argue that the risk of perceiving and treating recipients as objects rather than as persons is heightened by the

16. Leon R. Kass, "New Beginnings in Life," in *The New Genetics and the Future of Man*, ed. Michael P. Hamilton (Grand Rapids: Eerdmans, 1972), pp. 56-57.

17. Leon R. Kass, "Making Babies — the New Biology and the Old Morality," *Public Interest* 26 (Winter 1972): 53-54.

18. Immanuel Jakobovits, "Some Letters on Jewish Medical Ethics," *Journal of Medicine and Philosophy* 8 (1983): 217-24.

addition of yet another point of intervention.[19] On the other hand, initial widespread genetic intervention may actually decrease the need for later medical intervention, hence reducing rather than increasing the frequency of manipulation and its attendant risks. At this time many different methods of gaining access to genes for surgery are being investigated. Methods for introducing genes include, for example, injection, inhaling an aerosol, and removing cells for treatment and then placing them back in the body. The degree of concern about the coarsening effects of manipulation generally increases with the frequency and degree of invasiveness, particularly in any departure from the way human beings now come to be. A brief intervention after conception and before extensive development would not interrupt the loving bond and intimacy of intercourse at the start of life nor development in the womb. *In vitro* fertilization would be a more substantial departure, but might still be in support of a couple committed to each other and any children for life.

It is a serious charge that genetic intervention would turn the recipient into a man-made object for our use. But would it? Does surgery after birth for a harelip make the child "made, not begotten"? No. Physical intervention can be done out of love for the recipient; it can fully recognize and be motivated by concern for the recipient as a person. Early genetic surgery could someday correct the genetic code so that the child's palate and lips grow whole in the first place. Why would corrective surgery after birth not devalue a child, but before birth it would? Further, it is not the process of apparently random conception that makes us people or things. The Christian tradition describes angelic beings who are persons of significant dignity and worth without human begetting at all. Being a person is not limited to being born of a human being, and being a human being is not limited to a particular form of conception. Consider Jesus of Nazareth.

Feeling Rejected

Children need a great deal of unconditional acceptance. We expect a mother to love her baby wholeheartedly, even if the child "has a face

---

19. James F. Keenan, "What Is Morally New in Genetic Manipulation?" *Human Gene Therapy* 1 (1990): 293.

only a mother could love."[20] Prenatal testing assumes that the parents can withhold acceptance until the fetus is shown to be acceptable, and then fully engage it. The reality of parenthood is that if we abort for anencephaly, we might later have a child that loses conscious brain function due to oxygen starvation during birth. Having children is a risky commitment to another person, whatever the other person's condition turns out to be or become.

Torbjorn Tannsjo points out that the European Parliament that on January 26, 1982, affirmed a right to be born free of artificial intervention in one's genes, in the next paragraph clarified that this prohibition did not apply to therapeutic applications "since such therapy promises to make possible the elimination of certain hereditary diseases."[21] It is not a rejection of people hurt by polio to give children a polio vaccine. One can honor people who are differently abled, without affirming that loss of function is a good thing. It is not a rejection of particular persons with spina bifida to ensure that pregnant women have adequate B12 in their diet. Why should genetic intervention be perceived as a rejection of people afflicted by the unwanted condition? Genetic intervention need not imply a lack of care for a particular person. It may embody it. Those who by date of birth, mistake, or parental choices bear genetic disease that others have avoided will still need proper care. Moreover, they may contribute to God's self-revelation and grace to us. This later point is particularly prominent for Bouma and colleagues, who write from a Calvinist perspective that traditionally emphasizes God's pervasive providence. Those bearing handicaps have a needed role to play, for God's glory and provision are often revealed through dealing with suffering or weakness whether from a genetic handicap or the cross.[22] Suffering is not a good in itself, but suffering can be a necessary price for an end that is worth the suffering involved. In Mark 14:36 Jesus prays that he would not have to suffer the cross, but expresses most emphatically that he is willing to if there is no other way to achieve reconciliation. The point is to glorify God whatever one's estate, but that is not an excuse to acquiesce to a changeable condition.

20. Barbara Katz Rothman, *The Tentative Pregnancy: How Amniocentesis Changes the Experience of Motherhood* (New York: Norton, 1993), pp. 6-7.

21. Torbjorn Tannsjo, "Should We Change the Human Genome?" *Theoretical Medicine* 14 (1993): 239.

22. Hessel Bouma III et al., *Christian Faith, Health, and Medical Practice* (Grand Rapids: Eerdmans, 1989), pp. 266-67.

All human beings are of inestimable worth, but not all human characteristics are equally desirable.[23] Granted, God can allow and even use suffering to a positive service. Paul is described in Acts as being instrumental in numerous physical healings by God's intervention and is himself protected from a poisonous snake, yet a malady deeply bothered Paul (maybe poor eyesight) that God chose not to heal. He was required to live with his affliction and to grow in reliance and trust in God through the difficulty (2 Cor. 12:7-10). Purposeful suffering can be a point of identification with Christ, who purposefully suffered. Suffering is not always a complete enemy. It may also serve as a teacher. Yet all things being equal, it is better to be well than to be sick. At our end state that God intends for us, there will be no more sickness or pain (Rev. 21–22). If one has a headache, one may take aspirin and say a prayer, with gratitude for both. Preferring to end a disease is not casting aspersions on the worth of people who still have the disease. Avoiding heart disease does not mean that people who have experienced a heart attack are devalued. People who are well are not more important than people who are sick.

John Swinton makes the expressivist argument that to say that someone is welcome "and then to engage in social practices which are designed to ensure that their existence won't happen again is loveless and inhospitable."[24] But avoiding cancer does not mean that everyone with cancer is rejected. That would be to conflate a condition with the person. A person is far more than just the person's physical condition. Preventing a condition and caring for those who have it are not mutually exclusive. Vaccination against measles does not preclude caring for people with measles. We need to protect and nurture one another, yet we also should not leave unnecessary burdens that are hard to bear. Healing people of a disease does not disvalue people who cannot be healed. Avoiding a debilitative condition is manifestly different from denying a debilitated person his or her dignity, value, or right to live.

In contrast, the Nazi horror of killing people they deemed having "lives not worth living" of course threatened all others with similar conditions. Adrienne Asch argues that terminating pregnancy because the one developing has a disability undermines the life of older people who

---

23. Bruce R. Reichenbach and V. Elving Anderson, *On Behalf of God: A Christian Ethic for Biology* (Grand Rapids: Eerdmans, 1995), pp. 140-41.

24. John Swinton, introduction to *Theology, Disability, and the New Genetics: Why Science Needs the Church*, ed. John Swinton and Brian Brock (New York: T. & T. Clark, 2007), p. 19.

have the same disability.[25] Amy Laura Hall concurs.[26] However, protecting someone from a disability is another matter. It is better to hear than not to hear, better to have a capability such as sight than not to have it. That is not rejection of those who are already with us and differently abled. Theresia Degener reminds us that "disability must no longer be automatically equated with suffering, and non-disability must no longer be seen as the precondition for happiness."[27] That is true for child and parents. But wanting to free people from a particular condition or prevent them from developing the condition does not mean that people with the condition are devalued or rejected as people. People are far more than their physical abilities.

Staying Connected

Some people seek immortality in passing on their genes. The irony is that such a quest is both impossible and trivial. Genes quickly disperse over generations, and the physical form they embody is not our most important presence or legacy. The design of human genetics is one of dispersal and recombination. A child will carry only half of each parent's genotype, and even that half may not be what is manifest in the phenotype of the parent. A parent with green eyes could pass on a recessive gene for blue eyes. It would be from the parent's genotype but would not duplicate the parent's phenotype. By the fourth generation a child is equally related genetically to sixteen different people; in the fifth generation to thirty-two; and in the sixth to sixty-four. Doubling each generation compounds rapidly. My mother was pleased to tell me from her genealogical research that I am related to William Shakespeare. Although since Will's grandmother was sixteen generations back for me, barring intermarriage to simplify the calculation, I am equally related to about 65,536 other people of that generation.

25. Adrienne Asch, "Can Aborting 'Imperfect' Children Be Immoral?" in *Ethical Issues in Modern Medicine*, ed. John Arras and Bonnie Steinbock, 4th ed. (Mountain View, Calif.: Mayfield, 1995).

26. Amy Laura Hall, *Conceiving Parenthood: American Protestantism and the Spirit of Reproduction* (Grand Rapids: Eerdmans, 2008), p. 377.

27. Theresia Degener, "Female Self-Determination between Feminist Claims and 'Voluntary' Eugenics, between 'Rights' and Ethics," *Issues in Reproductive and Genetic Engineering* 3 (1990): 98.

For various motivations many societies have put great effort and importance into tracing and maintaining bloodlines. For example, the child as genetically connected property dominated Roman law. This may have been to reinforce distinctions of birth between slave and free.[28] Genetic parents could demand the return of a child that had been adopted a decade before and raised completely apart from them. The United States legal system has carried on this tradition in stressing genetic connections between people as paramount in issues of custody and inheritance. Children are sometimes treated as a form of property to be disposed of according to ownership rights. There have been cases of a child raised for years in mutual commitment and love with adoptive parents, only to be suddenly taken away because a man who contributed one sperm wished to claim his right to the child.

Thomas Murray recounts the story of Cara Clausen, who gave up her baby for adoption along with the written consent of the man identified as the father. A month later the man who had actually contributed the successful sperm discovered that Cara had a baby and demanded custody. He did not have an ongoing relationship with the mother, and he already had a fourteen-year-old son whom he had legally abandoned and a twelve-year-old daughter whom he had never met. He had not voluntarily paid child support for either. The local district court praised the parenting of the adoptive parents and ordered them to give the baby to the plaintiff even as it saw a need to order an investigation whether he would be a fit parent. Disagreements between the courts in Iowa and Michigan continued until the two-and-a-half-year-old child was taken by force from the only parents she had ever known and given to the plaintiff.[29] This travesty treated the child as property, not as a human being who should have been the first concern. There is normally a natural connection that comes with a genetic connection, especially when reinforced by carrying the child until birth. But the genetic connection is not a property right that overrides the commitments and well-being of the child.

The Christian Tradition and Adoption

Adoption is lauded in Christian tradition. Matthew and Luke state that God chose to be incarnated in a family where he had two parents but

28. Murray, *Worth of a Child*, p. 7.
29. Murray, *Worth of a Child*, pp. 41-44.

was not genetically related to his father Joseph. When during Jesus' public ministry his mother and brothers came to see him, he used their arrival as an opportunity to proclaim that all who followed God were his family (Matt. 12:46-50). Jesus as the eldest son undoubtedly had provided for his family and even while dying on the cross was making provision for Mary (John 19:26-27), yet he emphasized that one became part of his family by choice and commitment, not by genetics (Luke 8:19-21). One is adopted into God's family.

Adoption is characteristic of God's work through the Old Testament as well. God is the God of Israel by covenant, not birth. God chose to work through Abraham and his progeny, yet this is not an exclusive call to be God's people, this is a call to a particular task. Melchizedek and others completely unrelated genetically to Abraham are recognized as people of God (Gen. 14:18-20). This is a key theme in the book of Jonah. Even the "people of Israel" is a category that follows commitment to know and follow God, not mere bloodlines. Ruth from Moab (see book of Ruth) and Rahab from Jericho (Josh. 6:25)[30] are welcomed in while many in the bloodline are cast out (e.g., Exod. 32:25-28). The Davidic line is traced to Jesus not because it is the only one that God cares about, but as a sign to help recognize the Messiah when he comes. On into the time of the church, children are welcomed into the church community by dedication in some churches and by infant baptism in others. It remains for the child to understand and affirm for herself that she wants to become part of the church. That decision is publicly affirmed at a later age in baptism or confirmation. In essence, God has no grandchildren. It is not sufficient to be a descendant of someone in God's family. Each individual must choose to welcome that relationship or turn away. If one does receive that welcome provided by God, one becomes part of the body of Christ on earth. All human beings in God's family are welcomed as children by adoption. One is part of the people of God by conviction, not by physical descent.

The new life that begins now and extends forever includes immortality of the person, not of one's genes. There is no call from the tradition to be concerned about passing on one's genes into the future. Immortality is personal, not by progeny. Genes are important to physical and mental health. They matter because they matter to people. But

30. Note that Rahab and Ruth actually are part of the line leading to King David (Matt. 1:5).

they are not the point of this life or the next. Christians are to have children in order to share intimate love with new people, not in a doomed quest for genetic immortality. One is to love one's neighbor as oneself, not only one's genetic relatives. Adoption of children unrelated genetically is one of the closest human recapitulations of the life-giving adoption that has welcomed one into God's family. Whether genetically related or not, the most precious heritage that human beings can pass on to their children is to know God and receive life as it is meant to be in God.

When a couple discovers that one of them has an autosomal dominant condition yielding a 50 percent chance of severe harm for each conception, that raises several possible responses, including not having children, adoption, artificial insemination by donor, or selection of gametes or zygotes. Alternative ways of bearing children would also be a consideration if the couple faces a recessive condition that statistically would lead to a quarter of their children fully afflicted and half as carriers. The Christian tradition does not require a couple to have children, nor does it require them to be genetically related to their children. What is most central is what is best for the child, not duplicating some parental genes.

Caring for the Child

Leon Kass raises the concern that parents might abdicate responsibility for their children and the children for their parents if the genetic link is broken. Indeed, the genetic connection is "an indispensable foundation for sound family life."[31] He does not explain why it is indispensable. Of course, he is quite right that one has a responsibility to care for a child that one begins in sexual intimacy, yet if one of the couple that began that new life dies or flees, the child is not condemned to never experiencing "sound family life." Sharing genes may tap into sociobiological drive, but that is not the only possible grounds for committed love. Family resemblance may encourage the extension of self-love, but it is hardly determinative by itself. Is one more likely to sustain a relationship with another simply because one shares the same eye color or a

31. Leon Kass, *Toward a More Natural Science: Biology and Human Affairs* (New York: Free Press, 1985), p. 113.

similar nose? If such has any effect at all, it would be quickly overwhelmed by the responses and attitudes of the person. Phenotype matters for aesthetics and initial identification. Similarities imply connection between persons. But if there is no more connection between persons than a few physical traits, they quickly fade as a point of interest. Physical appearance helps us to identify persons, but it is the person that is worth identifying. A genetic link with parents does not guarantee care or safety. Susan Smith "feared that her two children, three-year-old Michael and fourteen-month-old Alex, stood in the way of her boyfriend's making a long-term commitment to her. In 1994 she strapped them into their child safety seats in her Mazda. Then she sent the car rolling down the embankment into the John D. Long Lake near Union, South Carolina. The two boys were drowned. . . . The safety and security of her children could not be guaranteed by the fact that they were in the care of their birth mother."[32] Sexual intimacy should embody a commitment to each other and any resulting child. If that is not honored due to death or irresponsibility, the resulting child can still be welcomed into a family. Sometimes the most loving thing a young single mother can do for a child is to give that child to a family that can better raise the child. Actual family care is often more formative than genetic connection for identification and commitment. Adopted and blended families can be examples of caring concern that does not rest on common lineage.

It might be noted as well that if continuity of genetic line is valued, intervention that follows conception and proceeds on the foundation of the given code could leave a substantial genetic link in place. Lee Silver estimated that by 1998 the total number of people alive in the United States who were conceived using artificial insemination by donor was about one million.[33] Studies have found such resulting families psychologically as healthy as traditional birth families. "Children conceived by ART [artificial reproductive technology] did not differ from naturally conceived children in emotions, behavior, or quality of family relations."[34] In fact, "adoptive parents and parents conceiving children

32. Ted Peters, *For the Love of Children: Genetic Technology and the Future of the Family* (Louisville: Westminster John Knox, 1996), p. 1.

33. Lee M. Silver, *Remaking Eden: How Genetic Engineering and Cloning Will Transform the American Family* (New York: Avon Books, 1998), p. 181.

34. Susan Golombok et al., "Families Created by the New Reproductive Technologies: Quality of Parenting and Social and Emotional Development of the

through ART expressed greater warmth and emotional involvement with children, as well as greater satisfaction with parenting roles, relative to birth parents."[35] The ART families may have a genetic link through one or both parents, the adoptive families no genetic link, and most function quite well.

Janet Fenton, the president of Concerned United Birthparents, has been quoted as saying that "if adoption were made into a kind of guardianship, children . . . would know who their real parents were and that they could go back to them at any time."[36] Fenton is equating being a genetic source with being the "real parents," and assumes that such parents who already gave up the child would take the child back at a later point. If not called the "real parents," sometimes those who provided the gametes are called the "biological parents." Even this adjective is misleading. The couple that raises a child, feeding, protecting, caring, and clothing the child for years, contributes more to the child's biological survival than one sperm or egg cell. With the growing potential for even more separation between types of genetic sources, gestation, and parenting, it may be that the best terms for each role in raising a child are: "gene sources," which would include whoever provides sperm, egg, nuclear material for an egg, or the nonnuclear egg; "gestational mother" for the woman who may be unrelated genetically yet intimately carries the developing child to term; and "parents" for the mother and the father who give the rest of their lives in permanent commitment to raising the child. Qualifying the latter with the adjective "social" mother or father neglects their essential and extended biological contribution. Being a mother or father in the fullest sense is about living out a lifelong commitment of love, provision, and care for someone who depends on you, not genetics.

Caring for a child with a disability can be rewarding; however, the divorce rate for parents of disabled children is much higher than for those who do not face such a challenge. Decreasing the instance of disability would help many families. Ronald Green suggests that actualizing some parental choice in genetic endowment might better match a

---

Children," *Child Development* 66 (1995): 285, 295; Frank van Balen, "Child-Rearing Following In Vitro Fertilization," *Journal of Child Psychology and Psychiatry and Allied Disciplines* 37 (1996): 687, 692.

35. Nancy L. Segal, "Behavioral Aspects of Intergenerational Human Cloning: What Twins Tell Us," *Jurimetrics* 38, no. 1 (Fall 1997): 61.

36. Janet Fenton, as quoted by Murray, *Worth of a Child*, p. 41.

child with what parents are able to do.[37] "People generally accept that parents have the right to involve their children in the parents' own most important dreams. Forbidding this, as Ruddick makes clear, would change the very meaning of parenting, deprive parents of some of their deepest aspirations for themselves and their children, and render children crosses too heavy for all but self-sacrificial saints to bear."[38] Children will have genetic influences whether parents choose them intentionally or not, and children will be able to channel their genetic influences to their own ends whether parents choose those ends or not. By analogy, one can express and follow through on one's preference for a certain appearance in a potential spouse, but once married there is a commitment to care for the person regardless of how the person's appearance may change. Parents could prefer a boy or a girl, or have one of each, without prejudice against siblings of either sex. Not long ago parents had no choice in the number or spacing of children. The use of contraception has not caused parents to love the children they do have any less. We expect parents to give the best start they can to their children. Genetic intervention may be part of that responsibility without reducing children to manufactured objects, devaluing people who are differently abled, or loosing the sense of family connection.

37. Ronald Green, *Babies by Design* (New Haven: Yale University Press, 2007), pp. 118-19.

38. Green, *Babies by Design*, pp. 126-27, working with William Ruddick, "Parents and Life Prospects," in *Having Children: Philosophical and Legal Reflections on Parenthood*, ed. Onora O'Neill and William Ruddick (New York: Oxford University Press, 1979), pp. 124-37.

6 The Present versus the Future

Meagan did the best she could to take care of her father. It was difficult. By his thirty-ninth birthday it had become clear that something was wrong. For the first time in his life he was bothered by increasingly serious mood swings. He had trouble concentrating. There was a twitch in his face and fingers that he attributed to nerves, but that did not explain his loss of balance. His speech slurred and he had difficulty swallowing. Just when he most needed the support of his family he began to have trouble even recognizing them and slipped into dementia. For his last years he could not control his body nor could he recognize anyone who helped him. Now he was dead at the age of forty-six. The doctors had warned Meagan that they knew of no way to slow the course of the disease. They also told her that she had a 50 percent chance of developing the same condition. About 150,000 people in the United States who have a parent afflicted with Huntington's disease (HD) are at that same risk.

A method to cure HD does not exist yet, but if there was a treatment for Meagan we would call it somatic. If the treatment affected her ova so that her descendants would not inherit the disease, the treatment would be called germ line. It is commonly argued that somatic treatment is welcome but germ-line treatment is not. Yet if in treating Meagan we could also protect her children, would that not be better? Some changes in the germ line could help our descendants. Should we provide that for them when we can?

142

Distinguishing Somatic and Germ-Line Intervention

There is a substantial physical difference between somatic cell intervention and intervention in the human germ line. Somatic cell intervention directly involves one recipient, whereas germ-line changes are inheritable. However, somatic cell intervention sometimes results in unintended germ-line effects. If a somatic intervention occurs early enough to affect basic body structure, it is likely to affect the gametes (sperm or eggs) as well. Further, it is not unusual for somatic interventions to extend a person's life long enough for childbearing. Genes are passed along that would not have been otherwise. That is a germ-line effect. The first directly intended germ-line intervention has already occurred. A team at the Institute for Reproductive Medicine and Science at St. Barnabas Medical Center in Livingston, New Jersey, thought a number of their patients were miscarrying due to defective mitochondria. By injecting ooplasm from donor eggs into patient embryos, the resulting eggs had mitochondrial DNA from two maternal lineages. Of the thirty women treated thus far for inability to carry pregnancy, fifteen have given birth. The resulting children would have genes from two mothers and pass those on to their children.[1]

Many think the distinction between somatic and germ-line intervention to be sufficiently clear to serve as a crucial ethical divide. By the mid-1980s there was already considerable consensus that somatic cell therapy was acceptable.[2] For the most part, it is contiguous with other therapies and had already received careful and convincing ethical analysis.[3] In contrast, germ-line intervention remains contested. On June 8, 1983, a diverse group of clergy from several faiths sent a letter

1. J. A. Barritt et al., "Mitochondria in Human Offspring Derived from Ooplasmic Transplantation," *Human Reproduction* 16, no. 3 (2001): 513-16.

2. Office of Technology Assessment, *Human Gene Therapy: A Background Paper* (Washington, D.C.: Superintendent of Documents, U.S. Printing Office, 1984), p. 47; National Institutes of Health, "Recombinant DNA Research: Proposed Actions under Guidelines," *Federal Register* 50, no. 160 (August 19, 1985): 33464.

3. Eve K. Nichols, *Human Gene Therapy* (Cambridge: Harvard University Press, 1988), p. 164; John C. Fletcher, "Ethical Issues in and beyond Prospective Clinical Trials of Human Gene Therapy," *Journal of Medicine and Philosophy* 10 (1985): 293-309; W. French Anderson and John C. Fletcher, "Gene Therapy in Human Beings: When Is It Ethical to Begin?" *New England Journal of Medicine* 303 (November 1980): 1293-97; Bernard D. Davis, "Ethical and Technical Aspects of Genetic Intervention," *New England Journal of Medicine* 285, no. 14 (September 30, 1971): 800.

to President Reagan asking for a ban on human genetic engineering. J. Robert Nelson clarified afterward that the involved clergy were not warning against somatic cell therapy. There were many examples of somatic cell therapy that most of the signers would affirm. What they wanted to discourage was modification of the human germ line.[4] Many philosophers and theologians described somatic cell therapy as acceptable but argued vigorously against germ-line intervention.[5] Government bodies emphasized the distinction as well. For example, a National Ethics Committee in France approved somatic cell therapy but recommended the complete prohibition of even research related to germ-line genetic therapy.[6] There have been other proposals for international law against any inheritable genetic modification,[7] and the United States governing body for gene intervention protocols emphasized the distinction in its "Points to Consider."[8] The widespread acceptance of somatic intervention, while germ-line intervention is often questioned, reflects the influential line drawn between the two. Granted, there is movement. In 2004 a Roman Catholic theological commission chaired by Joseph Cardinal Ratzinger, who is now Pope Benedict XVI, approved of genetically changing sperm stem cells for a therapeutic germ-line effect.[9] The emphasis was that while the intervention would benefit future generations, there must be no harm to embryos or the conjugal act.

---

4. J. Robert Nelson, "Genetic Science: A Menacing Marvel," *Christian Century* 100 (July 1983): 636-38.

5. Paul Ramsey, *Fabricated Man: The Ethics of Genetic Control* (New Haven: Yale University Press, 1978), p. 44.

6. National Ethics Committee, France, *Report Relative to Research Work on Human Embryos in Vitro and Use Thereof for Medical and Scientific Purposes* (December 1986), p. 24. Note Comité Consultatif National d'Ethique: 1984, "Problèmes d'ethique posés par les essais chez l'homme de nouveaux traitements" (Paris: Comité Consultatif National d'Ethique, 101 Rue de Tolbiac, 75654, 1984).

7. George J. Annas, Lori B. Andrews, and Rosario M. Isasi, "Protecting the Endangered Human: Toward an International Treaty Prohibiting Cloning and Inheritable Alterations," *American Journal of Law and Medicine* 28 (2002): 151-78.

8. Subcommittee on Human Gene Therapy, Recombinant DNA Advisory Committee, National Institutes of Health, "Points to Consider in the Design and Submission of Human Somatic-Cell Gene Therapy Protocols," *Federal Register* 50 (1989): 33463-467.

9. International Theological Commission, "Communion and Stewardship: Human Persons Created in the Image of God" (Vatican, 2004), section 90.

So Why Change the Germ Line?

What is contested by those who reject the distinction is not reasonable clarity of a physical difference, but moral relevance.[10] An intervention can usually be fairly characterized as primarily somatic or germ-line, but why does that matter ethically? To be early enough to help the individual, some genetic interventions will thereby be early enough to affect how the person's gametes develop. Considerable human suffering is physiologically untreatable by therapy with only somatic effects. Some cells such as those in the central nervous system cannot be reached unless the intervention is early in development. For example, Lesch-Nyan disease, which includes aggressive self-mutilation, does not appear to be treatable once it is in place. Replacing the disease-causing gene with a functional gene offers a better chance that it will express fully and cooperatively, plus have no competition with the old gene. Such a technique could correct dominant disorders.[11] Because the intervention would be early in development, one intervention would affect most body cells, including gametes, and it would not need to be repeated in the patient or the patient's descendants. LeRoy Hood has led researchers at California Institute of Technology in preventing tremors in shiverer mice and extending their life span to the normal range by inserting the gene they would otherwise lack into their parents before their conception and birth.[12]

Some conditions are treatable without germ-line intervention, but only marginally so. The gene for retinoblastoma is inherited as an autosomal dominant in 50 percent of the children of a parent with the disease. Genetic diagnosis at birth can lead to heightened vigilance that tempers the threat of retinal cancer, yet later these patients tend to develop osteogenic sarcoma, another type of cancer. Early intervention with germ-line effects would with one step eliminate more than one kind of cancer the patients would probably otherwise face.[13] For those patients there would be less suffering, financial cost, and risk.

The often-voiced concern about changing genes with potential

10. For example, R. Moseley, "Maintaining the Somatic/Germline Distinction: Some Ethical Drawbacks," *Journal of Medicine and Philosophy* 16 (1991): 641-49.

11. LeRoy Walters and Julie Gage Palmer, *The Ethics of Human Gene Therapy* (New York: Oxford University Press, 1997), pp. 72-74.

12. Walters and Palmer, *Ethics*, p. 61.

13. Walters and Palmer, *Ethics*, p. 79.

germ-line effects is that it may affect some descendants if it is passed on and expressed. This would compound good and bad results. However, harmful results need not be allowed to continue and interventions could be incremental in number and degree until proven, as with any other medical innovation. If the intervention has a damaging side effect, it could be modified or eliminated. If the effect is positive, many people could benefit on into the future from one intervention. That is markedly less invasive and more efficient than intervening in each generation.

Spotting PKU early and changing diet have kept many people from devastating mental retardation. On the other hand, sufferers find the bland and expensive diet hard to keep. Also, many have survived to childbearing age, hence increasing the number of children afflicted with the disease. A single germ-line intervention could eliminate a person's need for lifelong treatment and the risk of passing the condition on to children. Germ-line intervention requires fewer interventions with attendant costs and problems than lifelong treatment and retreatment in every generation. If it would be appropriate to treat one person for deliverance from HD, why not treat that one person in such a way as to deliver future children from the dreaded disease as well? One can argue that "the benefits of forever eliminating diseases such as spina bifida, anencephaly, hemophilia and muscular dystrophy would seem to make germ-cell gene therapy a moral obligation."[14] Prudentially, more people are affected by a germ-line intervention. In that sense the stakes are higher, but the procedure should not be done even for the first patient until its success and safety are substantially assured. Once it is clear that the procedure is helpful, provision for descendants is an advantage.

It has also been argued that zygote selection will almost always be superior to direct genetic alteration.[15] Why pursue direct germ-line intervention rather than zygote selection or selective abortion? There are a least three reasons.

1. Germ-line intervention values the zygote, embryo, or fetus that is treated rather than discarded. Selection methods usually lead to the immediate or eventual destruction of what is not chosen for implanta-

14. Art Caplan, "An Improved Future?" *Scientific American*, September 1995, p. 143.

15. Gerd Richter and Matthew D. Bacchetta, "Interventions in the Human Genome: Some Moral and Ethical Considerations," *Journal of Medicine and Philosophy* 23, no. 3 (1998): 314-15; Marc Lappe, *Ethical and Scientific Issues Posed by Human Uses of Molecular Genetics* (New York: Academy of Sciences, 1976), pp. 634-36.

tion. It would be more respectful and welcoming of developing life if it were treated rather than destroyed.

2. Germ-line intervention can enhance beyond what occurs in a particular family line. Two homozygous parents, both afflicted with cystic fibrosis, could not provide a healthy zygote to select. "Much more commonly, two prospective parents will both carry alleles causing milder forms of disease that do not typically prevent people from reaching adulthood or having children. Diabetes, heart disease, obesity, myopia, asthma, a predisposition to some cancers, and many other conditions that adversely affect the functioning of a human organ, tissue, or physiological system are examples. And preemptive cures for all could be achieved by genetic engineering."[16]

3. Germ-line intervention could potentially enhance beyond what occurs in *anyone's* family line.

Since germ-line intervention affects future descendants, it raises the question of what concern we should have for people in the future.

Concern for Future Generations

In the Christian tradition we are responsible to do the best we can with what we have. We have received the calling to support the flourishing of our physical world and ourselves. Does that include taking into account people of the near and distant future? Ethical systems usually include some degree of concern for the welfare of people, but does that include people in the future? Traditional theories of obligation have a basic problem in this case.[17] Future persons cannot make contracts or promises. The historic paradigm of "obligation" has three requirements: a specifiable service is required of one person; two parties are involved — one to provide the service and one to receive it; and a prior transaction has created the promise.[18] One who does not exist cannot fulfill

16. Lee M. Silver, *Remaking Eden: How Genetic Engineering and Cloning Will Transform the American Family* (New York: Avon Books, 1998), p. 268.

17. J. Brenton Stearns, "Ecology and the Indefinite Unborn," *Monist* 56 (1972): 613.

18. R. B. Brandt, "The Concepts of Obligation and Duty," *Mind* 73, no. 291 (July 1965): 387. Other examples include: Martin P. Golding, "Obligations to Future Generations," *Monist* 56 (1972): 85-99, and several articles in *Responsibilities to Future Generations: Environmental Ethics*, ed. Ernest Partridge (Buffalo: Prometheus Books, 1981).

the criterion of making a promise, so the usual description of obligation cannot apply. However, the term "obligation" may be broader than that. Obligations for those unable to speak for themselves but who are recognized persons, such as infants, can be as clear as for those who can speak. The obligations may be even clearer due to the recipient's need for special protection. *Having* claims does not require being able to *make* claims.[19] Claims can exist without mutual agreement. In many cases the obligation of one human being to another is extensive whether claimed or not. A requirement that comes with a position such as parent may be called a "duty," but it still exemplifies this broader sense of obligation.[20] One may have obligations to people who have not made a reciprocal promise.

While obligations to children who have not entered an agreement are relatively familiar, obligations specifically to those who do not exist yet have not been as carefully addressed. Can obligations extend to unnamed future human beings? Yes, some obligations may fall to unspecified persons.[21] One may have an obligation to build adequate brakes in a car even if one does not know who will eventually drive it.[22] One could say that people in the future should have clean air. If so, whoever now makes choices that affect air quality should consider that. Even those who do not recognize specifically "obligations" to future human beings still often argue for taking future needs into account.

Among those future needs are those of our children, but what do we owe *their* children? Led by powerful commitments and motivations such as love and hope, people often make tremendous efforts on behalf of their own children. That intervention for their children has effects for the children of their children. John Passmore argues that one should act deliberately to benefit the descendants of one's children.[23] However, he emphasizes how limited that beneficence could be. Human ignorance is great, capacity to change the future limited, and unintended effects are

19. Carol A. Tauer, "Does Human Gene Therapy Raise New Ethical Questions?" *Human Gene Therapy* 1 (1990): 414.

20. Brandt, "Concepts of Obligation," p. 387.

21. Galen K. Pletcher, "The Rights of Future Generations," in *Responsibilities to Future Generations*, p. 168.

22. Pletcher, "Rights of Future Generations," p. 170.

23. John Passmore, "Conservation," in *Responsibilities to Future Generations*, p. 54. For his complete argument see John Passmore, *Man's Responsibility for Nature* (New York: Scribner, 1974).

sometimes more influential than intended ones. Yet Passmore argues that we do cherish people such as our children and the institutions that are important to us. If one cares for other people, one will also care for what happens to them after one's own death. Concern from personal love extends into the future. According to Passmore, the extension depends on the usual, although not always present, commitment of parents to the happiness of their children. Witness the extensive efforts that go into trust funds and life insurance policies. One's children will probably be most happy if their children are happy, as those children are likely to be most happy if their children are happy. Passmore calls the resulting connections "a chain of love" from the present on into future generations. The progression continues making a chain of love that, if not directly broken, still does gradually diminish over time. Passmore suggests in this light that the best service for future generations is to create the best possible world now. However, this generation should be willing to forgo some enjoyments to better secure the needs of the near future, when we are able to project a higher degree of probability that the effort will be substantially beneficial. Love for people we do know and care for leads to concern and effort toward their future and beyond.

Passmore's chain of love calls for concern most directly for one's descendants. Is there a further case to care for those who are not closely and directly related? For Jonathan Glover, one's obligation is to whoever follows.[24] Glover argues from the principle of equality that the worth of each individual calls for equal consideration regardless of where or when that person lives. One should be concerned to aid and not harm others "even if one does not know their names." He cites the analogy of a bus with many passengers getting on and off. It would not be acceptable to leave a time bomb on the bus simply because one does not know who will be on board when the bomb explodes. One's place in time makes no more difference than one's place geographically. "The temporal location of future people and our comparative ignorance of their interests do not justify failing to treat their interests on a par with those of present people."[25] Harms should be avoided and recognized goods should be pursued for future generations.

24. Jonathan Glover, *What Sort of People Should There Be?* (New York: Penguin, 1984), pp. 143-44.
25. Gregory Kavka, "The Futurity Problem," in *Obligations to Future Generations*, ed. Sikora and Barry (Philadelphia: Temple University Press, 1978), p. 201.

149

For Daniel Callahan, to exclude any human beings, present or future, from our moral community invites abuses such as slavery or other oppression. He grants that "to state that we have moral obligations to the community of all human beings introduces its own problems. One of them turns on the practical impossibility of effectively discharging obligations to all human beings."[26] The problem is compounded if concern for future generations of human beings is included. Yet whenever human beings may live, they are still human beings. As human beings they warrant consideration if our actions can affect them.

Callahan goes on to emphasize that our actions will affect future human beings. The very existence of future generations depends on the present generation. The present generation has a responsibility to future people due to their biological dependency and their need as fellow human beings. Callahan argues as well that this biological link incurs a further obligation. As we have received from the past, so we have an obligation to pass on to the future. He uses the Japanese term *on* for this obligation.[27] One repays the care received from one's parents by taking equal or better care of one's children. With no exact correspondence in the English language, the term carries an idea of both gratitude and justice in passing on what the present has received in trust.

Thomas Sieger Derr sees concern for future generations as common to the worldviews of the Abrahamic religious traditions of Judaism, Christianity, and Islam.[28] Each refers to an idea of covenant, as in the case of Abraham, where individual choices have consequences for descendants as God interacts with children of the covenant on through the generations. Emphasis is placed on each generation fulfilling and carrying on that covenant. In the Christian tradition this is exemplified in the prominence of infant dedication or baptism. There the community welcomes newborns into the church to be raised as part of that community. The congregation promises to teach and encourage the children with the expectation that someday as adults they will publicly affirm their own commitment in baptism or confirmation and so seek to raise their children.

The Western traditions also usually describe history in a linear sense. Granting the laments in Ecclesiastes that complain of endless

26. Daniel Callahan, "What Obligations Do We Have to Future Generations?" in *Responsibilities to Future Generations*, p. 76.

27. Callahan, "What Obligations?" p. 77.

28. Thomas Sieger Derr, "The Obligations to the Future," in *Responsibilities to Future Generations*, pp. 41-42.

empty repetition (Eccles. 1:1-10), history is usually described not as a repeated cycle, but as having a beginning in creation, a consistent working of God within it, and a definite culmination to come. The future does not merely repeat the past. It can change and develop in substantially new ways. With that potential comes responsibility to contribute to positive change.

In Judaism and particularly in the Christian tradition, such responsibility is often summarized as love for one's neighbor as oneself.[29] Donald MacKay advocates that one should benefit one's neighbor, including neighbors in the future, with whatever tools are available. In the tenth chapter of Luke, where the command to love one's neighbor is affirmed, the question is immediately raised as to who is included in the category of neighbor. The response in the chapter is the story of the Good Samaritan. In that story one's neighbors are not just the family next door or the residents down the block. One's neighbor is whomever one is able to help. Neighbor love would then extend to future generations to the degree one is able to benefit them effectively. To love one's neighbor means to seek the best for others as one is able, whoever the other may be racially, culturally, geographically, or temporally. Such intervention for MacKay does not lead to salvation or perfection, yet human beings are responsible to God to improve life for one another rather than drift in complacency.[30] This is the model of Christ held up for imitation repeatedly, whether in the Gospels or in the apostolic letters (e.g., John 13:3-15 and Phil. 2:4-7).

For MacKay one should be motivated not only by love of neighbor, but also by "the fear of the Lord." Sins of omission are as serious as sins of commission, sloth as dangerous as pride. The steward who buried his talent rather than multiply it was rebuked for his inaction. Knowledge and neighbor love bring responsibility. Human beings will be held accountable for what they have achieved compared with what they could have done for the service of others and the glory of God. For McKay, planning and action on behalf of future human beings are not arrogant but a duty for the responsible steward.[31] Care for future generations is

---

29. Miroslav Volf, Ghazi bin Muhammad, and Melissa Yarrington, eds., *A Common Word: Muslims and Christians on Loving God and Neighbor* (Grand Rapids: Eerdmans, 2010), argues that this theme can be found in Islam as well.

30. Donald M. MacKay, *Human Science and Human Dignity* (Downers Grove, Ill.: InterVarsity, 1979), pp. 60, 79.

31. MacKay, *Human Science*, p. 58.

part of the mandate to do what we can to sustain, restore, and improve ourselves and our world.

Reasons for considering the needs of future generations have included love for one's children, the worth of all human beings, membership in the moral community of humanity, love of neighbor, and fear of God. However, none of these has been argued as an unqualified absolute. What else may counterbalance these claims or be distinctive about applying them to the future?

Three Often-Voiced Constraints

1. Do We Have a Right to Make Choices That Affect Future Human Beings?

As we have seen, Jürgen Habermas emphasizes that consent has to be taken into account.[32] Brent Waters echoes that "eugenic interventions violate the social relationships within which autonomy is formed; persons are free to modify themselves, but they have no right to modify others who cannot freely grant or withhold their consent."[33] This is an important challenge that will be addressed further in chapter 9, but here we can affirm that part of the difficulty of action or restraint on behalf of future generations is that members of current society cannot avoid making choices that affect future generations even though they cannot consult the people of those generations. To choose wisely on their behalf parallels the role of a parent making formative decisions for a child, but this would not be an instance of rightfully rejected ethical paternalism. "Paternalism may be defined as a refusal to accept or to acquiesce in another's wishes, choices, and actions for that person's own benefit."[34] One can act on behalf of future generations, but it is not possible to override the expressed wishes, choices, or actions of people who have not yet made any. Since they do not yet exist, to what degree can there

32. Jürgen Habermas, *The Future of Human Nature* (Cambridge: Polity Press, 2003), p. viii.

33. Brent Waters, "Disability and the Quest for Perfection," in *Theology, Disability, and the New Genetics: Why Science Needs the Church*, ed. John Swinton and Brian Brock (New York: T. & T. Clark, 2007), p. 208.

34. James F. Childress, *Who Should Decide? Paternalism in Health Care* (New York: Oxford University Press, 1982), p. 13.

still be concern for their autonomy?[35] Respect for persons should extend to whoever lives in the future. Whoever they may come to be in particular, they should have choices rather than be predestined to someone else's design. It is not possible to honor the autonomy of future individuals by consulting with them as we act; however, it is possible to be concerned about their autonomy as an end state. Current choices should avoid limiting the level of autonomy they will one day possess.

It is not enough to hope for ratification of our actions.[36] A later approval is problematic in that the intervention cannot be undone and the recipient may be substantially influenced by the received choices. Aldous Huxley referred to an extreme form of this problem in *Brave New World*. "That is the secret of happiness and virtue — liking what you've got to do. All conditioning aims at that: making people like their unescapable social destiny."[37] In Huxley's brave new world, all choices for the next generation were made and set by the controllers. People were shaped to their role rather than shaping roles and environment to their needs and desires. Such a concentration of choice in the hands of a comparative few who choose the conditioning could limit the self-determination of future generations. Does one generation have a right to make choices of such influence for future generations? The European discussion has at times led to a clear no. In an appeal to the French *patrimonie* or the German *Erbgut*, the broad collective environment of human beings must remain just as received. Mauron and Thévoz give the example that one cannot tear down a Gothic chapel for one's own convenience.[38] We should not in any way change our given heritage.

Yet in an important sense, the question of right to influence is inapplicable. "The human autonomy we are required to respect is not an absolute individual sovereignty. No one has created himself."[39] We do

---

35. "Autonomy simply means that a person acts freely and rationally out of her own life plan, however ill-defined" (Childress, *Who Should Decide?* p. 60).

36. Childress, *Who Should Decide?* p. 93; Alan Soble, "Deception and Informed Consent in Research," in *Bioethics*, ed. Thomas A. Shannon, rev. ed. (Ramsey, N.J.: Paulist, 1981), p. 364.

37. Aldous Huxley, *Brave New World* (New York: Harper and Row, 1969), p. 10.

38. Alex Mauron and Jean-Marie Thévoz, "Germ-Line Engineering: A Few European Voices," *Journal of Medicine and Philosophy* 16 (1991): 654-55.

39. Paul J. M. Van Tongeren, "Ethical Manipulations: An Ethical Evaluation of the Debate Surrounding Genetic Engineering," *Human Gene Therapy* 2 (1991): 74.

make formative choices that then shape who we become, but we start with a long list of givens bestowed on us by those who precede us. Past generations have made countless choices for the good and ill of the present generation. This generation's choices will unavoidably shape the world the next generation enters.[40] The choice is not whether this generation will shape the next or not, but rather to what degree and in what direction. Where we build our homes and cities shapes the environment that is passed on. Medical intervention that enables people with genetically based myopia, diabetes, retinoblastoma, and other diseases or disabilities to survive and bear more children spreads those genetic propensities and diseases through the population. The present generation could refuse to act deliberately on behalf of future generations, but it cannot escape its influence, nor the fact that by avoiding conscious intervention a different heritage is established from what could have been. Some risks are avoided and others are retained. When one generation builds beautiful Arcadian neighborhoods far from the smells and noise of manufacturing, most of the next generation has to drive to work.

Are there ways to protect the autonomy of future human beings? If our shaping of genetic heritage is incremental, no one generation would so change perception and experience as to determine all who follow. Over time one small initial change could lead to vast divergences as predicted by chaos theory, but each ongoing overlapping generation would have the opportunity to adjust before long-range implications became set. Intervention could increase choice rather than narrow it. Future generations might then be even more able to adapt to their unique environment and perspective. The current generation would not need to master the impossible task of predicting and balancing all the preferences of future generations.

Also, reversibility is a major concern for implementing change.[41] Future generations should not have to suffer indefinitely from an earlier mistake. If choices are incremental and reversible, future generations could restore a pattern that had been deleted or changed. It might be argued that some genetic heritage such as Tay-Sachs disease has little chance of being helpful in any scenario. Since we are finite beings con-

---

40. Willard Gaylin, *Adam and Eve and Pinocchio: On Being and Becoming Human* (New York: Viking Penguin, 1990), pp. 258-59.

41. James F. Childress, *Priorities in Biomedical Ethics* (Philadelphia: Westminster, 1981), p. 110.

sidering a distant future, there might be other changes that seem desirable now that would not be appreciated later. Vigilant caution is in order. Out of autonomy concerns, the future should not be predestined to one narrow vision.[42] Later chapters will describe standards and a process that would protect ongoing diversity.

2. Do We Really Know What Will Help Future Human Beings?

Brian Brock claims:

> In Christian theology, biological change is part of a larger story, one of the many subnarratives within a larger narrative of God's working, the end of which we do not see. We have no perspective from which to draw a definitive conclusion as to whether a biological change is part of the new creation or not. We therefore cannot say "this is superfluous genetic material" or "this is a defect, a mutation," unless we take up a totalitarian perspective in which we do not just claim to know parts of the logic of the whole, but that we exhaustively know the logic of the universe.[43]

Exemplifying Brock's argument, Job is understandably lost as to why events have so befallen him and is cajoled to accept that as part of his creaturely condition. Augustine counsels that what seems harmful is God-ordained to bless the larger picture. To eliminate suffering would lessen the whole.[44]

These and others have argued that as finite people we do not know the big picture and so may not know how harmful or helpful a present circumstance may be. One's place in time compounds the difficulty in considering the needs of others precisely because as one goes further into the future the circumstances and needs of future generations become harder to predict. The increasing uncertainty makes the weight of such concerns of less import. One cannot have an obligation

42. Robert Nozick, *Anarchy, State, and Utopia* (New York: Basic Books, 1974), pp. 313-14.

43. Brian Brock, Walter Doerfler, and Hans Ulrich, "Genetics, Conversation and Conversion," in *Theology, Disability, and the New Genetics*, p. 156.

44. Augustine, *City of God* 16.8.

to benefit remote future generations when one does not know what will benefit them.[45] Since we do not know all that the future holds, we might not know what would be a desirable genetic endowment for future generations. This is especially true for remote human generations. Even capacities that receive widespread acclamation now may not in the future. Even widely lauded and flexible capacities such as intelligence are controversial in their definition and measurement. Standard I.Q. tests measure only a narrow band of intellectual capability that reflects a "modern consciousness" of high abstraction.[46] Daniel Boorstin observed in his book *The Discoverers* that there was no prototype of one who greatly contributes. Those who have made important discoveries have ranged from mystics such as Paracelsus to establishment figures such as Harvey. There is a marked tendency for people under the different circumstances of various decades to emphasize different values.[47] Choices of any given generation may reflect more their temporary circumstances than future desires and needs.

While one does not know completely what will positively benefit future human beings, to a considerable distance in time one has a good idea what will harm them. We might begin with relieving burdens and in the process heed the Hippocratic tradition of *primum non nocere*, first do no harm. Granted, Thomas Szasz has written skeptically about such a commitment because he believes that often one person cannot be helped without hurting another.[48] He cites an example of prolonging the life of a patient who harms others, or correctly diagnosing a woman as psychotic to protect her husband and then seeing her lose her freedom to involuntary commitment. But the fact that one cannot predict all the effects of one's actions does not lead to the conclusion that all choices are equally desirable, nor that random choice would be as positive in its net effect as deliberately selected choices. Szasz is right that life is complex, but he also appears to be assuming that life is a zero-sum game with

45. Martin P. Golding, "Ethical Issues in Biological Engineering," *UCLA Law Review* 15, no. 267 (February 1968): 457.
46. Brigitte Berger, "A New Interpretation of the I.Q. Controversy," *Public Interest* 50 (Winter 1978): 29-44.
47. Charles Frankel, "The Specter of Eugenics," *Commentary* 57, no. 3 (March 1974): 31.
48. Thomas Szasz, "Ethics and Genetics: Medicine as Moral Agency," *Genetic Engineering: Its Applications and Limitations*, Proceedings of the symposium held in Davos, October 10-12, 1974, p. 114.

losers always in direct proportion to winners. Life may not always be a zero-sum game, and even if it sometimes is, justice might still come into play as to who might appropriately bear which burdens.

Faced with these human limitations, some argue that the wisest course is not to intervene at all.[49] Intervention should not take place where human beings lack complete knowledge to proceed. The argument at this point, however, appears to be not that such intervention is of itself immoral, but that it would be immoral to act imprudently. Acting with insufficient knowledge would be immoral, but if human beings gain sufficient knowledge so that an intervention is not imprudent, it would not then be immoral on that count. Unless one is convinced that human beings will never discern *any* correction or improvement (a counsel of enervating despair), this concern calls more for caution than for complete and permanent prohibition of intervention.

While it can be difficult to know exactly what will always be most beneficial to future generations or how to balance competing concerns, there is enough likely continuity to have some idea. It is unlikely that future generations will rebuke us for protecting some areas as wilderness or for wiping out smallpox. We have some idea of what would likely harm or help them. While we do not know the future situation and ideals, passing on capable and well-functioning bodies to future generations is likely to be helpful to them as well.

3. Are Not the Needs of the Present Already All-Consuming without Adding Concern about Future Human Beings?

Even if widely perceived as beneficial, important for equality of opportunity, and promising eventual cost advantage, the initial costs of extensive intervention would be high. How might the competing claims between needs of the present generation and needs of future generations be justly balanced? Would amelioration of current evils always be of the highest priority so that any effort on behalf of future generations would be postponed indefinitely?[50]

---

49. Leon R. Kass, "New Beginnings in Life," in *The New Genetics and the Future of Man*, ed. Michael P. Hamilton (Grand Rapids: Eerdmans, 1972), p. 62.

50. Golding, "Ethical Issues," pp. 458-59, and Glover, *What Sort of People?* p. 140.

John Rawls suggests a method for discerning fair warrants for re-source use between generations. One is to imagine deciding genera-tional duties without knowing which generation one will be in. The in-tent of deciding behind this "veil of ignorance" is simply to lead people to count people in other generations as of equal concern with them-selves. Each other person counts as much as oneself in such a calcula-tion because by the rules of the thought experiment one does not know which one *is* oneself. By such criteria reasonable people might choose to expect each generation to invest in some improvement for the future as long as it is at minimal cost to their generation. These savings would include that each generation would without sacrificing its own welfare set aside some resources and pass on information and culture to start the next generation off a little better than it did.[51] Each generation would be expected to contribute "justified savings" that, while of mini-mal cost to each generation, would add to an accelerating cumulative benefit. From such a policy every generation would benefit but the first.[52] If the first generation's sacrifice is minimal, it may not be too much to ask.

Such a rubric might provide a way to distribute justly between gen-erations the costs and benefits of genetic intervention. Rawls applies the standard specifically to genetic endowment. "It is also in the interest of each to have greater natural assets. This enables him to pursue a pre-ferred plan of life. In the original position, then, the parties want to in-sure for their descendants the best genetic endowment (assuming their own to be fixed). The pursuit of reasonable policies in this regard is something that earlier generations owe to later ones."[53] Of course, risk, surety of benefit, and other considerations would still need attention.

There are multiple reasons to be concerned about our descendants. The reasons considered in this chapter include love for one's children, the worth of all human beings, membership in the moral community of humanity, love of neighbor, and fear of God. The genetic heritage that we pass on to future generations should be a considered part of our cur-rent reflection as we make choices that will deeply affect our children and theirs. We should at least sustain what God has entrusted to us in or-

---

51. John Rawls, *A Theory of Justice* (Cambridge: Harvard University Press, 1971), pp. 284-93.
52. Ronald M. Green, "Intergenerational Distributive Justice," in *Responsibil-ities to Future Generations*, p. 95.
53. Rawls, *A Theory of Justice*, p. 108.

der to pass it on to them. Genetic heritage should not be worse for our presence. We should also improve what we can. Improvements are appropriate when the opportunities for them are clear. Such required clarity would recognize the immense interdependence of ourselves and the physical world, yet also the fact that it is not already ideal. The elimination of smallpox from the globe was an appropriate alteration of our environment. Wiping out Tay-Sachs, Huntington's disease, or Alzheimer's disease from our genetic heritage would be as well. Part IV offers four standards to help recognize appropriate intervention.

III Four Standards for Shaping Human Nature

7 Safe

Thick Standards

The prophet Micah wrote about twenty-seven centuries ago:

> What does the LORD require of you
> but to do justice, and to love kindness,
>   and to walk humbly with your God? (Mic. 6:8)

These expectations are paralleled in the standards I am proposing for genetic intervention in human beings. Human genetic intervention should proceed only when the intervention is

1. safe,
2. a genuine improvement,
3. an increase in the recipient's capacity, and
4. the best available use of limited resources.

The first standard of safety calls for protecting people from harm, and the second calls for genuine improvement for the recipient. These are both implications of Micah's call to love kindness. The third standard of increasing opportunity for recipients rather than trying to predestine them follows from walking humbly. We are to respect the needs and perspectives of others. They will not be predestined by our choices if our choices *increase their* choices. The fourth standard, to assure the best available use of limited resources, is required by Micah's call to do justice. That standard requires considering with due care and fairness the competing needs of varied individuals and communities. Micah 6:8 and my enumeration parallel as well the three fundamental norms that John Rawls described as undergirding liberal society: beneficence/ nonmaleficence, autonomy, and fairness.[1] There is also resonance in the principles articulated by Tom L. Beauchamp and James F. Childress in *Principles of Biomedical Ethics*.[2] As nonmaleficence, beneficence, autonomy, and justice, they dominate the practice of bioethics. Beauchamp and Childress write that they have abstracted these principles from our common morality. As referenced above, it is a common morality with a long tradition.

The four standards proposed in this chapter may receive wide affirmation as key questions, but I intend them to be particularly grounded and shaped in this work by Christian thought. Moral standards can be described as abstractions, what Michael Walzer calls a "thin" description, or with all the "thick" context and nuance of a particular tradition.[3] For example, the Beauchamp and Childress principle of beneficence, which states that one should generally contribute to the welfare of others, highlights an agenda more than it offers specific guidance. By itself it does not designate the ends needed to define what would indeed be beneficial. Its important contribution is more heuristic than material. I will use the call to beneficence more "thickly" as enabling genuine improvement, defined as helping others to grow and flourish in a way that knows and pleases God as that is understood in the Christian tradition. With respect for other traditions, my intent is to think through what members of the Christian tradition should do. Celia Deane-Drummond calls for the virtue of wisdom.[4] Appreciating that, I am trying to take the next step of actually thinking through how

---

1. John Rawls, *A Theory of Justice* (Cambridge: Harvard University Press, 1971).

2. Tom L. Beauchamp and James F. Childress, *Principles of Biomedical Ethics*, 4th ed. (New York: Oxford University Press, 1994).

3. Michael Walzer, *Thick and Thin: Moral Argument at Home and Abroad* (Notre Dame, Ind.: University of Notre Dame Press, 1994).

4. Celia Deane-Drummond, *Wonder and Wisdom* (West Conshohocken, Pa.: Templeton Press, 2006); *Genetics and Christian Ethics* (Cambridge: Cambridge University Press, 2006); *Creation through Wisdom* (London: T. & T. Clark, 2004); *Ethics of Nature* (Oxford: Wiley-Blackwell, 2004); *Biology and Theology Today* (London: SCM, 2003).

a wise person in the Christian tradition might address these issues. In that endeavor, principles can be useful tools for living out virtues such as wisdom. Virtues and principles are not antithetical.[5] Further, the virtuous use of principles can be deeply shaped by the understanding of reality and goals endemic to the Christian faith. For the third of the world's population that considers itself Christian, such a perspective should be formative. It may well be of interest as well to those who work with Christians or live alongside them.

Safety in Particular

From the beginning medicine has been committed to *primum non nocere* (first do no harm), or in other words, at least do not make the patient worse. The threat of making a patient worse is called risk. Risk is the composite of severity of a potential result multiplied by the likelihood of it taking place. An activity that could end in death might still be low risk if the chance of death is quite small. Driving to work might be an example. Being caught in a passing rain on an Oxfordshire summer day might be low risk, because while highly likely to happen, the damage from the adverse event would be quite low. We are generally willing to take greater risks for greater benefits. Once an intervention is proven from experience to have improbable or minimal harm, it can be extended to pursue lower benefits. The "precautionary principle" is sometimes cited; that counsels "when in doubt, don't." Actually, "when in doubt, don't" can sponsor inaction that is as decisive and risky as action. Inaction is not always the safest course. Living characteristically incurs risk. The case can be made that God takes risks in giving us choice and creativity. The very act of God speaking risks being misunderstood or ignored.[6] Safety requires care, not the elimination of all risk.

As with the introduction of any new drug, carefully observed and phased introduction embodies the maxim to first do no harm. Standard drug testing begins with gradually increasing amounts of the drug in ani-

---

5. For example, see the argument and practice of Edmund D. Pellegrino in *The Christian Virtues in Medical Practice* (Washington, D.C.: Georgetown University Press, 1996).

6. Donald M. Bruce, "Playing Dice with Creation," in *Re-ordering Nature*, ed. Celia Deane-Drummond et al. (London: T. & T. Clark, 2003), p. 155.

mal models. When the drug is shown to be safe for animals, then it is introduced in small amounts in just a few human beings. Then larger amounts are tested in larger numbers of human beings. The process is characterized by gradual implementation that puts each individual at incremental risk. Unfortunately some rare untoward effects will not be manifested until large numbers of people are involved over time, but such harms can be minimized by testing before introduction to the wider public and careful monitoring after.

Specifically in regard to human genetic intervention, multiple genes can influence one trait, even as one gene can have multiple influences. Nematodes have more genes than human beings, while human beings are much more complex. The extra complexity comes from individual genes having multiple uses. One intended change can have multiple ramifications, good or bad or mixed. Those effects can vary over the life span of interactions with environment and other genes being turned off or on. This helps to explain the spread of genes that are deleterious when one only has the harmful type, but useful when one has the harmful gene paired with a normal gene that covers for it. That is called being a carrier. It may be that the most common genetic disease for Caucasians, cystic fibrosis, helps to resist the effects of cholera when one inherits only one copy of the cystic fibrosis gene.[7] That can explain why the trait does not disappear. If it was only harmful, one would expect it to die out. Tay-Sachs carrier status may offer some protection against tuberculosis.[8] Sickle-cell anemia seems to resist malaria in carriers while being quite harmful when homozygous. Granted, a mutation that is not particularly helpful can randomly dominate, especially in a small interrelated population. Twenty-five percent of the Amish in Lancaster County, Pennsylvania, have the last name Stolzfus.[9] I am not aware of an adaptive advantage to the name Stolzfus, unless perhaps it is considered highly attractive to potential mates. The propensity of that last name probably tracks back to a few large families by that name that came early to the area and had a large number of sons rather than daughters, a random event.

7. Sherif E. Gabriel et al., "Cystic Fibrosis Heterozygote Resistance to Cholera Toxin in the Cystic Fibrosis Mouse Model," *Science* 266 (October 7, 1994): 107-9.

8. Jared M. Diamond, reply to "Tay-Sachs Carriers and Tuberculosis Resistance," *Nature* 331, no. 6158 (February 25, 1988): 666.

9. Masha Gessen, *Blood Matters* (Orlando: Houghton Mifflin Harcourt, 2008), p. 209.

Safety is complicated not only by the interaction of genes with other genes and environment, but also by inheritance. The stakes are higher when a genetic intervention is inheritable because more people are involved, but intervention should not be done even for the first recipient until its success and safety are substantially assured. Once it is clear that the procedure is helpful, provision for descendants is an advantage. Reversibility of genetic change, more by switching genes on or off than by removing them, would be a further welcome safeguard.

Someone to Protect

Derek Parfit has argued that an individual cannot be harmed by alterations before birth because the person altered is not who later comes into existence. The individual that does come into existence would not exist without the intervention, so to object to an intervention would imply that the person who results would be better off not existing than existing with the intervention.[10] This is far too low a standard. It is better to consider the intervention effect for the whole class of newborns, whoever they may turn out to be.[11] This can be seen as well in narrative identity.[12] The child born is not identical to the one born if there had been no intervention, but is still eventually the child that received the alteration.

A crucial but controversial point for protecting recipients is to recognize when a recipient is present as a human person. This is not an esoteric question in that genetic intervention is most formative early in development. Many genetic conditions can be rejected or altered only if the intervention is at an early stage of life. Further, it is easier to read the genome than to change it. If an embryo is not yet a fellow human being, it can be set aside without the loss of any existing person. Parents who love their two children with cystic fibrosis but cannot imagine how they could also manage to care for a third child with the condition could test, say, four embryos and only implant the two that are not carrying the disease. If embryos have the potential to be fellow human beings but are not yet people, setting aside the two embryos that would

10. Derek Parfit, *Reasons and Persons* (Oxford: Clarendon, 1984), p. 359.

11. Philip G. Peters Jr., *How Safe Is Safe Enough? Obligations to the Children of Reproductive Technology* (Oxford: Oxford University Press, 2004), p. 32.

12. Janet Malek, "Identity, Harm, and the Ethics of Reproductive Technology," *Journal of Medicine and Philosophy* 31 (2006): 83-95.

produce the disease would not be a double murder. The selection would assure that any children born from the remaining two embryos would not have the disease. Granted, there is no guarantee that the remaining two embryos would lead to birth. Only about one-third of naturally occurring embryos manage to implant in the uterus. Two-thirds of embryos that are conceived never establish a pregnancy.[13] The only way to avoid the routine loss of most embryos is not to have sexual intercourse at all. Further, when the two healthy embryos are implanted, it is still not clear how many children will result, because sometimes embryos naturally split into two, resulting in identical twins. Sometimes two distinct embryos merge and lead to the birth of one child who is genetically a mosaic of the first two embryos. Individuality is not settled until about two weeks after the egg and sperm meet. For that matter, even after the egg and sperm meet it takes twenty-four hours for the genetic material to gather together in a process called syngamy. Early human development is a complex process of many steps.

The Christian tradition has from the beginning emphasized neighbor love as inclusive, not exclusive. Love should seek to extend care as widely as practicable to fellow human beings, but of course that does not tell us when a fellow human being is present to love. Early members of the Christian movement were noticed for their taking in abandoned babies and caring for the sick and vulnerable. Neighbor love extends to the most vulnerable but does not of itself tell when a neighbor is present to love. When a Christian realized that she was pregnant, she was to nurture that developing life. However, early church fathers Tertullian, Lactantius, Jerome, Augustine in the *Enchiridion*, Cyril of Alexandria, Theodoret, and the most influential shaper of Roman Catholic doctrine, Thomas Aquinas, all wrote that there was no soul or person in the womb until there was a body present to ensoul.[14] This view parallels the widespread gut-level reaction of people to modern ultrasound images. When, albeit with needed magnification, something starting to resemble a human body can be seen in the womb, most people realize there is

13. See, for example, N. S. Macklon, J. P. Geraedis, and B. C. Fauser, "Conception to Ongoing Pregnancy: The 'Black Box' of Early Pregnancy Loss," *Human Reproduction Update* 8 (2002): 333-43. For women in their forties, probably 90 percent of embryos do not implant, according to D. Gareth Jones, *A Tangled Web: Medicine and Theology in Dialogue* (Oxford: Peter Lang, 2008), p. 151.

14. John Connery, *Abortion: The Development of the Roman Catholic Perspective* (Chicago: Loyola University Press, 1977), pp. 40, 50-52, 56.

a developing child present to protect. Most people do not have the same immediate recognition earlier in the process if they see a microscopic sphere consisting of identical cells. The church fathers called the point where a body was formed "formation." Before formation there was developing life of a human type, but not yet a person, a soul. That preformation period was simply not addressed by exhortation to avoid abortion. Abortion was an act that a woman might consider once she missed her period. It is during the first two weeks after sperm and egg meet that many genetic interventions might occur, before a missed period, before individuality is settled, and before formation.

There are important arguments for the position that the single cell that starts to form when the egg and sperm meet is already a fellow human being, a person, a soul. However, that conviction is not found in the Apostles', Nicene (325), or Chalcedon (451) creeds that stated classic Christian doctrine for the early church. It is not taught by Scripture.[15] It is not the traditional teaching of the Christian churches. It is not a scientific statement. How did so many current evangelicals come to think of it as a standard of science or their faith?[16] Such would be an important study. This book cannot take the time to unpack all the involved cultural history, but I note for this chapter how much such a conviction affects in some cases whether the method of intervention is safe for the recipient.[17] If an intervention kills a fellow human being, that would of course be abhorrent. If an intervention occurs before a fellow human being is present and helps a person who later does come to be, then it is safe, and by that standard welcome.

15. For example, the often cited text Jer. 1:5 says that God chose Jeremiah *before* Jeremiah was conceived. This is a description of God's knowledge and plan, not of when Jeremiah came to be. If it was about when the person Jeremiah first came into existence, it would be teaching that Jeremiah had a preexistence before being conceived. That is not a teaching of Scripture or the church. D. Gareth Jones thinks through some other misappropriated passages in *Designers of the Future* (Oxford: Monarch Books, 2005), pp. 81-82.

16. See, for example, Edwin C. Hui, *At the Beginning of Life: Dilemmas in Theological Bioethics* (Downers Grove, Ill.: InterVarsity, 2002).

17. To see the involved arguments for embryo status, an insightful place to start with a wide range of views thoughtfully pursued would be Brent Waters and Ronald Cole-Turner, eds., *God and the Embryo* (Washington, D.C.: Georgetown University Press, 2000), or my brief overview in "The Ethics of the Altered Nuclear Transfer Proposal to Obtain Embryonic Stem Cells," *Perspectives on Science and Christian Faith* 58, no. 4 (December 2006).

Safety as a Spur to Action

> We can fully expect to see the old proposals for eugenic "improvement" to the human species . . . rationalized this time, not as species "improvement" but as individual "risk reduction" — the reduction of the risks of growing old, of having children with unpalatable physical and behavioral traits, and so on. Everyone seems to agree on the value of avoiding "harm," and it is around this value that the technological amelioration of the human condition is most effectively pursued.[18]

Conrad Brunk is concerned that widely appreciated harm avoidance may become a spur for society to pursue human genetic intervention. He is quite right that there is substantial agreement that we do not want people to be harmed. "Increasingly, 'expert' formulas are dominated by considerations of harm and the risk of harm that are most amenable to the quantifiable, empirical methods of analysis that are most favored by the technological mind itself."[19] For example, the Supreme Court of Canada has made a number of recent decisions articulating that it cannot prohibit an action unless that action can be shown to cause "provable harm." But as Brunk points out, there is a remarkable range of actions that can be cast as harm avoidance. This is akin to the challenge that we saw for distinguishing cure and enhancement. All cures can be described as a kind of enhancement. Enhancements can be described as cures. Avoiding harm could become a major driving force toward enhancement. Ronald Green, for example, already advocates that we have an obligation not to bring into the world a child who will suffer genetically.[20] What is safe in a given case requires a thick and contextualized assessment, as this work is pursuing.

18. Conrad G. Brunk, "Religion, Risk, and the Technological Society," in *The Twenty-first Century Confronts Its Gods: Globalization, Technology, and War*, ed. David J. Hawkins (Albany: State University of New York Press, 2004), p. 46.

19. Brunk, "Religion, Risk," p. 48.

20. Ronald Green, "Parental Autonomy and the Obligation Not to Harm One's Child Genetically," *Journal of Law, Medicine and Ethics* 25 (1997): 5.

8 Genuine Improvement

What Is Indeed Better?

It is said that you can never be too rich or too thin. To the contrary, have you seen anorexia? Too rich may be harder to discern, but it is flagged in 1 Timothy 6:10. "For the love of money is a root of all kinds of evil, and in their eagerness to be rich some have wandered away from the faith and pierced themselves with many pains." One can have too much of a good thing if it begins to crowd out what is most important. There are concerns that genetic intervention would be trying to improve on God's plan for human life.[1] Apparent goods from genetic intervention might replace or distract from God's best. Such abuse is well worth taking into account, but I have argued along with Irenaeus that God's plan includes the improvement of human life. It may be that some physical enhancement can be a small part of that development.

Generally an improvement is an improvement. We do not usually question whether it is good to improve. Our definition of improvement will stem directly from what we understand to be the purpose of our lives. Education, athletic training, and proper diet are examples of long-lauded attempts toward enhancement. We go to great lengths in education to try to develop ability and health. Morally and spiritually as well, by God's grace one is to train to be closer and closer to the image of Je-

---

1. Donal P. O'Mathuna, "Genetic Technology, Enhancement, and Christian Values," *National Catholic Bioethics Quarterly* 2 (2002): 227-95.

sus Christ.[2] If these goals are legitimate, the question that remains is one of justified means, not whether it is appropriate to try to improve. Enhancements might enable us to process what we experience, understand, and remember more effectively. They might also make us less slaves to illness, pain, premature death, even less dependent on medical science and physicians.[3] Growth is part of the mandate to sustain and improve what is entrusted to us. That includes our physical selves and the rest of the physical world.

What is crucially at issue for this standard of improvement is whether a given genetic change actually *is* an improvement and whether it is a net improvement when all its implications are considered. On the one hand, injecting a genetically produced vaccine to increase the body's immunity against a debilitating or even lethal disease is easy to recognize as a genuine improvement. On the other hand, because genetics are so basic to human structure and function, apparently small changes can have surprisingly pervasive and varied effects. These can quickly complicate the evaluation of an intervention. The stakes are particularly high in genetic intervention in that it can alter the brain and in so doing alter the person.[4] The role genetics play in cognition, affec-

---

2. James Keenan describes this process in the Roman Catholic tradition as one of pursuing "perfection," which is the fulfillment of what one is called to be. For Keenan, properly used genetic enhancement might aid that goal. See "A Virtuous Consideration of Enhancement," *Christian Bioethics* 5, no. 2 (August 1999): 104-20.

3. John Harris, *Enhancing Evolution: The Ethical Case for Making Better People* (Princeton: Princeton University Press, 2007), p. 2.

4. The book edited by Warren S. Brown, Nancey Murphy, and H. Newton Malony, *Whatever Happened to the Soul? Scientific and Theological Portraits of Human Nature* (Minneapolis: Fortress, 1998), has been influential in describing the human soul as a distinct yet emergent property of the physical body. J. P. Moreland and Scott B. Rae have responded with *Body and Soul: Human Nature and the Crisis in Ethics* (Downers Grove, Ill.: InterVarsity, 2000), that the body and soul are two distinct entities intimately related to each other. To the contrary, the New Testament scholar Joel B. Green argues that dualism is not found in Christian Scripture. In *Body, Soul, and Human Life: The Nature of Humanity in the Bible* (Grand Rapids: Baker Academic, 2008), he finds monism a much more apt description from a biblical worldview. The 2009 September issue (61, no. 3) of *Perspectives on Science and Christian Faith* (the journal of the American and Canadian Scientific Affiliations) has a lively exchange in Rae's review of Green's book, followed by a response from Green (pp. 191-96). For our discussion here, whether preferring types of dualism or monism, there is substantial consensus that the physical body affects what is often called the soul, and that the soul affects the physical body.

tive regulation, personality, and central system disorders is receiving increasing investigation and established connections.[5] The physical brain and the genes that found its structure deeply shape our perception and behavior.[6]

Resulting characteristics are often double-edged. If one intervenes genetically to emphasize one particular temperament, one may lose another with its attendant advantages. Compulsiveness can be an annoying trait and in sufficient degree a psychiatric disorder, yet a deep sense of responsibility, vigilance, and attention to detail can be virtues.[7] They are necessary traits for earning a Ph.D. Different cultures reward different personality constellations. Drugs that alter personal styles may not so much be improving the person as helping the person better fit a particular society's expectations.[8] The compulsive industry that one culture may admire may be spurned as narrow hyperactivity by another. What one person considers laudable acting on principle can be seen by another as stubbornness; cooperativeness as seen by one can be collaboration in another's eyes, or rugged individualism can be seen as feckless egoism.[9] Moreover, some genetic predispositions lead to positive outcomes given certain types of environmental influences and to negative outcomes given other circumstances. "There are no genes specific for criminal behavior. Instead, there are genes that predispose children to impulsive, compulsive, hyperactive, and aggressive behaviors, and when these behaviors persist for a lifetime, the affected individuals are at a greater risk of becoming involved in various illegal behaviors. Of course, some of these same individuals may also become congressmen, senators, entrepreneurs, and CEOs."[10]

Kay Redfield Jamison has argued that many artists have had

5. Terry E. Goldberg and Daniel R. Weinberger, eds., *The Genetics of Cognitive Neuroscience* (Cambridge: MIT Press, 2009).

6. For example, Byron C. Jones and Pierre Mormede, eds., *Neurobehavioral Genetics: Methods and Applications* (Boca Raton, Fla.: CRC Press, 2006), and W. Jordan et al., eds., *Psychiatric Genetics: Applications in Clinical Practice* (Washington, D.C.: American Psychiatric Publishing, 2008).

7. Peter D. Kramer, *Listening to Prozac: A Psychiatrist Explores Antidepressant Drugs and the Remaking of the Self* (New York: Penguin Books, 1993), p. 35.

8. Kramer, *Listening to Prozac*, p. 41.

9. Charles Frankel, "The Specter of Eugenics," *Commentary* 57, no. 3 (March 1974): 31.

10. David E. Comings, "Both Genes and Environment Play a Role in Antisocial Behavior," *Politics and the Life Sciences* (March 1996): 84.

symptoms of manic depression, but any heightened creativity would not justify their suffering.[11] One can take Prozac (flurocine) to relieve psychic pain. Flurocine limits serotonin uptake, which leaves more serotonin available in the system. It is not manufactured by gene transfer techniques, but exemplifies one of the important questions that the multiplication of genetic pharmaceuticals will raise more emphatically. Such treatment could be quite helpful or it might mask needed attention to what is causing the pain.[12] We would do well to recognize if the pain is a warning sign of something that needs correction before the damage is worse. One of the most feared aspects of leprosy is the inability to feel pain. While not being able to feel pain sounds wonderful to anyone experiencing chronic pain, that loss makes it difficult to defend the body from injury. Physical pain usually warns that something is wrong and needs immediate attention before the damage worsens. Not feeling the warning of pain results in a gradual wearing away of body parts as they are injured and lost. Now psychic pain can have a purely physical cause, in which case a physical response is quite appropriate; however, it might alternatively stem from a destructive pattern embedded by years of abuse or bad choices. Like physical pain, emotional pain can also be a sign that something is wrong and emphatically needs our attention in our physical, psychological, social, or spiritual life. To turn off the warning light without dealing with the actual problem might be devastating over time. Granted, if psychic pain is signaling an overwhelming underlying need, there may be times when it is helpful to temporarily postpone that need chemically until one is able to handle it better.[13] But simply because drugs can provide relief does not mean that the problem was merely physical. The drug may mask a warning signal about something deeper. Solving the problem and taking Prozac might both increase levels of serotonin in the brain, but the more important change might be in priorities, convictions, and character, not just brain chemistry. We need to be careful that we do not settle for counterfeit fixes that

11. Kay Redfield Jamison, *Touched with Fire: Manic Depressive Illness and the Artistic Temperament* (New York: Free Press, 1993).

12. James Peterson and Kelvin Mutter, "Discerning Pain for Its Alleviation," *Journal of Spirituality and Mental Health* (forthcoming).

13. Michael J. Boivin, "Finding God in Prozac or Finding Prozac in God: Preserving a Christian View of the Person amidst a Biopsychological Revolution," *Christian Scholar's Review* 32, no. 2 (Winter 2003): 159-76.

turn off the warning light instead of addressing the reason it is calling for our attention. As spiritual beings in a school for souls, we are here to learn, not for maximum comfort.

Ritalin has become the drug of choice in some places for many young children. It seems to be helpful for a genuine condition of attention deficit disorder. It may also be a convenient way to pacify large ill-taught classes or to temper the results of widespread dependence on the rapid images and passive entertainment of television as a babysitter for young children. A genetically designed pill might release the same neuro-transmitters in the brain as prayer, so that there is a parallel feeling. But for the Christian tradition, prayer is not about pursuing a physical sensation; prayer is about a relationship with God. A pill might duplicate one physical side effect of prayer but not its purpose. If the drug comes to re-place prayer, it has been a distraction from what most mattered.

The point is a good life, not just a good time. Thoughtful hedonists realize that the best net effect of maximum pleasure and minimal pain over a lifetime might require forgoing some immediate pleasure. A hedonist might give up the pleasure of rich desserts to extend life for other pleasures that are less life-shortening. But from a Christian perspective, a good life is not the pursuit of passing pleasure at all. Pleasure is not the point. This brief life on earth is a place of growth, a place of learning and becoming the kind of people that can glorify and enjoy God forever. If one wants to be miserable, try to be happy. Joy is found in giving up pleasing oneself as the central project. Jesus was characterized by abundant joy, yet apparently lived under often dismal circumstances and ended that time in a torturous death. He is a model for all that human beings can be. The good life is not in amassing and securing personal comforts and prizes. It is about abiding joy, not just moments of happiness. It is about living in a way that pleases God and is suitable for the life to come. That needed growth in character becomes embodied in the human brain. Our brain is structured by our choices over time in physical connection patterns that encourage angles of perception and response. That is character, mental reflexes to see and value and do what is right.

In light of the above, what would be an example of an improvement? Ability is not relative to normal species functioning, rather to possible alternatives.[14] John Harris gives the following example: If the

14. Harris, *Enhancing Evolution*, p. 92.

ozone layer someday disappears, there could come a time when white skin could be a devastating disability in its vulnerability to skin cancer. It would be quite normal for many people, but a substantial handicap that could be overcome by darker skin. There would be a clear identifiable advantage to receiving a genetic intervention to increase melanin. Would a genetic intervention that increased quickness and facility of memory be an enhancement? Yes, in the sense that it would be immensely helpful for learning languages and other memory-intensive endeavors that are crucial to communication and community across national borders or even for tasks as simple and important as a teacher learning student names. Would memory enhancement make a painful memory difficult to forget? Improved ability to recall does not require one to recall. One still has a choice in what one chooses to revisit. What of capacity overload? Like a computer's memory chip or a full cup, is there simply no room for more information if one's brain is already filled to capacity? It is possible that most people already have storage that they have not tapped, or storage capacity that could be effectively expanded. Increasing information does require increasing search capabilities in order to use it well, as seen in the explosion of information on the Web and search engines to retrieve it. So for some enhancements to be helpful, they would have to progress in tandem with others. Whether the effect a genetic intervention offers is a genuine improvement will often be a complex judgment.

Prejudiced sex selection does not meet the standard of genuine improvement. In India, ultrasound has been so commonly used for sex selection that birth ratios of male to female are running in some areas at 135 to 75.[15] At least this horrific loss of daughters is likely to be self-correcting. If one sex is selected more than half of the time, the status of the rejected sex should rise as natural shortages follow. Families seeking gender balance are a different case where both genders are valued. The Baylor School of Medicine is tracking the results when parents can choose a girl or boy to see what results accrue in their context.[16]

John Rawls's notion of primary goods that every rational person should value includes goods such as liberties, opportunities, income and

15. Allen Buchanan et al., *From Chance to Choice: Genetics and Justice* (Cambridge: Cambridge University Press, 2000), p. 183. Ronald M. Green cites 130 males to 100 females in some regions of India, in Green, *Babies by Design* (New Haven: Yale University Press, 2007), p. 199.

16. Ronald M. Green, *Babies by Design*, p. 203.

wealth, health, intelligence, and imagination.[17] By Rawls's estimation, it would be irrational not to want any of these. Along the same lines, Ronald Lindsay argues that "If there ever were a way to enhance mental acuity, mathematical and spatial reasoning, language faculties, creativity, musical abilities, and the like, I would propose that we should do so."[18] After a survey of the varied Christian traditions on genetic enhancement, Ted Peters advocates that enhancement of mood, memory, or executive capabilities in themselves could lead to an improvement in human well-being without raising ethical objections.[19]

Lauding Suffering

For Nancy Mairs, interventions that relieve suffering are not improvements. She writes, "[P]erhaps because I have embraced a faith with crucifixion at its heart, I do not consider suffering an aberration or an outrage to be eliminated at any cost, even the cost of my life. It strikes me as an element intrinsic to the human condition. I don't like it. I'm not asked to like it. I must simply endure in order to learn from it. Those who leap forward to offer me aid in ending it, though they may do so out of the greatest compassion, seek to deny me the fullness of experience I believe I am meant to have."[20] Physical suffering is not a new issue for the Christian tradition. In parts of the West where the church is well established, suffering is not automatically associated with church membership, yet persecution has been the case through most of the church's history and even today in many parts of the world. Most of church history has been characterized by great suffering. It was not even legal to be a Christian in the Roman Empire until the Edict of Milan in 313, almost three hundred years after the church began. To this day Christians are severely persecuted for their faith in many parts of

17. John Rawls, *A Theory of Justice* (Cambridge: Harvard University Press, 1971), pp. 54-55.
18. Ronald A. Lindsay, "Germ-Line Genetic Enhancement and Rawlsian Primary Goods," *Kennedy Institute of Ethics Journal* 15, no. 1 (2005): 50-52.
19. Ted Peters, *Anticipating Omega: Science, Faith, and Our Ultimate Future* (Göttingen: Vandenhoeck & Ruprecht, 2006), p. 128.
20. Nancy Mairs, "Sex, Death, and the Crippled Body: A Meditation," as quoted by Amos Yong, *Theology and Down Syndrome: Reimagining Disability in Late Modernity* (Waco, Tex.: Baylor University Press, 2007), p. 179.

the world. Current slavery in Sudan and burnings in Orissa are examples. This is not a surprise to members of the tradition. The central symbol is the cross, an instrument devised to inflict pain. Since Christ was allowed to suffer, it is not surprising that such might befall his people as well. This is not perceived as in some sense a deserved suffering as in karma. Karma was assumed when people brought a man born blind to Jesus. They asked him, "Who sinned, the man born blind or his parents?" The puzzle was in their assumption that surely someone had sinned for the man to suffer in this way. If it was his parents, it was not fair for their child to suffer the ill consequences. If it was the child's own sin, how could he be guilty at birth? Jesus replied that it was neither (John 9:1-3). At another point he noted that a recent building collapse had crushed people who were no more guilty than others (Luke 13:4-5). Bad things can happen to people whether they are predominately good or bad.

Why then does God allow suffering that God could have stopped? There have been countless opportunities to reflect on that question. They have generated as many responses. The following is a brief list of ten possibilities that have been cited, none of which is exclusive to the others.

1. A great deal of suffering may be self-inflicted in varying degrees. If one embezzles at work and then is caught, life in jail is a great loss, but it is a self-inflicted one. One cannot blame God for one's incarceration. If one commits adultery, the loss of one's spouse and children is not an affliction from God. That is the result of one's own devastating actions.

2. In the two examples above the perpetrator is not the only one hurt. Many people are hurt by someone else's abuse of free will. This includes God (Eph. 4:30). Why then allow it? Free will exacts a high price. It must be endemic to what is most important to be worth its cost.

3. Other writers attribute some suffering to chance. If individuals want God to leave them alone, God honors that choice and leaves them alone. In that case they cannot blame God for not protecting them in an often dangerous world.

4. Suffering may serve to draw our attention to something that needs to be addressed before the damage is worse.

5. While suffering can obscure everything else if it overwhelms or is allowed to dominate one's life, it can call the sufferer to take stock of

what most matters. Clear and right priorities are worth a significant price.

6. Søren Kierkegaard wrote that suffering is a powerful medicine that either kills or heals the patient. One's response is all-important. Suffering can build character that comes in no other way. To strengthen a muscle one must exercise it. Suffering is not always only an enemy. It can sometimes be a teacher (1 Pet. 1:6-7). Coal can become diamonds under pressure.

7. Over the centuries Christians have taken some consolation that God suffers too (Eph. 4:30). While some theologians have argued that God is impassible (cannot suffer), most agree that at least in the person of Jesus Christ and in his people God suffers. This was central, for example, to Julian of Norwich's meditations on the cross as so many people around her died of the plague.[21] In the cross she could see both God's firsthand understanding of human suffering and God's compassion going to such lengths to relieve it.

8. Suffering can be on behalf of others. This has its most clear example in Jesus Christ. When he faced the time of his crucifixion, Jesus prayed for that cup to be taken away from him if there was another way to achieve God's purpose. But he was willing to pay the necessary price to free his people. His later followers often counted it a privilege to share with him in everything, including that price (Phil. 1:29-30). It appears that almost all the original disciples died for their faith, as did countless others.

9. Suffering on this earth is temporary. It is said that Abraham Lincoln used to keep perspective through celebration and trial by repeating to himself that "this too will soon pass away." Somehow things are more bearable if one is confident that their duration is finite. The Christian tradition is confident that there can be horrendous moments, but they are but a fraction of time compared to the eternity promised to God's people (2 Cor. 4:17).

10. The most prominent response to suffering in the biblical tradition is to trust in God's character. God knows what God is doing and that is enough. This is the response to suffering found in the book of Job. When Job asks God why he is suffering so, God begins to reminisce with him about creating the great creatures of the sea and laying the founda-

---

21. Julian of Norwich, *Showings*, ed. Edmund Colledge (Ramsey, N.J.: Paulist, 2002).

tions of the continents. The point is not that God is more powerful than Job. That is overwhelmingly true. The point is that Job does not have the big picture. Job cannot even conceive of all that God has done or is doing (Job 42:1-6). It might be akin to the first time I took my twin daughters in for their immunizations. They looked at me with disbelief when I allowed them to be stabbed with a needle by the strange woman in a white coat. Yet they had nowhere else to turn for comfort and still toddled back to me. I so wished that I could explain that the shot was necessary to protect them from great harm in the future, but they could not yet speak sufficiently to understand the concept of immunization. Also, I would have gladly suffered the pain in their place.

Suffering can serve an important role, yet by definition it is painful. Following Jesus' example, his people should look for ways to relieve it. If suffering is relieved, is some good lost that would have been achieved through it?[22] Human life is fragile. There will always be sufficient opportunities to suffer to achieve those ends. Healing on all human levels of being was central to the ministry of Jesus Christ and remains characteristic of his people. The physical world is a place to choose reconciliation and healing.

Differently Able

Allen Buchanan and his coauthors argue that when genetic intervention is available to correct a disability, it would be wrong not to use it.[23] Yet some argue that people who are differently abled are always so for a worthy reason.[24] Sharon Betcher argues that the Holy Spirit should be seen "not as the power to rescue and repair according to some presupposed 'original state' or ideal form, but as the energy for 'unleashing multiple forms of corporeal flourishing.'"[25] Amos Yong adds that the

22. Hans Ruh, "Die ethische Verantwortung des Naturwissenschafters," *Reformatio* 32 (April 1983): 156.

23. Buchanan et al., *From Chance to Choice.*

24. John Swinton and Brian Brock, eds., *Theology, Disability, and the New Genetics: Why Science Needs the Church* (New York: T. & T. Clark, 2007); Yong, *Theology and Down Syndrome.*

25. Sharon Betcher, "Monstrosities, Miracles, and Mission: Religion and the Politics of Disablement," as quoted by Yong, *Theology and Down Syndrome,* pp. 181-82.

180

Spirit values and nurtures the full range of human embodiment,[26] and Stanley Hauerwas concludes that "Our greatest nobility as humans often derives from the individual's struggle to make positive use of his or her limitations."[27] There can be a beauty, an admirable accomplishment, in what we do with what we have. God knows what we face and how we deal with it. Augustine argued further that what can seem harmful is nevertheless God-ordained to bless the larger picture. To eliminate such suffering lessens the whole.[28]

Discernment is required then to know what to allow to continue and what to relieve. In the incarnation, the second person of the Trinity was severely limited for a time, disabled in regard to his divine attributes. Granted, the self-limitation was by choice. Paul was to remain content with his thorn in the flesh. God accommodated Moses' stammer. Jacob had a limp and Jesus' resurrection body still bore scars (John 20:24-28).[29] Were Christ's scars essential for Thomas to identify him at that moment or a precedent for all time of how God will resurrect us? Luke heralds that the poor, maimed, blind, and lame are welcomed to the heavenly banquet, but do they remain permanently poor, maimed, blind, and lame (Luke 14:15-24)? Jesus did not leave the man born blind as he was (John 9). Among the joys Isaiah describes as a sign of God's future reign are hearing for the deaf and sight for the blind (Isa. 29:18). The point is not perfection,[30] just freeing people to be all they can be.

This raises a theological issue that is particularly sensitive for Amos Yong's tradition. Classic Pentecostals believe that all illness has been relieved on the cross, so continuing disability or illness always tracks back to sin or lack of faith. Yong argues to the contrary that his own brother with Down's is part of God's plan for a diverse human community. Waters argues in parallel in the Swinton volume, "May not the scholar disabled by critical cynicism, for instance, be graced by the

26. Yong, *Theology and Down Syndrome*, p. 182.

27. Stanley Hauerwas, *Suffering Presence* (Notre Dame, Ind.: University of Notre Dame Press, 1981), p. 172.

28. Augustine, *City of God* 16.8.

29. See also Nancy Eiesland, *The Disabled God: Toward a Liberatory Theology of Disability* (Nashville: Abingdon, 1994), p. 98.

30. Michael J. Sandel, *The Case against Perfection: Ethics in an Age of Genetic Engineering* (Cambridge: Harvard University Press, Belknap Press, 2007), and Leon Kass, "Ageless Bodies, Happy Souls: Biotechnology and the Pursuit of Perfection," *New Atlantis*, Spring 2003, pp. 9-28.

gift of simplicity offered him by the Down's syndrome person?" For Waters, as for Yong, Down's is part of the different gifting God has designed for the edification of all. For Yong, Down's is God's design for his brother now and for eternity. John Swinton tells the story of a woman "who has a rich spiritual life and who feels special *because* of her disability, not in spite of it."[31]

While it is essential to make peace with what one has, she is special because she is, not because she has a disability. We need not make a virtue or end goal of necessity. If disability is a blessing, as described above, why not provide it for everyone? If the point is to be passive in regard to genetics as God-ordained, why not be passive for every other genetically endowed characteristic such as some types of being born blind? Even if God ordains a condition, cannot God ordain its relief?

As mentioned concerning risk, it has been argued that almost any genetic endowment is preferable to not existing. Hence being a child that was designed to be deaf is better than not being at all. If the only alternative is nonexistence, almost any state should be acceptable. This argument seems to have the implication that a child has no place to complain if it is born with fetal alcohol syndrome to a mother abusing alcohol while pregnant, if the only alternative is never having been born at all. On the contrary, the standard should concern whether the parents have done everything they morally and reasonably can to bless a child they bring into the world.[32] We should and do make significant efforts to prevent intellectual disability. For instance, lead has been reduced in paint and gasoline to limit brain damage during pregnancy. By law, alcoholic beverages carry warnings that drinking alcohol during pregnancy can lead to fetal alcohol syndrome. Some parents have tried to bless their children by using prenatal diagnosis to screen for or against certain genetic conditions. One is already making a decision like this when, for example, deciding whether or not to have children that are likely to share one's potentially lethal or debilitating genes. If an adult with Huntington's disease chooses not to have genetically related children, is that significantly different from only implanting embryos that do not have the disease? The answer depends on whether or not a

31. John Swinton, introduction to *Theology, Disability, and the New Genetics*, p. 5.

32. Jonathan Glover discusses the related issues at length in "Parental Choice and What We Owe Our Children," in *Choosing Children, Genes, Disability, and Design* (Oxford: Oxford University Press, 2006), pp. 37-72.

fellow human being is yet present at the embryonic stage. Any human should be welcomed and cared for. A crucial question then is when a human being is present, an important discussion that I have referenced in the last chapter.

We have always had some control over both the timing of children and their later development. Preimplantation diagnosis makes possible some guidance of the child's genetic heritage as well. Our responsibility remains whether we intervene or not. With the availability of the new technology comes responsibility for selecting the child's genetic endowment or for not doing so. Genetic heritage becomes increasingly less fate and more parental choice. There is less surprise and more opportunity to help or harm. The availability of the technology does not leave us the option of not choosing. Even if the embryo is not yet a fellow human being, some have expressed concern that choosing one set of genes over another kills a potentially great figure with the rejected genetic start. One may be avoiding Beethoven because his genes showed a predisposition to someday go deaf. But by this speculation, the selection of an embryo could also be avoiding Mao or Stalin, each responsible for the systematic death of tens of millions of people. We just cannot tell that level of prediction from reading genetic endowment. Genes create terrain, not destiny. A good genetic start does not guarantee a good outcome; it just makes such more likely. As in most of life, one does not have guarantees, but one can improve the likelihood of a more capable life.

Officially, prenatal genetic testing is offered in standard medical care to enhance preparation and choice. In practice, what is most often available currently is abortion well into pregnancy to prevent the birth of children with disabilities, most often with Down's syndrome.[33] Shuman and Volck estimate that from 70 to 90 percent of Down's syndrome fetuses are aborted in North America.[34] Termination rates after prenatal diagnosis of Down's range from 67 to 95 percent in Europe.[35]

---

33. Hugo W. Moser, "A Role for Gene Therapy in Mental Retardation," *Mental Retardation and Developmental Disabilities* 1 (1995): 4-6. Ruth Schwartz Cowan does describe the use of prenatal genetic testing in Cyprus to avoid some abortions for thalassemia. *Heredity and Hope: The Case for Genetic Screening* (Cambridge: Harvard University Press, 2008).

34. Joel Shuman and Brian Volck, *Reclaiming the Body* (Grand Rapids: Brazos, 2006), p. 81.

35. Celia Deane-Drummond, *Genetics and Christian Ethics* (Cambridge: Cambridge University Press, 2006), p. 90.

Down's is caused by a trisomy at chromosome 21 and affects far more than just mental agility. It is associated with "much higher incidences [of] potentially fatal conditions like cardiovascular diseases, pulmonary vascular abnormalities, hematological (blood-related) and gastrointestinal disorders, leukemia, pneumonia, diabetes (and all of its side effects), thyroid disease, epileptic seizures, osteoporosis (bone fragility), and insomnia."[36] These vary in combination and severity. Developed countries have been able to raise average life expectancy for those with Down's syndrome to about fifty-five, still far less than the average of those without trisomy 21.[37] Within that shortened life span the incidence of Alzheimer's is four times as high as for the general population.[38] Down's syndrome children vary in capability. Most of them learn, though usually not as quickly as, and possibly by different methods from, the average. They can live fulfilling, but relatively short, lives.

The writers of the Swinton and Brock anthology are agreed that the abortion of Down's pregnancies is a travesty for at least three reasons. First, by the time a diagnosis of Down's is made, a fellow human being is already with us and should be welcomed. If the one diagnosed in the womb with Down's has already developed to the point of being a fellow human being, protection and nurture should follow as much as for people at any other age. Since the diagnosis is usually not available until several months into pregnancy, it is held by many that a child is already present and should be welcomed whatever his condition.

Second, aborting Down's pregnancies disparages those who live with Down's. This concern quite appropriately considers how people perceive themselves and long-term societal momentum. People are embodied, but they are also more than their bodies. Most can distinguish who they are from a condition that affects them. Avoiding the condition does not say that those who still deal with it are thereby worth less. But killing someone who already does exist because that person has a condition is threatening to others who also have it.

Third, God has a purpose in people being born with Down's. When they are not, the world is poorer for missing them and the individual for not fulfilling a personal calling. This contention parallels an Augustinian view of providence that God ordains even the darkest

---

36. Yong, *Theology and Down Syndrome*, p. 62.
37. Yong, *Theology and Down Syndrome*, p. 73.
38. Yong, *Theology and Down Syndrome*, p. 74.

threads of our lives for their role in the greater picture we do not yet see. Modesty in what we think we know is needed, yet would one be willing to apply this understanding to brittle bone disease where a little girl breaks ribs when she sneezes and her femur if she tries to skip rope? She suffers for God's plan?

Thomas Reynolds recognizes the real challenges that people face with disabilities, but emphasizes the present worth of those with disabilities.[39] He is particularly concerned that impairments not be exacerbated by societal expectations into disabilities.[40] "Deformity is in the eyes of the beholder."[41] Nearsightedness is not often thought of as a disability because society has developed tools such as eyeglasses that negate it as an issue. The Americans with Disabilities Act of 1990 has mandated that public buildings be wheelchair accessible so that such mode of locomotion offers relatively free movement. The Accessibility for Ontarians with Disabilities Act of 2005 pursues that end as well. Individuals should do their best to take part, and society can do much to make that possible. Disability is an opportunity not only for an individual to adjust, but also for wider society and the church in particular to make a way. But impairment is not just socially constructed. Reynolds has written a heartfelt book spurred by his son facing Tourette's, Asperger's, bipolar, and obsessive-compulsive disorders. He writes that "we frequently had to negotiate our way through anxieties or embarrassing eruptions in public places like church, a restaurant, or the local grocery store, which always elicited condescending gazes and suspicious whispers . . . of bad parenting or a toxic home environment."[42] Then there is the difficulty in discerning which behaviors that limit his son's ability to function result from developmental disability and which from developmental immaturity.[43] One set must be worked around, the other should not be infantilized where genuine growth can occur.

Philip Ferguson writes:

39. Thomas E. Reynolds, *Vulnerable Communion: A Theology of Disability and Hospitality* (Grand Rapids: Brazos, 2008), p. 187.

40. Reynolds, *Vulnerable Communion*, pp. 14-15, 210.

41. Brian Brock and Stephanie Brock, "Being Disabled in the New World of Genetic Testing," in *Theology, Disability, and the New Genetics*, p. 41.

42. Reynolds, *Vulnerable Communion*, pp. 12-13.

43. Reynolds, *Vulnerable Communion*, p. 75.

> The point is not so much whether . . . a blind person cannot enjoy a Rembrandt . . . but whether social arrangements can be imagined that allow blind people to have intense aesthetic experiences. . . . People in wheelchairs may not be able to climb mountains, but how hard is it to create a society where the barriers are removed to their experiences of physical exhilaration . . . ? Someone with Down syndrome may not be able to experience the exquisite joy of reading bioethics papers and debating ethical theory, but . . . that person can experience the joy of thinking hard about something and reflecting on what he or she really believes. . . . The challenge is to create the society that will allow as many different paths as possible to the qualities of life that make us all part of the human community.[44]

A genetic impairment of a function is most severe if the structure of society requires that function to participate. Sometimes the most effective service may be in removing the structural demand. Genetic research has great promise to enable better understanding of one facet of who we are. It cannot bring utopia, but increasingly it can enable us to make life better for many people. That is a worthy endeavor, yet one that needs to be balanced with research into other promising ways of helping people flourish.

People faced with impairment or illness are never just cases of the disease or disability. They are unique persons, part of the body of Christ, no less for what they face. We can still ask and should ask, "Are there ways you can contribute?" Almost always the answer is yes, and both they and the body of Christ are better for it. A person with a visible disability might not consider that difference to be his or her greatest concern. Jesus did not assume such. When presented with people paralyzed or blind, he asked, "What would *you* like me to do for you?" (Luke 18:40-41). Alasdair MacIntyre writes, "Disability and dependence on others are something that all of us experience at certain times in our lives and this to unpredictable degrees, and . . . consequently our interest in how the needs of the disabled are adequately voiced and met is not a special interest . . . , but rather the interest of the whole politi-

---

44. Philip Ferguson, as quoted in Erik Parens and Adrienne Asch, "The Disability Rights Critique of Prenatal Genetic Testing," *Hastings Center Report* Special Supplement 29, no. 5 (1999): S13-S14.

cal society, an interest that is integral to their conception of the common good."[45] As is often said, the able-bodied are only temporarily so.

We can often learn from dealing with difficulty, but this is not a warrant to intentionally deafen one-half of the population and blind the other half for the good of our souls. Even if we do our best to approach full functioning, there will still be no lack of obstacles in life to teach us to cope and to help. We do not need to create, laud, or acquiesce to impairment. Would we leave a child unable to walk because it seems to be good for his character? Should we leave correctable conditions untreated as a moral lesson for those afflicted and those not? The recognition of different abilities helps one to deal with unchangeable situations, but personal hardship that could be relieved should not be retained. The neighbor who has limitations, and we all do, varying with type and time, should be just as treasured as one who has fewer limitations. This does not mean however that one should abstain from seeking to free people as much as possible, all other things being equal. Even for those holding Augustine's view that God ultimately is the cause of each affliction, God may also lead us to heal when we can.

Improvement of Relative Position

Some genetic changes might be not so much advantages in and of themselves as positional leverage over other people. An editorial in the *Lancet* argues concerning growth hormone treatment that it is better to change society's attitudes than the physical height of the individual.[46] Here the argument is assuming a case where the intervention does not concretely help the recipient except to greater social acceptance or in social competition. In such a case it would be more humane for society to welcome and respect all as they are than to insist on aesthetic conformity or an antiquated connection of leadership with physical dominance. Simply seeking positional advantage against others results in an arms race, for example, of who can be tallest for basketball. If all take steroids, all are at greater risk and no one has a resulting advantage. As athletes dedicate their lives to physical performance at the

---

45. Alasdair MacIntyre, *Dependent Rational Animals: Why Human Beings Need the Virtues* (Chicago: Open Court, 1999), p. 130.

46. Editorial, *Lancet* 335, no. 8692 (March 31, 1990): 764.

highest levels, many will risk taking performance-increasing drugs to stay competitive. A generation of East German women athletes were given male steroids without their knowledge to increase their performance. That resulted in many cases of sterility and other endocrine problems. In the late 1980s about twenty Dutch and Belgian cyclists who were taking erythropoietin (EPO) to increase their blood's oxygen-carrying capacity went into cardiac arrest from their EPO-thickened blood.[47]

Strict restriction of such substances allows people to compete on an even playing field without taking such risks. But what can be used to restore tissue damage can often be used to augment tissue. Off-label uses are common practice. If correcting to normal, why not to better than normal? Treatments for muscle loss from muscular dystrophy can potentially be used for greater muscle mass to the high end of normal range or beyond. Standards and monitoring methods for steroids and other drugs have been developed to enforce fair competition.[48] Genes create a more difficult case. They affect natural body products that occur in varying degrees in different people by genetic heritage. As discussed in chapter 4, it is normal for capacities to be found in a range. Eero Maentyranta of Finland won two gold medals in cross-country skiing at the 1964 Winter Olympics. It was later discovered that he had a naturally occurring genetic mutation that increased the number of his red blood cells. The human body makes EPO to spur the production of red blood cells. Maentyranta's genes lacked the instructions to turn off EPO, hence his innate aerobic capacity was much higher than for most people.[49] EPO can be made synthetically and be injected into the body to increase red blood cell count. It is difficult to tell if genetic products are inherited or artificially introduced. Training at high altitude can also boost the number of red blood cells, as can pregnancy. Athletic commissions already sort out competitors into various classifications such as sex, weight, and age. To assure relatively even competition in the future, new distinctions may be needed that measure what is present in

47. Ronald M. Green, *Babies by Design*, p. 21.

48. George Khushf argues that performance-enhancing drugs are not only unfair, but more importantly they are inherently dehumanizing. However, he states repeatedly that it is difficult to say why they are dehumanizing. "Thinking Theologically about Reproductive and Genetic Enhancements: The Challenge," *Christian Bioethics* 5, no. 2 (1999): 171, 179 nn. 29-30.

49. Nicholas Agar, *Liberal Eugenics* (Oxford: Blackwell, 2004), p. 98.

the body, not how it came to be there. Otherwise the competitive edge in athletic competition may become more a matter of chemistry than of training and skill.

We can praise athletic achievement for accomplishment or for what is done with what one has. The Paralympics are a case in point, as are senior athletic competitions. The Paralympics may someday surpass performance of unaided Olympics. See the progress of the blade runner who has no feet. Repairing sport injury can end a career or may sometimes result in improved performance. It would then be an advantage to have been injured, such as when bone heals and is stronger where a break occurred. Yet many athletic activities are done for the sheer joy of movement and action, such as rock climbing. In those cases people getting better at the activity might heighten enjoyment without anyone being treated unfairly. There are also nonsports endeavors where enhanced ability could benefit all involved. It is highly competitive to become a surgeon. If genetic intervention and competition combined to bring forward surgeons with unusually precise and steady hands, that would bless them and their patients.

9 Increase Choice for the Recipient

C. S. Lewis is often quoted as saying that "what we call Man's power over Nature turns out to be a power exercised by some men over all other men with Nature as its instrument." "Each new power won by man is a power over man as well. Each advance leaves him weaker as well as stronger. In every victory, besides the general who triumphs, he is a prisoner who follows the triumphal car . . . the power of Man to make himself what he pleases means, as we have seen, the power of some men to make other men what they please."[1] Cameron and DeBaets write that "We have the power to instill our flawed and culturally conditioned genetic preferences and values in the next generation and so exercise a tyranny over all future generations of human beings, who would become the genetic products of our own devising."[2] Jürgen Habermas elaborates that genetic enhancement "commits the person concerned to a specific life-project or, in any case, puts specific restrictions on his freedom to choose a life of his own."[3] "Eugenic interventions aiming at enhancement, reduce ethical freedom insofar as they tie down the person concerned to rejected, but irreversible intentions of third parties."[4] Habermas is concerned that while each generation unavoidably shapes

1. C. S. Lewis, *The Abolition of Man* (New York: Collier Books, 1962), pp. 70-77.

2. Nigel Cameron and Amy DeBaets, in *Design and Destiny: Jewish and Christian Perspectives on Human Germline Modification*, ed. Ronald Cole-Turner (Cambridge: MIT Press, 2008), p. 115.

3. Jürgen Habermas, *The Future of Human Nature* (Cambridge: Polity Press, 2003), p. 61.

4. Habermas, *Future of Human Nature*, p. 81.

the next, socially induced change such as a person's first language, location, and education can be affirmed, rejected, or modified by the developing individual. In contrast, genetic assignment is set, hence the recipient has no choice in what genes are carried in her body. Habermas is quite right to be concerned about people making choices for themselves and others about their future, but he is not taking fully into account the human condition and the limitations and capabilities of social and genetic shaping. Consider the following:

1. It is the human condition that individuals cannot choose their birth genes. The alternative to a parent deciding for the child is not self-design; it is random chance.

2. Social assignment is more formative than Habermas admits. Granted that an adolescent can make decisions about how to carry on or modify social assignments, the language such thoughts are composed in will be the first language the child learns at someone else's direction. The developing adolescent does not begin with a clean slate. Choices made socially on the child's behalf are deeply formative of what the child then accepts or rejects.

3. Genetic assignment is less formative than Habermas fears. Genetics are not as determinative as is often assumed. Increasing eyesight acuity does not determine what one chooses to look at. Further, epigenetics, the study of how genes activate or turn off, is a rapidly developing field that may well allow intervention in the future to turn on or off genes without having to add or remove them from the body. Such techniques could reverse or implement some kinds of genetic changes in a competent adult.

4. Some social assignments increase an individual's choices, such as the ability to read. Devoting a substantial part of a child's early years to literacy increases the child's opportunities. It does not decrease them. Some genetic decisions could also increase future choices rather than decrease them. Assuring the ability to hear increases what the developing person can take in or ignore; it does not determine what the person listens to. Parents cannot avoid shaping their children, but they can offer more possibilities rather than fewer.[5] That would provide power to others, not over others, for a more open future.[6]

5. Dena S. Davis, "Genetic Dilemmas and the Child's Right to an Open Future," *Hastings Center Report* 27, no. 5 (September-October 1997): 5.

6. Joel Feinberg, "The Child's Right to an Open Future," in *Whose Child? Chil-*

Kirsten Finn Schwandt reports of a couple who desired to be parents and who each had achondroplasia. Inheriting this gene from both parents is lethal, but one normal gene from one parent and the achondroplasia allele from the other result in dwarfism. Such parents have a one-in-four chance of a child inheriting the lethal form, a two-in-four chance that the child will receive a mix resulting in dwarfism, and a one-in-four chance that the child will inherit the normal alleles from both parents resulting in more typical height. The couple specifically requested that zygotes be tested so that they might select only the ones who would be dwarfs to carry till birth. They believed that achondroplasia was not a defect but a way of life that they wished to share fully with their children.[7] Tom Murray cites a parallel case of deaf parents wanting to implant only zygotes that would lead to a deaf child.[8] While people with achondroplasia or hearing loss are full and welcome citizens, it is difficult to picture how deliberately seeking that condition for children would increase opportunities for them.[9] John Harris asks if it would be plausible to have someone say to us, "I have accidentally deafened your child; it was quite painless and no harm was done so you needn't be concerned or upset."[10]

People often make choices that limit their own future options. Some seem trivial and are never noticed. An arbitrary turn down one store aisle can lead to meeting a future mate or not. There are consciously chosen life commitments such as to marriage or a monastic order that make possible great goods, but for most decisions it is an advantage to keep options open. Circumstances or one's vision may

---

dren's Rights, Parental Authority, and State Power, ed. William Aiken and Hugh LaFollette (Totowa, N.J.: Rowman and Littlefield, 1980).

7. Kirsten Finn Schwandt, "Personal Stories: Cases from Genetic Counseling," in *Genetic Testing and Screening: Critical Engagement at the Intersection of Faith and Science*, ed. Roger A. Willer (Minneapolis: Kirk House Publishers, 1998), pp. 45-46.

8. Thomas H. Murray, *The Worth of a Child* (Berkeley: University of California Press, 1996), pp. 115-16.

9. A parallel discussion is whether cochlear implants should be provided for the children of hearing-impaired parents. A number of deaf parents have refused permission for the treatment, preferring that their children be fully part of their deaf world and culture. See L. Swanson, "Cochlear Implants: The Head-on Collision between Medical Technology and the Right to Be Deaf," *Canadian Medical Association Journal* 157, no. 7 (October 1997): 929-32.

10. John Harris, *Enhancing Evolution: The Ethical Case for Making Better People* (Princeton: Princeton University Press, 2007), p. 103.

change. Genetic pharmaceuticals usually lend themselves to this reversible caution. One can stop taking the drug and return to one's initial state. People often practice temporary self-medication to their benefit and no one's harm. For example, caffeine is a common choice. While it is mildly dehydrating, it offers measurable improvement in concentration for focused tasks. It is open, not predestining. One can use the heightened awareness for a task of one's choice and when one stops taking in the caffeine, it leaves the body eventually. Some genetic interventions may be reversible as well. Genes cannot be removed from the body, but some can be turned on or off as desired. Other drugs and interventions have irreversible effects. For example, powerful sterilizing drugs may not offer the chance to return to fertility. When an intervention is irreversible, one should be dramatically more certain of its use, just as one should take care for example in choosing a tattoo. The "lizard man," as termed in the news for filing his teeth, adding implants under his skin, and tattooing his entire body to more closely resemble a lizard, will find it difficult to return to a more typical appearance if he someday finds his earlier choices less interesting. The value of an open future is especially important for children who have not yet had the opportunity to make their own life-shaping choices.[11] Human beings are far more complex than genetic heritage, but human beings cannot avoid being shaped by genetic heritage, early childhood, and later socialization. No one springs forth one's own creation. Rather the question is whether interventions have increased choice or decreased it.

Because genetic intervention is likely to be costly when first introduced,[12] offers to intervene in children are likely to be pitched to the desires and needs of the parents who choose the intervention and pay the bills.[13] Even as they want to help and do help, parents will need to make a conscious effort to be sure that any intervention benefits the child, not just themselves. An important criterion to assure that focus is

11. Feinberg, "The Child's Right to an Open Future."

12. For example, human growth hormone currently costs about twenty thousand dollars a year for daily injections.

13. Elisabeth Beck-Gernsheim recounts this historical development particularly for the roles of women in *Die Kinderfrage: Frauen zwischen Kinderwunsch und Unabhängigkeit* (The question of children: Women between the wish for children and independence) (Munich: Beck Verlag, 1988), and *Mutterwerden — der Sprung in ein anderes Leben* (Becoming a mother: The leap into another life) (Frankfurt: Fischer Verlag, 1989).

that any genetic intervention must increase the child's capacity, hence future choices. Otherwise the child might have reason to feel predestined. As described above, some parents want their children to be deaf or dwarfs like themselves. Such interventions would decrease the choices eventually available to their children. External influences could be so direct and pervasive as to encourage the abdication of personal responsibility or could actually limit future choices.[14] But genetic intervention does not have to be determinative. External shaping can be freeing. As cited, enabling a child to read increases future choices; it does not preclude them.

If people are enabled to live longer, what they do with that time can be highly valued and is not predetermined. One hundred years ago in the United States, a girl who reached the age of ten had a life expectancy of about sixty-two. In 2004, a girl of ten could expect to live to eighty-one. That is an increase in life expectancy of 31 percent.[15] The apostle Paul said, "For to me, living is Christ and dying is gain" (Phil. 1:21). In the Christian tradition death is a transition, not a feared end, but we are expected as good stewards to do the best we can with what we have while we are here. So we eat right, exercise daily, and follow doctor's advice to extend our lives. Our lives here are longer now than they used to be. If we extend them further, they will still be the tiniest fraction of the life to come, but important for what can be done uniquely here. Even if time in the womb was only a start, it was an important start that one should not leave prematurely. Longer lives do require society to adjust. For example, concerns have been raised that England is becoming overcrowded. That feeling is not surprising considering it is the most densely populated country in Europe. Overcrowding does not have the same resonance in Canada with thirty million people spread over ten million square kilometers. Some of that territory is a bit brisk, but each family of three could still have its own square kilometer if the population spread out over the land. Actually Canada is highly urban with most of the population concentrating in ten metropolitan areas by choice, and immigration is welcomed.

Genetic intervention need not be predestining or harmful.[16] The

14. Hessel Bouma III et al., *Christian Faith, Health, and Medical Practice* (Grand Rapids: Eerdmans, 1989), p. 185.

15. Ronald Green, *Babies by Design* (New Haven: Yale University Press, 2007), p. 103.

16. Bernard Häring, *Manipulation: Ethical Boundaries of Medical, Behavioral,*

intervention might increase capacities and choice rather than attempt programming, and be publicly known as such. Bernard Häring's concern is that "the essential point" (p. 14), "final concern and criterion" (p. 50), "key word" (p. 57) for guiding such intervention is freedom. For Häring such freedom is the unique dignity and capacity of humanity (p. 55). Human beings find their highest state in self-transforming love relationships that are founded on freedom and characterized by a longing for ever growing knowledge of what is good and truthful, the capacity to love what is good and put it into practice (p. 57). Human beings are not just to preserve freedom, but rather to enhance it. Human beings may intentionally shape their environment and themselves as long as this furthers the sacredness of each person and the growth of freedom for all. Consciously shaping ourselves and accepting the influence of others are part of our modern society of hospitals and schools.[17] Such can serve freedom. Intentional shaping of others takes place best with free consent if the recipient is able to consent, and if it creates future freedom of choice for those who have yet no will to exercise. For Häring, then, the constructive use of genetic intervention to that end should be pursued cautiously and responsibly as a God-given and God-empowered mandate.

In contrast, Alasdair MacIntyre has described seven virtues that people would want their children to have. Among these is a commitment not to manipulate others. He then argues that if parents have those virtues themselves, they will not want to manipulate their children genetically to have them.[18] In response, it is important first to clarify that genes do not encode virtues.[19] Virtues stem from a higher level of reasoning and commitment than is carried in our genes. Also, virtuous parents will seek to encourage virtues in their children through education, modeling, and conversation. To raise a child with no guidance until she is of age to decide for herself is to raise a hellion that will not have the ability to choose when the time comes. An open future has to

---

and Genetic Manipulation (Slough, U.K.: St. Paul Publications, 1975). Page numbers have been placed in the text.

17. Roger L. Shinn, "Genetic Decisions: A Case Study in Ethical Method," *Soundings* 52 (Fall 1969): 308-9.

18. Alasdair MacIntyre, "Seven Traits for the Future," *Hastings Center Report* 9, no. 1 (February 1979): 7.

19. Bruce R. Reichenbach and V. Elving Anderson, *On Behalf of God: A Christian Ethic for Biology* (Grand Rapids: Eerdmans, 1995), pp. 206-8.

do with helping children build skills of discernment, which free them to evaluate and apply as persons in their own right. "[O]ur children are not our children: they are not our property, not our possessions. Neither are they supposed to live our lives for us, or anyone else's life but their own. To be sure, we seek to guide them on their way, imparting to them not just life but nurturing, love, and a way of life; to be sure, they bear our hopes that they will live fine and flourishing lives, enabling us in small measure to transcend our own limitations. They are sprung from a past, but they take an uncharted course into the future."[20] There are gifts such as health that we can develop in our children that do not predestine them except to more opportunity than they would have had otherwise. Such abilities increase the choices before them. Such do not set their future; they respectfully open it. That is a godly use of power, to empower. Genetic intervention should be put to that use.

---

20. Leon Kass, "The Wisdom of Repugnance: Why We Should Ban the Cloning of Humans," in *The Human Cloning Debate*, ed. Glenn McGee (Berkeley, Calif.: Berkeley Hills Books, 1998), pp. 171-72.

10 Best Use of Always Finite Resources

The bumper sticker read "If you think education is expensive, try ignorance." While many good things in life may indeed be relatively free, most are not. Resources such as time, attention, and money are always finite for individuals and societies. The choice for one investment means that the applied resources are not available for another. In the Christian tradition everything belongs to God, who freely gives that we might share. Investing then in genetic intervention, as any other investment of entrusted resources, requires that we consider if it is the best use for that stewardship. We should hone our skills and character to serve more effectively. This was entailed in the parable of the stewards described earlier. Adults should eat a diet that supports their health. Safe vaccinations should be used to help protect ourselves and our children from crippling or even lethal disease. There is much that we can do to support and augment our lives as adults and as parents helping children to the best available start.[1]

Just as important as the physical start for children is sharing life with parents. Parents provide the steady base that frees the child to become and explore. My own daughters as toddlers explored most boldly when they could regularly toddle back to hug my knee before the next foray. They would naturally check their base and seemed to think, "O.K.

---

1. On the responsibilities of the family in the Christian tradition, see Stephen G. Post, "Marriage and Family," in *Christian Ethics: Problems and Prospects*, ed. Lisa Sowle Cahill and James F. Childress (Cleveland: Pilgrim Press, 1996), pp. 265-83. Also, see Rodney Clapp, *Families at the Crossroad: Between Traditional and Modern Options* (Downers Grove, Ill.: InterVarsity, 1993).

Daddy is right here. It is safe to explore out from this point." The way parents treat their children through the opening years of their lives in being with them and caring for them is far more influential than anything they will be able to do genetically. It would be counterproductive to spend little time with one's child because one worked a second shift to pay for a genetic intervention to increase her average intelligence by 10 percent. One would probably contribute more to her intelligence by interacting with her during that time. Human beings can augment intellectual ability by training and use. Genetics is only part of physical health, and physical health is only part of what we support for ourselves and our children as we grow and develop, yet genetics can make a genuine difference. Intervention should proceed only when it is the best service available from that portion of our always finite resources. When this balance is pursued at the community level, it raises issues of social investment.

While genetics have a pervasive influence, they do not in any sense constitute all the factors that affect human health. Environmental insult can interact with genetic susceptibility.[2] Personal choices are formative. Social factors may play a prominent role as well.[3] Wealthy governments around the world are continuing to invest a large percentage of medical research funds in genetic research. This is already having substantial therapeutic benefits through genetic testing. It is easier to read the genome than to change it. Some critics are concerned that genetics draws funds away from more effective research and direct social services. For example, concern has been raised that the hypothesis of a "thrifty" gene in some minorities drew attention away from social factors that were causing high rates of obesity. Public health services could have more quickly and directly helped through education and employment efforts in that case than through genetic studies.[4] Paul Edelson

2. Stuart L. Shalat, Jun-Yan Hong, and Michael Gallo, "The Environmental Genome Project," *Epidemiology and Society: A Forum on Epidemiology and Global Health* 9, no. 2 (March 1998): 211-12.

3. Examples of articles emphasizing this aspect include: N. Kreiger et al., "Racism, Sexism, and Social Class: Implications for Studies of Health, Disease, and Well Being," *American Journal of Preventative Medicine* 9, no. 6 (1993): 82-122; J. W. Frank, "The Determinants of Health: A New Synthesis," *Current Issues in Public Health* 1 (1995): 233-40.

4. R. McDermott, "Ethics, Epidemiology and the Thrifty Gene: Biological Determinism as a Health Hazard," *Social Science and Medicine* 47, no. 9 (November 1998): 1189-95.

198

thinks the quick adoption of phenylketonuria (PKU) testing supplanted more effective interventions for the vast majority of the mentally challenged. The state-mandated testing prevented mental retardation in those who carried the genetic anomaly. Prevention is better than attempts at repair after the disease has had devastating effects. The change for people with PKU has been dramatic. But the vast majority of cases of mental retardation are not PKU-related. Edelson is concerned that social policy should not be distracted from education and services for those who are already with us and continue to arrive.[5]

One of the strongest motivators for genetic intervention may well be equality of opportunity. This is not an issue for those who are skeptical of the potential service in genetic intervention, lest one be like the guest at the resort who complained that "the food was inedible and the portions were too small." Fair distribution is only a question for desired goods. Equality of opportunity can be seen as a subset of a wider discussion of distributive justice. Many material standards have been argued for the just distribution of resources including equal share, need, merit, past contribution, and voluntary exchange. For example, in North America each of these methods is used for different goods: equal share for one vote per person in civil elections, need for emergency room treatment, merit for college admission, past contribution for awards such as the Pulitzer Prize, and voluntary exchange for consumer goods. Conflict over what is just in a given situation is often at root about which material standard is appropriate in that case.

There are at least three points where equality of opportunity comes into contact with genetic intervention.[6] First, some religious and philosophical traditions emphasize the priceless worth of each human being. Hence as much as possible an important advantage should be available as much to one as another. If forms of genetic intervention become important goods that can help pursue basic life plans, as education and medical care do, the opportunity to benefit from them should be as available as possible to all.

---

5. As cited by Diane B. Paul in "Appendix 5: The History of Newborn Phenylketonuria Screening in the U.S.," in *Promoting Safe and Effective Genetic Testing in the United States: Final Report of the Task Force on Genetic Testing*, ed. Neil A. Holtzman and Michael S. Watson (Baltimore: Johns Hopkins University Press, 1998), p. 141.

6. I am not limiting "equality of opportunity" to concerns about institutional discrimination. For a description of different uses of the phrase, see John Roemer, *Theories of Distributive Justice* (Cambridge: Harvard University Press, 1996).

Second, equality of opportunity for the citizens within a particular country can be grounded in an affirmation of fairness. Equality of opportunity is often cited to justify large disparities in the distribution of goods. The assumption is that this is fair because in a free market society all people have ways available to develop their skills and work. That rewards vary is not unjust in that each person has a substantially equal opportunity. Those who have gained more have in some degree earned it. As one maximizes the opportunities that one has, one is likely to gain more opportunities. There is often truth to the old saying that the harder one works, the luckier one gets. So equality of opportunity cannot mean lifelong equal options. The person who works hard for high grades in chemistry and then to complete medical school will have opportunities not available to someone who skipped classes for other pursuits that mattered more to him then. The ideal of equality of opportunity is a societal effort to elevate starting access with basic education and medical care. As time passes, opportunities will tend to increase or decrease according to the individual's use of previous opportunities.

A major factor that this theory has traditionally not had to take into account is the natural lottery of starting capacity. Some people have genetic advantages of health and other capabilities far superior to others. If a society is able to readdress some of that imbalance by genetic intervention and claims to support equality of opportunity, there will be pressure to implement universal intervention to approximate the claimed equal opportunity more closely.

Third, if genetic intervention is available only to a few, the recipients could claim a meritocracy of measurably superior abilities. Claims to that end have been actively pursued without any basis in physical reality.[7] Aristocracies have often claimed to merit their position by superior attributes, whether actually present or not. To in fact have a physical distinction of one group over another would lend itself to such oppression. Enhancement of capacity, if available to only a few, could increase stratification. There might be reinforcement of already harmful social evils such as heightism and racism. The response can be one of prohibition of anyone having access or provision so that all have access. By the latter approach of making genetic intervention widely available,

---

7. Mark H. Haller, *Eugenics: Hereditarian Attitudes in American Thought* (New Brunswick, N.J.: Rutgers University Press, 1963), p. 5.

the population would not have to be homogenized if the choice whether and how to use it is left up to the adults who receive it or parents on behalf of their children. There might be a "genetic decent minimum" that is almost universally recognized and provided as helpful to the recipient.[8] Yet beyond that, the multiplicity of decision makers would lead to a variety of choices and results. Variation is healthy for a society in offering complementary traits for complex daily life and more adaptive pathways when circumstances change. One could observe as Winston Churchill did, that he was always a bit out of sync before brilliantly leading Great Britain through World War II. Treasured during the war for his unique combination of traits to lead his country through those dark hours, he was quickly retired by the voters when it was over. The evaluation of genetic traits is shaped by context. Equality of opportunity does not require that all be the same. We would be poorer for it.

Paul Lauritzen thinks the recognition of human rights stems from fellow feeling. The recognition of human rights is based on our recognizing ourselves in the other. We have compassion for one another because we can imagine ourselves in the other's place. If genetic intervention is widespread in different directions, people may lose that sense of identity with others, hence also the sense of common needs and concerns of all human beings. The ground for honoring universal human rights would be lost.[9] By this view, genetic intervention that is proven to be helpful must be widely provided to protect the very foundation of our common society, but is such affordable?

Maxwell Mehlman is sure that genetic enhancement could not be provided to all citizens because of the prohibitive expense.[10] Mehlman teams with Jeffrey Botkin to offer one cost solution: genetic services should be available only by lottery. Every set of parents would have an equal chance at being selected randomly for full genetic services. This would not protect equality of results or capability, but would at least se-

---

8. Allen Buchanan et al., *From Chance to Choice: Genetics and Justice* (Cambridge: Cambridge University Press, 2000), pp. 81-82.

9. Paul Lauritzen, "Stem Cells, Biotechnology, and Human Rights: Implications for a Posthuman Future," *Hastings Center Report* 35, no. 2 (March-April 2005): 25-33.

10. Maxwell Mehlman, *Wondergenes* (Bloomington: Indiana University Press, 2003), pp. 126-27, and "The Law of Above Averages: Leveling the New Genetic Enhancement Playing Field," *Iowa Law Review* 85 (2000): 517-93.

cure equal chance of genetic help. Society would benefit from gene-enhanced abilities in the workforce, but no one group could monopolize the technique and take over almost all positions distributed by merit. Genetic intervention would be limited in its share of the medical economy.[11] If genetic intervention is offered officially only by lottery, only the wealthy will have the means to circumvent the imposed shortage. In parallel, if citizens of Ontario are wait-listed for care and can afford to do so, it is not uncommon to pay cash for the service in India or the United States. Ronald Lindsay suggests that if indeed it becomes clear that the rich are using genetic purchasing power to unfair advantage, rather than trying to limit the rich purchasing advantageous genetic services, it would be better not to allow anyone to be rich. Redistribution of wealth is a more effective limitation on advantages for the wealthy than legal constraint. The wealthy have a long history in every culture of being able to use economic power to circumvent or leverage control systems to their own advantage. With a redistribution of wealth, the rich could not abuse what they do not have.[12] Lindsay's proposal has not been viable when it has been tried.

If a lottery for genetic intervention could maintain equal chance of success, such a lottery would be superior to the unfairness and social disruption of generations of compounding disparate access. However, it is likely that once it is clear that some genetic interventions are safe and efficacious for the improvement of physical life, most parents will want them for their children. Simply a chance at the service would not be any more sufficiently consoling to the losers than everyone having an equal lottery chance for the first twelve years of education, instead of assured access to it. Equality of opportunity calls for all to be able to receive the resource, not just have a go at it in a lottery. Once it is clear that intervention is safe and works, demand will soar and the costs per intervention will decline, particularly as less labor intensive techniques are developed. Most of the objects and services that we now consider standard have moved to that status from originally luxury categories. A primary school education was a luxury unaffordable for many for much

11. Maxwell J. Mehlman and Jeffrey R. Botkin, *Access to the Genome: The Challenge to Equality* (Washington, D.C.: Georgetown University Press, 1998), pp. 124-28.

12. Ronald A. Lindsay, "Enhancements and Justice: Problems in Determining the Requirements of Justice in a Genetically Transformed Society," *Kennedy Institute of Ethics Journal* 15, no. 1 (2005): 33.

of the history of North America. Now education through the twelfth grade is a guaranteed provision and considered a necessity.

Already back in 1998, the pharmaceutical executive John Varian estimated that it took about 280 million dollars to bring an idea for a drug on through development to market availability.[13] Such expenses have compounded. Developing genetic pharmaceuticals and other interventions could be a societal drain from other, more effective strategies.[14] However, genetic interventions are likely to be paid for initially by the wealthy as a hoped-for advantage for themselves or their children. This would come not from tax revenue but from their own discretionary income. If they can spend such funds on college tuition, a personal trainer, or gambling in Las Vegas, why not spend them to increase their physical capacity? This also means that relatively high start-up risks fall on volunteers who pay for the intervention's development. When it becomes clear that it is safe and advantageous, government will probably be called upon to provide it for all. A current example in this process might be laser eye surgery to correct to 20/20 vision. Further, writing began as an elite activity. Books could be afforded by only a few and read by only a few more, yet now literacy is widespread and crucial to our society. What if the technology of writing and reading had been banned at the beginning because it was too expensive and only for the elite?[15] Why deny a benefit to some because it is not yet available to all? Taken consistently, this would require dismantling most of the infrastructure of the global north and sending it south of the equator.

While the issue of cost has been raised as a limit to widespread intervention, cost will probably become an incentive for intervention rather than a restraint. The onetime cost of genetic intervention could be considerably less than the cost of repeated hospitalization and lost work. Combining the economic advantage of less needed care with citi-

---

13. John Varian, "Genetics in the Marketplace: A Biotech Perspective," in *Genetic Testing and Screening: Critical Engagements at the Intersection of Faith and Science*, ed. Roger A. Willer (Minneapolis: Kirk House Publishers, 1998), pp. 64-65.

14. Karen Lebacqz, "Bioethics: Some Challenges from a Liberation Perspective," in *Faith and Science in an Unjust World*, ed. Roger L. Shinn (Geneva: World Council of Churches, 1980), p. 279, and Jean Porter, "What Is Morally Distinctive about Genetic Engineering?" *Human Gene Therapy* 1 (1990): 423.

15. John Harris, *Enhancing Evolution: The Ethical Case for Making Better People* (Princeton: Princeton University Press, 2007), p. 14.

zens probably being capable of more taxable productivity, it would be in the government's economic interest to make genetic intervention available to all. Intervention could be an economic boon, freeing resources for other services. While it would probably be technically intensive and expensive at first, through improving techniques it would be progressively less so. After the initial bulge in start-up costs, reduction in other medical care costs would begin immediately. Myopia, diabetes, trisomy 21, Huntington's, Alzheimer's, and many other diseases and conditions treated at great expense to the sufferer and society are genetically caused or related. A onetime intervention to eliminate these diseases and disabilities might become economically desirable. If such a situation develops, the economic issue of genetic intervention may become more an autonomy issue of whether a society should require it to avoid the greater expense of not doing it. Economic costs will initially pressure against government provision and then probably eventually for it. Genes can do only so much, but in some cases they may reduce the need or pressure for state-initiated solutions that require pervasive government intervention. Genetic intervention near the beginning of a life may eventually preclude the necessity of more frequent, costly, and invasive government provision later.

IV Who Applies These Standards?

11 The Devastating History of Coercion, Racism, and Eugenics

Coercion, Racism, and Eugenics

Can human genetic intervention help to protect, even increase, human freedom and diversity? The eugenics movement, after all, was used to justify some of the most horrific abuses of the last century.[1] There are minority groups who worry to this day that any genetic measurement or change will be used against them.[2] A genetic program that sets human development toward one ideal would be at risk of such abuse. Pursuing one ideal would narrow the diversity of possibilities and values carried on. While group consensus may have the advantage of eliminating some mistakes, it can also lead to "group think" that is less careful and more group aggrandizing. Since human beings tend toward self-interest, one prevailing ideal would probably be placing the self-interest of one group over that of others. Daniel Boorstin suggests that this is an evident observation from even the most cursory reading of history.[3] There are

---

1. For example, Benno Muller-Hill, *Tödliche Wissenschaft: Die Aussonderung von Juden, Zigeunern und Geisteskranken 1933-1945* (Lethal science: The exclusion of Jews, gypsies, and the mentally ill, 1933-1945) (Rowohlt: Reinbek, 1984).

2. Herbert Nickens notes a parallel that today a substantial portion of African American adults in the USA blame a racist conspiracy for high rates of drug abuse, AIDS, crime, broken families, and teen pregnancy in the black community. "The Genome Project and Health Services for Minority Populations," in *The Human Genome Project and the Future of Health Care*, ed. Thomas H. Murray, Mark A. Rothstein, and Robert F. Murray Jr. (Bloomington: Indiana University Press, 1996), p. 59.

3. Daniel Boorstin, in *Washington Post*, August 5, 1984, p. C3.

multiple examples from recent history of groups using genetic concern in particular as a weapon against other groups. Paul Ramsey contends that "the culmination or abuse of eugenics in the ghastly Nazi experiments would seem to be sufficient to silence forever proposals for genetic control."[4] Others, too, have cited this fear.[5] This argument is so pervasive in discussion about genetic intervention, and appropriately so, that it warrants extended analysis. In recent history a highly educated culture applied genetic concern in a horrific way. What can we learn from that experience?

Arguing from historical analogy, such as Ramsey's reference to the Nazi experience, is fraught with difficulties. It depends on establishing the historical detail needed for an accurate comparison and showing that the case is close enough to draw an effective parallel.[6] With the Nazi movement as the prime exhibit, the history of human attempts to improve human genetic endowment, often called "eugenics," has been abhorrent in its interference with the choice of marriage partners, sterilization programs, and deadly racism. On the one hand, the parallel of proposed genetic intervention with eugenic sterilization or coerced marriage partners is not directly applicable, in that genetic intervention as now contemplated does not require those means. In fact, freedom in the choice of mates and whether to have children would be increased by genetic technology, since the extensive elimination of inheritable diseases would allow many people to have children who would otherwise be unable to. On the other hand, there may be a relevant link be-

---

4. Paul Ramsey, *Fabricated Man: The Ethics of Genetic Control* (New Haven: Yale University Press, 1978), p. 1.

5. These include Martin P. Golding, "Ethical Issues in Biological Engineering," *UCLA Law Review* 15 (February 1968): 448-50; Hans Schwartz, "Theological Implications of Modern Biogenetics," *Zygon* 5 (September 1970): 264; Arno G. Motulsky, "Government Responsibilities in Genetic Diseases," in *Genetics and the Law II*, ed. Aubrey Milunsky and George J. Annas (New York: Plenum, 1980), p. 238; World Council of Churches, Church and Society, *Manipulating Life: Ethical Issues in Genetic Engineering* (Geneva: World Council of Churches, 1982), p. 9; and W. French Anderson, "Genetics and Human Malleability," *Hastings Center Report* 20 (January/February 1990): 24.

6. The *Hastings Center Report* has organized two discussions of this problem specifically as it applies to the analogy of Nazi practices with current choices: "Biomedical Ethics and the Shadow of Nazism: A Conference on the Proper Use of the Nazi Analogy in Ethical Debate," 6 (August 1976): special supplement, and "Contested Terrain: The Nazi Analogy in Bioethics," 18 (August/September 1988): 29-33.

tween genetic concern and racism. At least such an argument is cited so frequently that it warrants a particularly thorough appraisal. The first question then to test the analogy is, to what degree has past genetic concern been racist?

Eugenics and Racism

"Eugenics" was first studied, and coined as a term, by Sir Francis Galton in his *Inquiries into Human Faculty and Its Development.* Galton's interest was sparked by the work of his cousin Charles Darwin on natural selection. Darwin warned that helping "the weak" human beings to survive and propagate was "highly injurious to the race of man."[7] Galton responded with a program to purposefully encourage the positive evolution of human beings through marriage choice.[8] He defined that positive evolution as follows: "We would include among our standards of eugenic value sound physical health and good physique, intelligence, and moral qualities which make for social cohesion. The latter would comprise courage (but not aggressiveness), serenity or contentment, and cooperativeness. We would also here include the quality described above as genophilia (love of children)."[9] It is noteworthy that eugenics did not start with race as the ideal nor with race listed as the epitome of the ideal.[10] According to Mark Haller's study of how eugenic ideas began in the United States, eugenics "began as a scientific reform in an age of reform," which was pursued by the more liberal leadership.[11] For example,

7. Charles Darwin, *The Descent of Man and Selection in Relation to Sex,* 2nd ed. (New York: D. Appleton, 1922), p. 136.

8. C. P. Blacker, *Eugenics: Galton and After* (Cambridge: Harvard University Press, 1952), pp. 107-8.

9. Blacker, *Eugenics,* p. 289.

10. As typical of his period, Galton did begin to articulate also an imperialist motivation for eugenics. Part of the purpose for eugenics became "to give the more suitable races or strains of blood a better chance of prevailing speedily over the less suitable than they otherwise would have had." Quoted by Golding, "Ethical Issues," p. 464.

11. Mark H. Haller, *Eugenics: Hereditarian Attitudes in American Thought* (New Brunswick, N.J.: Rutgers University Press, 1963), p. 5. Diane Paul traces this pattern across Europe in "Eugenics and the Left," *Journal of the History of Ideas* 45, no. 4 (1984): 567-90. Gunnar Broberg and Mattias Tyden found this connection specifically in Sweden in *Eugenics and the Welfare State: Sterilization Policy in Denmark, Sweden, Norway, and Finland* (East Lansing: Michigan State University Press, 1996).

Harry Emerson Fosdick, famous for his sermon at Riverside Church in New York City "Shall the Fundamentalists Win?" was a member of the advisory board of the American Eugenics Society.[12] Amy Laura Hall has traced the enthusiasm for eugenics through mainline Christian denominations. She gives one example after another, from eugenic sermon contests to articles in denominational magazines.[13] Edward J. Larson writes that eugenics was less popular in the more traditional American South in part because "The concept of salvation and sanctification for all, solely by divine grace, challenged eugenic doctrines of fixed, inherited degeneracy and superiority."[14] In many places, however, people began to use eugenics to explain poverty in terms of bad inheritance. Studies of family lines such as the "Jukes," "the Tribe of Ishmael," and "the Kallikaks" were published as proof that no environmental reforms could salvage some family lines.[15] From finding some family lines incorrigible, it was a small step to rejecting the wider families of particular races.

Legislation that claimed the justification of eugenics was enacted to restrict immigration from certain countries. A number of prominent citizens connected the quality of the American character with the propagation of "superior races," namely, northern European whites. Francis A. Walker, the president of MIT and director of the 1870 census, warned that massive immigration of inferior stock was overwhelming the "native" Anglo-Saxon stock.[16] Henry Cabot Lodge wrote in 1891 that "immigration of people of those races which contributed to the settlement and development of the United States is declining in comparison with that of races far removed in thought and speech and blood from the men who have made this country what it is."[17] In the spring of 1894 several young Harvard University graduates started the Immigration Restriction League, and in 1895 Henry Cabot Lodge introduced

12. Nathan Hallanger, "Eugenics and the Question of Religion," in *The Evolution of Evil*, ed. Gaymon Bennett et al. (Göttingen: Vandenhoeck & Ruprecht, 2008), p. 311.

13. Amy Laura Hall, *Conceiving Parenthood: American Protestantism and the Spirit of Reproduction* (Grand Rapids: Eerdmans, 2008). See also Christine Rosen, *Preaching Eugenics: Religious Leaders and the American Eugenics Movement* (New York: Oxford University Press, 2004).

14. Edward J. Larson, *Sex, Race, and Science: Eugenics in the Deep South* (Baltimore: Johns Hopkins University Press, 1995), p. 13.

15. Haller, *Eugenics*, pp. 106-7.

16. Haller, *Eugenics*, p. 139.

17. Haller, *Eugenics*, p. 56.

the Immigration Restriction Law, which limited immigration by race. The law was passed with strong support by the United States Congress. It was vetoed by President Grover Cleveland, but the immigration restriction movement continued to gain strength as well as the attention of the eugenics movement.[18]

E. A. Ross, a leader in the eugenics movement, raised the alarm that the continuing immigration of inferior races would produce a diminution of stature, a depreciation of morality, an increase in gross fecundity, a considerable lowering of the level of average natural ability, and a falling off in the frequency of good looks in the American people.[19] The Second International Eugenics Congress, which met in New York City in 1921, laid heavy emphasis on racial issues, reflecting the concerns of the wider American culture at the time. The racially based Immigration Restriction Bill passed again in the United States Congress in 1925, and this time it was signed into law. Two years before, the Canadian Parliament had passed the Chinese Immigration Act that banned any Chinese from immigrating to Canada and remained in force until it was repealed in 1947. Across the Atlantic, the eugenics movement also reflected the racist tack of the Second International Eugenics Congress and the wider culture. In England the emphasis was not so much on limiting immigration as on subjugating the "lesser races" in colonies for "their own benefit."[20]

At about the same time, Nazism began to gain power in Europe and pursued a racial policy combining a drive for racial purity with a quest for racial dominance that then elevated both to a level of unrestrained terror. It has become a paradigm for the abuse of power and is intertwined with eugenics in the perception of many. "No other historical experience has the place in our ethical discourse as the Nazi one. It is as though in a relativist and pluralist society this is our single absolute evil."[21]

While being held in the Landsberg am Lech prison (1923-24),

18. Kenneth Ludmerer, *Genetics and American Society: A Historical Appraisal* (Baltimore: Johns Hopkins University Press, 1972), p. 84.

19. Paul Bowman Popenoe and Roswell Hill Johnson, *Applied Eugenics* (New York: Macmillan, 1918), p. 301.

20. Geoffrey Searle, *Eugenics and Politics in Britain, 1900-1914* (Leiden: Noordhoff International Publishing, 1976), pp. 35, 42-43, 74. Also Haller, *Eugenics*, pp. 13-14.

21. Peter Steinfels, "Biomedical Ethics and the Shadow of Nazism," *Hastings Center Report* 6 (August 1976), special supplement, p. 1.

Adolf Hitler wrote in *Mein Kampf* his vision for the future. "Everything we admire on this earth today — science and art, industry and invention — is the creative product of but a few peoples, perhaps originally of one race. Upon them the subsistence of this whole civilization depends. If they are destroyed, the beauty of this earth will be buried with them."[22] For Hitler, "the triumphant advance of the best race" is "the sine qua non of all human progress." The world is a struggle where "it is necessary and just for the best and strongest man to be victor."[23] According to Hitler, that strong man on whom civilization depends is the Aryan race.

> So it is no accident that the first civilizations arose where the Aryan, encountering lower races, subjugated them and made them do his will. They were the first technical tools to serve a dawning civilization. . . . Thus the road which the Aryan must travel was clearly marked. As a conqueror he subjugated the inferior peoples, and regulated their practical activity under his orders, according to his will, and for his own purposes. But in thus setting them to a useful if a hard task, he not only spared the lives of the conquered, but gave them a fate which perhaps was actually better than their previous so-called "freedom."[24]

For Hitler, these were not idle concepts to be left in the abstract. From a 1933 speech: "Implementation of the fundamental political concept of race, which has been reawakened by National-Socialism and expressed in the phrase 'blood and soil' implies the most far reaching revolutionary transformation that has ever taken place. The fundamental necessity for consolidation of the racial foundation of our people, which is implicit in these words . . . governs all the aims of National-Socialism both externally and internally."[25] The "purity of the Volk" was intended to be — and indeed became — the center point of Hitler's policies. Disease was defined to include racial judgments.[26] Nazi eugenics de-

---

22. Adolf Hitler, *Mein Kampf*, trans. Ludwig Lore (New York: Stackpole, 1939), p. 281.

23. Hitler, *Mein Kampf*, p. 281.

24. Hitler, *Mein Kampf*, p. 287.

25. Werner Maser, *Hitler's Mein Kampf: An Analysis* (London: Faber and Faber, 1970), pp. 133-34.

26. William E. Seidelman, "Mengele Medicus," *Milbank Quarterly* 66, no. 2 (1988): 223.

manded racially purifying the health of the people of Germany as individuals and as a society.[27] The systematic means were already developed in Germany in the 1930s. Beginning with the Nazi Party coming to power in 1933, panels of three physicians reviewed paperwork to designate children born with severe birth defects as having "lives not worth living." Once these children were murdered, the families were given certificates with a falsified cause of death.[28] By October 1939 the program, now called T4, was officially expanded to adults, medically murdering 65,000-80,000 patients who were demented, psychotic, developmentally challenged, or otherwise deemed "undesirables."[29] Physicians were not required to take part. There were no repercussions if they did not, yet they did in substantial numbers.[30] The medical ideology was that some people had to die for the health of the whole. Physicians became accustomed to systematically killing individual patients to improve the heritage of the German Volk. The routines that were developed for these medical murders, including lethal gas in apparent shower rooms, were ramped up for "the final solution." Hitler planned that "it will be the first task of the People's State to make race the center of the life of the community."[31] In the racist practice of eugenics, Hitler found a "scientific" cloak and dagger for his destruction of "international Jewry," "gypsies," and others. When Germany came under his power,

> the eugenics movement became inextricably interwoven with the Nazi regime. Hitler's Minister of the Interior, Wilhelm Frick, proclaimed, "the fate of race-hygiene, of the Third Reich and the German people will in the future be indissolubly bound together." Prominent eugenicists became Nazi officials, and Hitler filled his government with other men who at least sympathized with the eu-

27. Ludmerer, *Genetics and American Society*, p. 116.

28. United States Holocaust Memorial Museum, "Final Solutions: Murderous Racial Hygiene, 1939-1945." *Holocaust Encyclopedia*, at http://www.ushmm.org/wlc/article.php?lang=en&ModuleId=10007064 (accessed September 5, 2009). Thanks to David Gushee for leading me to this and the following source.

29. Doris L. Bergen, *War and Genocide: A Concise History of the Holocaust* (Lanham, Md.: Rowman and Littlefield, 2003), pp. 126-29.

30. Shmuel Reis, "The Holocaust and Medicine" (lecture at McMaster University, Hamilton, Ontario, June 6, 2008).

31. Hitler, *Mein Kampf*, pp. 338-39.

genics program. Many of the private organizations concerned with eugenics education were reorganized as government agencies, the most prominent of which was the Kaiser Wilhelm Institute for Anthropology, Human Genetics, and Eugenics, directed by Fischer.[32]

The eugenics movement became a racist movement in Nazi Germany, as it did largely in the American and Canadian movements for immigration restriction, and in the British eugenists' support for colonialism.

Using the Analogy

Are racism and the murder of those differently abled somehow inherent to the idea of eugenics? Rainer Hohlfeld charges that they are. "All concepts of a positive eugenics are therefore constant expressions of the class and race thinking of a ruling elite."[33] Amitai Etzioni continues the concern, "Even before genetic engineering developed very far, the mere question of how it might be used would invite a resurgence of racist ideologies and conflicting racist camps, each advocating its version of the desired breed."[34]

Here Etzioni has pointed, perhaps unintentionally, to a key distinction between eugenics and racism. As Cynthia Cohen has emphasized, for the Nazi analogy to retain its power, it must be used with precision where it most accurately applies.[35] It is accurate that eugenics, like racism, depends on the valuation of some genetic endowments as more desirable than others. For example, it would be preferable to be born with healthy eyes than with a genetic susceptibility to retinoblastoma that leads to blindness and death. On the contrary, Theresia Degener and others, as cited in chapter 8, argue that disability is actu-

32. Ludmerer, *Genetics and American Society*, pp. 115-16.
33. My translation of "Alle Konzepte einer positiven Eugenik sind daher stets Ausdruck eines Klassen und Rassendenkens einer herrschenden Elite." Rainer Hohlfeld, "Jenseits von Freiheit und Wurde: Kritische Anmerkungen zur gezielten genetischen Beeinflussung des Menschen," *Reformatio* 32 (May 1983): 220.
34. Amitai Etzioni, "Biomedical Ethics and the Shadow of Nazism," *Hastings Center Report* 6 (August 1976), special supplement, p. 14.
35. Cynthia B. Cohen, "Contested Terrain: The Nazi Analogy in Bioethics," *Hastings Center Report* 18 (August/September 1988): 33; also, in more detail "'Quality of Life' and the Analogy with the Nazis," pp. 113-35.

ally a neutral condition, rendered difficult only by society's discrimination. Society should adapt to whatever one's abilities are.[36] Granting that society should welcome and adapt to its members, whatever their abilities, it would still be to the individual's advantage and society's benefit to increase each one's physical capacity. Those who are blind should be welcomed. But if the genetic option is available not to be blind, sight would be helpful for the individual and society. Pope Pius XII has written that "The fundamental tendency of genetics and eugenics is to influence the transmission of hereditary factors in order to promote what is good and eliminate what is injurious. This fundamental tendency is irreproachable from the moral viewpoint."[37] If one is attempting to improve in some sense the genetic endowment of newborns, one must have some goal as to what a better or ideal genetic endowment would be. Without such a goal there would be no direction or point to genetic intervention. It is in the choice of the ideal that racism has often entered eugenics.

If "normal" health is the ideal, eugenics will not be racist unless health is defined as the distinct characteristics of one particular race. If intelligence is the ideal, eugenic attempts will not be racist unless "intelligence" is defined in an inherently racist manner, such as through a culturally biased test. Only if the ideal is defined by the characteristics of a particular race will eugenics be racist. While the term "eugenics" has been used to refer to coercive breeding and racist policies, its literal definition is simply "good birth." In that sense eugenics is the attempt to improve the genetic endowment of newborns. The ideal goal of eugenics is from outside eugenics, from a philosophy of life or worldview. That is what determines the racist or nonracist intent of the particular eugenics program. Hitler could exploit the eugenics movement not because eugenics is inherently racist, but because so many German eugenists were willing to adopt his Aryan race model as the ideal genome.

The harmful use of a technology does not automatically prove that such use is inherent to the technology. Josef Mengele, the Nazi "doctor of death," claimed to be doing medical research as he tortured

36. Theresia Degener, "Female Self-Determination between Feminist Claims and 'Voluntary' Eugenics, between 'Rights' and Ethics," *Issues in Reproductive and Genetic Engineering* 3 (1990): 94, 98.

37. Pope Pius XII, "Moral Aspects of Genetics" (September 7, 1953), in *The Human Body: Papal Teachings*, ed. the Monks of Solesmes (Boston: St. Paul Editions, 1979), p. 256.

prisoners. While his acts are abhorrent and justly condemned, they are not of themselves an argument that all medicine and medical research are sadistic; rather they call for careful safeguards against abuse such as rules of informed consent and institutional review boards for human subjects research. Nazi racism, in the name of a healthy genetic endowment, does not prove that seeking a healthy genetic endowment is pursuing an inherently racist ideal.

The analogy's most powerful warning may be the one described by Gary Crum: "I believe we should strive to see Nazis as individual persons such as ourselves; persons whose rationales and actions were sometimes despicable, but not always so. We should make an effort to stop using the experience of Nazism as a metaphor for 'The Cosmic Evil' and instead try to read it like a warning label on a bottle under our own kitchen sinks."[38] Self-deception can be powerful. There were people who convinced themselves that they were morally upstanding even as they were drawn into the Nazi programs. Milton Himmelfarb has argued that many in the theologically leftist branch of German Protestantism supported Nazism initially.[39] The Roman Catholic resistance to the destruction of mentally or physically handicapped people, yet considerable compromise with Nazism at other points, has been described by Donald J. Dietrich.[40] It is a chilling warning to take care in what physical goals are chosen. As we have examined, societies have in the past repeatedly made race a part of their ideal. It is not logically necessary, but is it socially avoidable? A possible defense might be the dissemination of choice to the point where it could not be used as a weapon of one racial group against another. The Ashkenazi Jewish community, for example, that was devastated by the Nazis in the name of eugenics has embraced genetic screening to substantially eliminate a number of genetic diseases that used to be common in their community. Genetic intervention does not have to be used by one group against another.

38. Gary E. Crum, "Contested Terrain: The Nazi Analogy in Bioethics; Commentary," *Hastings Center Report* 18 (August/September 1988): 31.

39. Milton Himmelfarb, in *Hastings Center Report* 6 (August 1976), special supplement, p. 11. Paul Weindling found eugenics advocates within the political left, which was working against Nazism (*Health, Race, and German Politics between National Unification and Nazism, 1870-1945* [Cambridge: Cambridge University Press, 1989]).

40. Donald J. Dietrich, *Catholic Citizens in the Third Reich: Psycho-Social Principles and Moral Reasoning* (New York: Transaction Books, 1988).

Welcoming Diversity

Encouraging variety in the use of genetic intervention is important not only for defense against group abuses, but also for human flourishing. Genetic intervention directly addresses the physical form that is so central to being human. Deciding what is appropriate is then related to the most basic questions of the purpose and place of human life. Our physical nature is foundational to our very existence. It should be changed only with great care, yet it is probably not now the best expression of what human beings can be physically. Physical change can be for the better. While genetic intervention should be incremental in an area of such implications, it should also take place in the light of considered long-range goals, lest small steps culminate in unwanted results. Since long-range goals tend to reflect deeply held values and worldviews, a working consensus is even more difficult to obtain than immediate cooperative choices. A detailed social consensus on what human beings should be is unlikely in our pluralistic setting.

For example, "the United States, like many other societies, is morally pluralistic: no one set of beliefs about how it is good or fitting for human beings to live their lives prevails in American society. Although some quite general beliefs about human good are widely shared in American society, many beliefs about human good are widely, deeply, and persistently disputed."[41] By pluralistic I do not mean secular. A secular worldview is only one of many competitors for shaping our perception and commitment.[42] Members of our society in all their varied conceptions of the purpose of being human, of justice and autonomy, of benefits and harms,[43] are likely to continue to respond to genetic intervention in a plethora of different ways.

While the conception of what is most human varies dramatically, there are at least four widely affirmed characteristics of human beings that could structure a response to the question of direction: human beings are finite, fallible, self-concerned, and diverse. First, human beings are finite in that they do not have access to all information, nor could

41. Michael J. Perry, *Love and Power: The Role of Religion and Morality in American Politics* (New York: Oxford University Press, 1991), p. 8.

42. John R. Pottenger, *Reaping the Whirlwind: Liberal Democracy and the Religious Axis* (Washington, D.C.: Georgetown University Press, 2007).

43. James F. Childress, *Who Should Decide? Paternalism in Health Care* (New York: Oxford University Press, 1982), p. 48.

they comprehend it if they did. As finite beings, people tend to have varied and incomplete sets of knowledge that lead to different choices. One set of knowledge may lead toward different solutions than would another or partially overlapping set.

Second, human beings are fallible in that even when all applicable information is available, they may still make mistakes in understanding and judgment. Fallibility multiplies the diversity of choices from fact sets by further varying the responses to any one set. Even if there were one clear choice that followed from a shared set of information and values, a variety of choices would probably be made. Human fallibility is further compounded by the human tendency to misjudge the degree of one's finiteness when pursuing a desired goal.[44]

Third, it is widely held that human beings tend primarily to be self-concerned. In the Christian tradition this is seen as a corollary of sin. Yet even apart from sin, each person tends to be more concerned with his or her own personal welfare than with that of others. While there are many instances of exception and tempering, such as in the care of offspring, the tendency is nevertheless prevalent. Choices made on behalf of others bear the risk of being made more for the benefit of the one choosing than for those receiving the intervention. That is as much from the impinging proximity of one's own needs and desires as from any intentional priority. The self-interest of one often calls for a choice that is different from the self-interest of another. Rarely do the self-interested choices of all completely coincide. Even choices that are harmful for most people usually benefit someone. Since there are many different individuals and interest groups, choices of direction will vary further.

Fourth, people are diverse. The United Nations' *Declaration of Universal Human Rights* shows a remarkable global consensus on some basic values, yet there is variation in the definition and weight given to each value from one person or group to another. People often have different end goals as to what is desirable. Faced with the same information, logic, and joint interests, they may still weigh them differently for different ends. Considering these characteristics of human beings, complete consensus on direction for intervention in human genetics is unlikely. A probable lack of consensus in this case is not a pessimistic expectation. Consensus might be undesirable even if it could be obtained.

44. James B. Nelson, *Human Medicine: Ethical Perspectives on New Medical Issues* (Minneapolis: Augsburg, 1973), p. 94.

In light of the above human characteristics, it may be that complete consensus concerning the best direction for human genetic intervention would not be helpful. One enforced ideal too easily lends itself to the loss of enriching diversity, and even worse to one group oppressing another. Latitude for different choices is preferable. What is both needed and possible for implementation in the wider community is a process of dispersed choice within the broad bounds of limited societal consensus, not a unanimous and enforced ideal. Such a process of decision is described in the next chapter.

12 Checks and Balances

Detailed society consensus on the direction of genetic intervention is both unlikely and undesirable. Rather than one set conclusion for all, a process of who decides may be our best community response. There are a number of proposed arbiters.

Chance

Currently genetic assortment from two parents appears to be primarily by chance. Some theological perspectives would argue that God sets genetic endowment through apparent chance and so should not be interfered with. Others argue that God could exercise providence through human genetic choice or allow random assortment. An advantage to chance is the diversity of combinations it presents. Any intentional and effective influence on human genetics would be likely, by definition, to lessen the range closer to those endowments deemed desirable.[1] The exception to such narrowing would be if choice is widely disseminated and those who choose make substantially different choices.

Robert Sinsheimer argues that human genetic endowment is not best left to chance. By intervening, human beings could enlarge collective freedom and concurrent responsibility.[2] He goes on to argue that much of

1. Jonathan Glover, *What Sort of People Should There Be?* (New York: Penguin, 1984), p. 47.
2. Robert L. Sinsheimer, "Genetic Intervention and Values: Are All Men Cre-

220

human progress has been the consequence of human effort to reduce the role of chance in exposure to hunger, cold, attack, and plague. By limiting chance, human beings have increased their choices and freedom.[3]

Future Generations

Directional choices could be left to future generations, but this generation cannot avoid the choice of intervening or not. If the choice is not to intervene, future generations will start with a different set of givens than if this generation begins intervention. Such reticence would probably reduce future choices by not enhancing abilities, hence losing their attendant opportunities. If most advantages of intervention are ever to be realized, some present generation must begin on behalf of the next. Always leaving genetic intervention to future generations would lead to infinite deferment. Instead of trying to honor future choices by quixotically trying not to make any decisions currently, genetic intervention could emphasize the increase of capacity to expand future generation choice. Change could be incremental and reversible to lessen any unexpected harm.

Research Scientists

If genetic intervention is begun within a given generation, a number of candidates might guide the process. Genetic scientists would have the best grasp of the involved technical information and possibilities. They would be the experts on what is materially feasible. For E. O. Wilson, this expertise in empirical knowledge, particularly of the theory of evolution, is the only sure and worthy guide for human choice. Wilson argues that "like everyone else, philosophers measure their personal emotional responses to various alternatives as though consulting a hidden oracle."[4] The irony according to Wilson is that a person's emotional-ethical responses or "oracle" is part of the survival kit bequeathed by

ated Equal?" in *Modifying Man: Implications and Ethics*, ed. Craig Ellison (Washington, D.C.: University Press of America, 1978), pp. 122-23.

    3. Sinsheimer, "Genetic Intervention and Values," pp. 122-23.

    4. Edward O. Wilson, *On Human Nature* (Toronto: Bantam Books, 1982), p. 6.

the natural selection of evolution to aid survival and propagation. The authority of emotions in ethical matters is that in general they help their bearer make choices that will help that bearer or near relatives propagate, hence spreading the genes for that emotional-ethical response. Since scientists, indeed sociobiologists, best know the mechanism of such evolving thought processes, they would be the appropriate ones to guide future selection.

Empirical knowledge of our biological nature does reveal the limits of what physical change is currently feasible, but it does not offer guidance for what is desirable. It demarcates what is physically possible but does not demarcate clearly what should be sought. The perspectives of geneticists and other scientists would probably not be representative of the concerns of the population at large, and they would be as subject to the vicissitudes of self-interest as any other group. Considering the pressure to win research grants, pursuing finance and personal prestige could gain inordinate influence.

Physicians

Fowler, Juengst, and Zimmerman advocate extending the patient-centered ethic of clinical therapy to decisions about genetic intervention.[5] They argue that the medical model is already in place and effective. Genetic intervention would begin as help for the presenting patient to overcome a reproductive health problem of possibly conceiving children with genetic disease.[6] Decisions would be made by patients or parents with physician guidance. As characteristic of clinical medicine, the focus would be on compassion for those immediately present with little if any concern for long-run implications.[7] Treatment selection would depend on negotiation between a particular doctor and patient.[8]

5. Gregory Fowler, Eric T. Juengst, and Burke K. Zimmerman, "Germ-Line Gene Therapy and the Clinical Ethos of Medical Genetics," *Theoretical Medicine* 10 (June 1989), prepublication copy, pp. 1-31.

6. Eric T. Juengst, "The NIH 'Points to Consider' and the Limits of Human Gene Therapy," *Human Gene Therapy* 1 (1990): 430.

7. Arthur Zucker and David Patriquin, "Moral Issues Arising from Genetics," *Listening: Journal of Religion and Culture* 22, no. 1 (Winter 1987): 65-85.

8. Mark Siegler, "The Doctor-Patient Encounter and Its Relationship to Theories of Health and Disease," in *Concepts of Health and Disease: Interdisciplinary Per-*

Eric Juengst argues further that the involved physician as a professional should be the one who sets intervention limits. Questions of what genetic intervention is appropriate would be "ultimately questions for professional conscience and vision, not public policy."[9] The driving conviction is that only fellow professionals can fully understand and guide the practice of the profession, hence they set the appropriate standards. Lantos, Siegler, and Cuttler seem to assume this for example in their prescription for the parallel case of human growth hormone. They conclude that when faced with new therapies, "If pediatricians do not respond to these dilemmas thoughtfully, carefully, and forcefully, other decision makers, whose decisions may reflect political, social, or market forces, may then respond in ways that do not reflect the best interests of children."[10] Undoubtedly pediatricians will be affected by "political, social, or market forces" as well, but they at least have a professional commitment to put their patients first.

The authors' concern is perceptive and laudable for all involved in such choices, including physicians. Traditionally physicians have had complete control of medical decisions because they have technical expertise and purport to have solely the patient's best interests in mind. Fortunately, this may often be substantially the case. Unfortunately, medical expertise does not guarantee it. Physicians are as subject to the vicissitudes of humanity as any other human beings. Troyen Brennan writes to his fellow physicians that they need to take care to follow "a truly ethical stance consistent with just doctoring and not merely, as it appears they have in the past, turn these ethical propositions to their own advantage."[11] Apparent beneficence, particularly if practiced unilaterally, can mask self-interest. "Motivating reasons can diverge from justifying reasons."[12] One can see advantages to the current clinical model such as the working out of these issues in the privacy of the doctor-patient relationship. Choices could be made personally with minimum

---

spectives, ed. Arthur L. Caplan, H. Tristram Engelhardt Jr., and James J. McCartney (Reading, Mass.: Addison-Wesley, 1981), pp. 628, 643.

9. Juengst, "NIH 'Points to Consider,'" p. 431.

10. John Lantos, Mark Siegler, and Leona Cuttler, "Ethical Issues in Growth Hormone Therapy," *JAMA* 261, no. 7 (February 17, 1989): 1024.

11. Troyen A. Brennan, *Just Doctoring: Medical Ethics in the Liberal State* (Berkeley and Los Angeles: University of California Press, 1991), p. 238.

12. James F. Childress, *Who Should Decide? Paternalism in Health Care* (New York: Oxford University Press, 1982), pp. 43-44.

outside interference, yet professional expertise would guide the process. Problems such as the general public's tendency "to underestimate familiar risks and overestimate risks that are unfamiliar, hard to understand, invisible, involuntary, and/or potentially catastrophic," would be tempered by knowledgeable and professional counsel.[13] Such evidence-informed practice should best remember that physicians bring values, not just facts, and that patients bring facts, not just values. A dialogue of values shapes the gathering and interpreting of facts that is too pervasive to eliminate statistically. Double-blind review is a powerful tool, but not an all-encompassing one. While gathered and precise experience can be quite helpful, there is more to any particular case than what has usually worked before. Further, all the limits of current medical practice might be carried over such as lack of access or accountability.[14]

How one describes the goals of medicine is more than an intramural debate. Medicine in our society has considerable prestige, institutional power, and financial endowment. How it states and pursues its goals is widely influential. The goals of medicine have been described in a number of ways. Relief of suffering and increase of capacity have been commonly cited, with of course the traditional commitment to *primum non nocere* (first do no harm). In all, serving the patient is the priority. How a patient is served is not by complete consensus. Colleagues already offer cosmetic surgery such as face-lifts and tummy tucks. In some jurisdictions instances of intentionally ending life have been delegated to physicians.[15] There is also extensive health care outside the traditional system, from herbs to acupuncture. Even if some enhancements are not carried out by the medical establishment, that does not eliminate other people offering those services. The massive alternative health care industry is a case in point. James Lindemann Nelson has coined the term "schmoctors" for a whole new group of providers who might practice "schmedicine."[16] These schmoctors might specialize in

13. W. French Anderson, "Human Gene Therapy: Why Draw a Line?" *Journal of Medicine and Philosophy* 14, no. 6 (December 1989): 691.

14. For an example of a modified structure for clinical medicine, see Brennan, *Just Doctoring.*

15. Professor Dave Leal of Brasenose College, Oxford University, reminded me of this parallel.

16. Erik Parens, "Is Better Always Good? The Enhancement Project," in *Enhancing Human Traits: Ethical and Social Implications,* ed. Erik Parens (Washington, D.C.: Georgetown University Press, 1998), p. 11.

providing the genetic enhancements if they are not offered by others. While physicians cannot as a group control all the uses of their expertise, they can choose what they will endorse as a group. What the medical establishment offers has an imprimatur effect of a prestigious and pervasive system. Physicians cannot unilaterally determine all uses of genetic intervention, but they are still responsible for their part. The medical establishment has been richly endowed by public and private payment and charity and has a rich heritage built from the service of many. If it speaks with a unified voice, its influence will be substantial.

Expert Panel

A wider-based group of experts could be assembled to include, along with genetic scientists, other leaders such as clergy, ethicists, and political scientists to deliberate and choose. Such a body would have the advantage of sustained, careful, and more comprehensive reflection on the involved questions. It would still however lack the breadth of society, for no one committee can have representatives for everyone. This would be true even if the committee was as broadly based as the Public Policy Advisory Committee proposed by Jeremy Rifkin and his Foundation on Economic Trends.[17] He has argued that such an expert advisory committee should include one or more experts in each of the following fields: protecting medical care and insurance consumers, workplace discrimination, women's rights, rights of minorities, disabled rights, and legal rights to privacy and civil liberties. While such a committee would presumably care for people's rights, it could not possibly represent all perspectives and concerns. No committee could be aware of all concerns, nor express them in ways recognizable to all participants. Attempts to speak for diverse constituencies tend to abstract out to the lowest common denominator.[18] The consensus that has come to be called "the Georgetown mantra" (nonmaleficence, beneficence, autonomy, and justice) is more fruitfully heuristic than able to guide practical

17. Foundation on Economic Trends, "Proposed Amendment to the National Institutes of Health Guidelines for Research Involving Recombinant DNA Molecules to Establish a Public Policy Advisory Committee," *Human Gene Therapy* 2 (1991): 133.

18. John H. Evans, *Playing God? Human Genetic Engineering and the Rationalization of Public Bioethical Debate* (Chicago: University of Chicago Press, 2002).

choices when standing alone. This is the problem of thin and thick descriptions discussed in chapter 7.

A further issue for expert panels is how clients evaluate conflicting advice. As new genetic tests have become available, caregivers and legislatures have struggled to determine which tests should be added to the standard of care. In response, the American College of Medical Genetics (ACMG) gathered a panel of leading experts and published a report in 2006 that was endorsed by groups such as the American Academy of Pediatrics and then applied substantially in state legislation across much of the United States. Concern was then expressed that the ACMG task force was shaped by the expertise of its members — some having developed certain tests and others working as advocates for particular diseases — so that the committee recommended too many newborn genetic screening tests.[19] Prescribing too many tests would not necessarily be from nefarious self-interest; members could be just acting out the priorities that cause them to develop valued expertise in the first place that was then sought for the committee. A carefully constructed alternative was offered by another panel of experts.[20] This second report was funded by the National Human Genome Research Institute of the National Institutes of Health and organized by the Hastings Center, an august bioethics think tank near New York City. When faced with dueling expert panels, should policy makers and the public summon a new expert panel to arbitrate?

Committees by definition do not include everyone. Committee work could lend itself to self-interested manipulation and would, if it could choose for all, potentially eliminate some traits that are highly valued by minority groups or subsets of the groups that do have representation. To the degree that such an expert committee gave specific recommendations, it would centralize the thrust of intervention. Observing the allotment of kidney dialysis by a Seattle committee, Sanders and Dukeminier wrote that "the Pacific Northwest is no place for a Henry David Thoreau with bad kidneys."[21] Given centralized power to choose, even a committee of minorities threatens diversity.

19. Mary Ann Baily and Thomas H. Murray, eds., *Ethics and Newborn Genetic Screening: New Technologies, New Challenges* (Baltimore: Johns Hopkins University Press, 2009).

20. Baily and Murray, *Ethics and Newborn Genetic Screening*.

21. David Sanders and Jesse Dukeminier Jr., "Medical Advance and Legal Lag: Hemodialysis and Kidney Transplantation," *UCLA Law Review* 15 (1968): 378.

Such a council could serve as a long-range adviser, but not well as the sole locus of decision.[22] No matter how erudite and empathic the committee, it could not match the best efforts and innovations of millions of people all trying to do the best for themselves and their children. Insights can come from countless unheralded corners.

Parents

Societal diversity adds not only valued variety to life, but also greater societal adaptability and room for minority perspectives.[23] Garland Allen has written that science and technology both in research and application have always been controlled by whichever class was in power.[24] By disseminating choice, minority perspectives are protected as required by respect for those who hold them and as potential precursors for views that could someday be adopted by the society at large. Disseminating choice eliminates the possibility of unified movement but also maximizes lived options for the future. Diversity would probably be served best by dispersing intervention choices to the widest level, the choices of persons for themselves and of parents for their children. There is precedent for the latter in that parents already make most decisions on behalf of their children, and reproductive freedom is widely and deeply valued.[25]

Note that, in a public policy context, arguments against the prominence of autonomy in our liberal culture are often misdirected. Support for individual autonomy is not to thin decisions to isolated individuals, but rather it is to make space for thick decisions that are not dictated by the broader public. Individual autonomy allows the individ-

---

22. For a parallel with past bioethics commissions established by the federal government, see John C. Fletcher and Franklin G. Miller, "The Promise and Perils of Public Bioethics," in *The Ethics of Research Involving Human Subjects: Facing the 21st Century*, ed. Harold Y. Vanderpool (Frederick, Md.: University Publishing Group, 1996), pp. 155-84.

23. Richard A. McCormick, *The Critical Calling: Reflections on Moral Dilemmas Since Vatican II* (Washington, D.C.: Georgetown University Press, 1989), p. 268.

24. Garland Allen, "Genetics, Eugenics, and Class Struggle," *Symposium on the History and Teaching of Genetics: XIII International Congress of Genetics* (June 1975): 29.

25. Nicholas Agar, *Liberal Eugenics* (Oxford: Blackwell, 2004), p. 15.

ual to consult and express a community not designated or required by the broader public. Thin public discussions that are striving for consensus and hence usually end with the lowest common denominator, could be superseded by parental decisions fully reflecting the accumulated wisdom and life experience of their particular traditions.[26]

> But the parent-child relationship is not just a matter of individual well-being. The broader community also depends on this structure to accomplish the enormous, long-term, and labor-intensive tasks of child rearing. These include material support, daily physical and emotional care, basic education in language and culture, and socialization into the customs and norms of the community. There is no failure as costly to a society as a failure in this primary arena of nurture and formation, none so difficult to repair or compensate for the breakdown of this most fundamental social relation. Those who do not learn to bond and empathize with other human beings through this interpersonal connection, who do not learn how to function within the group of which they are part, are at best handicapped in their social relations. At worst, they are dangerous.[27]

Recognizing the importance of family is not to absolutize isolated family autonomy. Reinhold Niebuhr wrote an influential classic called *Moral Man and Immoral Society*.[28] It has been observed that from what he wrote it should have been titled *Immoral Man and More Immoral Society*. Individuals and societies comprised of individuals are prone to self-interest, self-deception, and abuse of others. Dispersing decision making among parents is not assuming their perfection. It would be to protect families and communities in some degree from state domination. When the common good is entrusted solely to the discernment and enforcement of government, communities are crushed. A large state simply cannot conceive, let alone nurture, the variety of perspectives and insights of its citizens. The state can constrain and empower,

26. John H. Evans has noticed this possibility in his sociological description of the de-theologizing of the public bioethical debate (*Playing God?* p. 155).

27. Sondra Wheeler, "A Theological Appraisal of Parental Power," in *Designing Our Descendants: The Promises and Perils of Genetic Modification* (Baltimore: Johns Hopkins University Press, 2003), p. 241.

28. Reinhold Niebuhr, *Moral Man and Immoral Society* (New York: Scribner, 1932).

228

but it is too coercive and blunt an instrument to be allowed or invited to act unilaterally in the name of the common good.

On the one hand the same freedom that is advocated to protect parents from coercion may be turned to unbridled choices of too much intervention. "If the changes that will be achieved are sufficiently desirable so that they not only avoid social harms but also facilitate individual success in a high-technology, post industrial society, then the genetic changes will be desired by individuals for their children."[29] In traditions that emphasize personal freedom, genetic intervention might be pushed more aggressively by autonomous individual parents than by the authoritarianism often feared. Decisions will vary in import. For human genetic intervention, "either such traits as hair colour, gender, and the like are important or they are not. If they are not important why not let people choose? And if they are important, can it be right to leave such important matters to chance?"[30] On the other hand, parental objection to needed intervention has been raised as a potential problem. Genetic intervention could be expected for some cases as efficacious medical treatment is required in some cases for children now.[31] Conflicts between parental choice and what society comes to regard as a decent minimum could develop. Parental choice may be limited to be sure that the child is protected from intervention or lack of intervention known to be overwhelmingly harmful.[32] Granted, such legislated requirements could raise concerns of past eugenic coercion.[33]

Other problems with parental choice might include intentional or unintentional usurpation of parental choice by the counselors who present the possible options, a lack of understanding and foresight when faced with complicated and technical choices,[34] or self-centered choices

29. H. Tristram Engelhardt Jr., "Human Nature Revisited," in *Ethics, Politics, and Human Nature*, ed. Ellen Frankel Paul, Fred D. Miller Jr., and Jeffrey Paul (Oxford: Basil Blackwell, 1991), p. 189.

30. John Harris, *Clones, Genes, and Immortality* (Oxford: Oxford University Press, 1998), p. 191.

31. Hardy Jones, "Genetic Endowment and Obligations to Future Generations," in *Responsibilities to Future Generations*, ed. Ernest Partridge (Buffalo: Prometheus Books, 1981), p. 250.

32. World Council of Churches, Church and Society, *Manipulating Life: Ethical Issues in Genetic Engineering* (Geneva: World Council of Churches, 1982), p. 8.

33. Juengst, "NIH 'Points to Consider,'" p. 430.

34. Bo Lindell, "Ethical and Social Issues in Risk Management," in *Faith and Science in an Unjust World: Report of the World Council of Churches' Conference on*

by the parents. Having a child who suffers from the genes one has passed on by chance or choice is devastating and disorienting. David Biebel writes, "to experience genetic disease in one's children is to be immersed in a boiling cauldron of almost pure pain, with a generous helping of surprise, confusion, disappointment, anger, and guilt thrown in."[35] Through the stress and hope, our society counts on parents having the best interest of their children in mind.

Legislatures

There are four prominent arguments for a government role in genetic intervention. First, William Vukowich advocates that legislatures alone should make the involved choices for more effective unity of effort. Legislation should be passed that sets standard intervention for each child.

> The selection of desirable and undesirable traits can be left to the legislature. Indeed, legislatures have enacted negative eugenic laws in the past. Although legislative selection of genetic traits could open the door for oppressive practices, traditional constitutional limitations should insure against abuses. Legislative rather than parental choice would provide greater unity of effort: it would be a more effective means of diminishing detrimental genes and propagating superior ones than parental choices that would vary from couple to couple.[36]

The legislature as sole decider could grant an efficiency of unified vision and development, and may be less finite than one set of parents, but it may be more fallible than all parents acting separately. It takes time to build sufficient public consensus to write coercively enforced law. The cumulative effect of investment and results from individual or group decisions can be revealing but can also make stopping or redirecting cer-

---

Faith, Science, and the Future, Massachusetts Institute of Technology, Cambridge, USA, 12-24 July, 1979 (Geneva: World Council of Churches, 1980), p. 126.

35. David B. Biebel, "The Riddle of Suffering," in *Genetic Ethics*, ed. John F. Kilner, Rebecca D. Pentz, and Frank E. Young (Grand Rapids: Eerdmans, 1997), p. 3.

36. William Vukowich, "The Dawning of the Brave New World — Legal, Ethical, and Social Issues of Genetics," *University of Illinois Law Forum* 2 (1971): 202.

tain practices quite difficult. As a starting point legislation could assure safety as it already does for other medical interventions. This would include insisting on incremental steps. Our history has been to use new methods and products before we know their full effects. That has included untoward effects from aerosols on the ozone layer to DDT and eagle eggs. But at least the mistakes of parental decisions would be spread out for potentially less possible maximum gain of unified development, but also less chance of unmitigated disaster of everyone enhanced in a deleterious way. Usually acting by majority decision, a legislature as sole decider would probably limit diversity and be more easily manipulated by one group's self-interest. "Nations, like individuals, are endlessly tempted to claim that they are more moral than they are."[37]

Second, for Margery Shaw, the legislature has a duty to protect public health. "It should be incumbent upon the law to control the spread of genes causing severe deleterious effect just as disabling pathogenic bacteria and viruses are controlled."[38] This is not only for the sake of the treated individual, but also the effect on all the other individuals in society. Fewer individuals incompetent to care for themselves and hence in need of protection means more talent and more productivity for one another. Such a legislated requirement would lead to direct conflict with institutions and individuals that do not accept genetic intervention. In North America the state needs significant cause to override parental wishes, yet such can be evoked to protect children from significant harm.[39] Such legislation would probably be quite difficult to enforce. The best chance for state implementation of guidelines would be through licensing providers.[40]

Third, others expect a right to intervention that would probably require public provision and enforcement. "It seems quite certain that with further advances in genetics our concept of human rights, and our concern with the quality of life, will be enriched with a new right: that

---

37. Kenneth Thompson, *Morality and Foreign Policy* (Baton Rouge: Louisiana State University Press, 1980), p. xi.

38. Margery Shaw, "Conditional Prospective Rights of the Fetus," *Journal of Legal Medicine* 5 (1984): 63-116, as quoted by Neil A. Holtzman, "Recombinant DNA Technology, Genetic Tests, and Public Policy," *American Journal of Human Genetics* 42 (1988): 628.

39. Maxwell Mehlman, *Wondergenes* (Bloomington: Indiana University Press, 2003), pp. 127-33.

40. Mehlman, *Wondergenes*, pp. 155-59.

of being born without the handicap of a readily preventable serious genetic defect."[41] To date, many children are born with genetic conditions
that cause pain and disability. When nothing can be done about it, that
reality is unfortunate but not unjust.[42] However, if the means is available to increase greatly the chance that a child will be born with a
healthy genetic endowment, and we do not do that for the child, that
omission may indeed be unjust and uncaring. There might be a "genetic
decent minimum" that is widely recognized and should be provided as
helpful to any human being.[43] Is refusing to take available B vitamins
during pregnancy that results in spina bifida (granted, this is not the
only possible cause) as culpable by omission as the commission of
drinking alcohol during pregnancy that causes fetal alcohol syndrome?
For that matter, is choosing not to take an available vitamin for the sake
of your developing child an act of commission? Is not availing oneself of
counsel and avoiding alcohol while pregnant an act of omission? The
often-made distinction between omission and commission in this case is
not as helpful as it might first appear.

The feminists Goerlich, Krannich, and Degener each argue that
individuals and society should adapt to given genetic endowments, not
genetic endowments to individual or social desires,[44] yet many genetic
disabilities would reduce choice in any society. "Huntington's is, above
all, a disease of endless replication, reducing the wonderful multiplicity
of human lives to a dreary, deadening sameness, repeating over and over
again the same awful saga."[45] Disease lessens diversity by decreasing opportunity for different choices. There is little variety among the life-

41. Bernard D. Davis, "Ethical and Technical Aspects of Genetic Intervention,"
New England Journal of Medicine 285, no. 14 (September 30, 1971): 800.

42. Leonard Fleck writes of this shift in "Justice, Rights, and Alzheimer Disease
Genetics," in *Genetic Testing for Alzheimer Disease: Ethical and Clinical Issues,* ed.
Stephen G. Post and Peter J. Whitehouse (Baltimore: Johns Hopkins University Press,
1998), p. 202.

43. Allen Buchanan et al., *From Chance to Choice: Genetics and Justice* (Cambridge: Cambridge University Press, 2000), pp. 81-82, 174.

44. Annette Goerlich and Margaret Krannich, "The Gene Politics of the European Community," *Issues in Reproductive and Genetic Engineering* 2 (1989): 214;
Theresia Degener, "Female Self-Determination between Feminist Claims and 'Voluntary' Eugenics, between 'Rights' and Ethics," *Issues in Reproductive and Genetic Engineering* 3 (1990): 94, 98.

45. Alice Wexler, *Mapping Fate: A Memoir of Family, Risk, and Genetic Research* (New York: Random House, 1995), p. xxv.

style choices of corpses. Alive and valued people who suffer genetic disabilities make important choices in how they leverage what they can do, yet they do not have as many choices as people who have more capable bodies. There may be consensus that government should reduce the most horrific genetic harms for the sake of the individual.

Walters and Palmer argue that it is preferable that genetic disease be eliminated by voluntary genetic screening and therapy. They are aware that "if a voluntary program has been tried and has failed because of public inertia or unreasonable resistance, a mandatory program might seem to be morally justifiable in this case, even to a civil libertarian, as a reasonable means to a highly desirable end."[46] Walters and Palmer are thinking specifically about an attempt to rid a population of cystic fibrosis, a laudable goal. However, the phrase "unreasonable resistance" is fraught with dangerous precedence. Walters and Palmer argue then that such a campaign may well be offered and would probably be widely accepted as are current screening programs, but it should not be required by any state. Such would violate a basic human right.[47] Yet many jurisdictions do mandate immunization for the sake of a child, even against parental wishes.

The fourth community concern likely to draw legislative interest is long-term mass effects. What might be advantageous for individuals could have a negative impact when widely practiced. Parents would not necessarily be trying to change society; they would just be trying to give their children the best possible start. Individuals and society already work sometimes successfully, sometimes not, at building communities that encompass substantial differences in levels of ability. Depending on how it is implemented, genetic intervention could lessen the distance between people's opportunities or increase it. Issues of direction and distribution would be crucial. Lee Silver has projected that if only an elite group has access to the technology, two classes of human beings could eventually differentiate as species. They might be called the "Naturals" and the gene enriched, or "GenRich."[48] Actual divergence would require population isolation. As long as there is intermarriage, genes introduced to the GenRich would disperse to the Naturals. To

46. LeRoy Walters and Julie Gage Palmer, *The Ethics of Human Gene Therapy* (New York: Oxford University Press, 1997), p. 87.

47. Walters and Palmer, *Ethics*, p. 88.

48. Lee M. Silver, *Remaking Eden: How Genetic Engineering and Cloning Will Transform the American Family* (New York: Avon Books, 1998), p. 4.

become separate species would probably require an isolated colony such as on Mars, spurred by selection for the Martian environment. Long before there could be differentiation into separate species, government would be challenged on its commitment to equality of opportunity discussed in chapter 10.

What is allowed by public policy has an influence as something within the range society does not make an effort to prohibit, but that is quite different from society advocating that it should be done. Having a right to do something does not mean it is the right thing to do. Society can create space for individuals and their communities to choose. "Public sentiment is everything. With public sentiment, nothing can fail; without it nothing can succeed. Consequently he who molds public sentiment, goes deeper than he who enacts statutes or pronounces decisions. He makes statutes and decisions possible or impossible to be executed."[49]

Utopias generally have been optimistic about government leadership. Plato's guardians and Wells's samurai would be examples. In contrast, Justice Brandeis has written that "experience should teach us to be most on our guard to protect liberty when the government's purposes are beneficial. Men born to freedom are naturally alert to repel invasion of their liberty by evil-minded rulers. The greater dangers to liberty lurk in insidious encroachment by men of zeal, well-meaning but without understanding."[50] Joseph Fletcher counsels that in dystopias such as the one in *Brave New World*, totalitarian regimes abuse human engineering but human engineering does not necessarily lead to totalitarianism.[51]

National legislatures can also be contested by international borders. The World Trade Organization permits exclusion of a product or service only if there is a credible scientific study showing that the import poses "unacceptable risk." Even if a country has built a substantial consensus that as a society it does not want a particular product or practice, it must prove measurable harm to block the import.[52] There is a

---

49. Abraham Lincoln, August 21, 1858.

50. Justice Louis Brandeis, *Olmstead v. U.S.*, 277 U.S. 479 (1928).

51. Joseph Fletcher, "New Beginnings in Life: A Theologian's Response," in *The New Genetics and the Future of Man*, ed. Michael P. Hamilton (Grand Rapids: Eerdmans, 1972), p. 84; Aldous Huxley, *Brave New World* (New York: Harper and Row, 1969).

52. Conrad G. Brunk, "Religion, Risk, and the Technological Society," in *The Twenty-first Century Confronts Its Gods: Globalization, Technology, and War*, ed. David J. Hawkins (Albany: State University of New York Press, 2004), p. 49.

decided tendency when seeking consensus to screen out what many groups within the society might consider their most deeply held convictions. Since biotechnology is developing the capacity to alter nature in general and human nature in particular, to an unprecedented degree it highlights our foundational understanding of who we are and what we should be doing.

The sociologist Dorothy Wertz has observed that Japan, China, and India have the technology for enhancement efforts and few internal cultural barriers to them. For example, there is little concern about limiting contraception or abortion.[53] Wertz was not surprised to hear the president of the East Asian Society of Bioethics argue that we should use recombinant DNA techniques to promote "artificial evolution-positive eugenics."[54] Prebirth tests are already very popular in China, where many parents know they will be able to have only one child. That child carries all their dreams and every advantage they can provide. The leadership of Singapore has created policies to encourage well-educated citizens to marry and have many children.[55] It is doubtful that the more extensive and precise techniques of genetic intervention would be eschewed. Interest in genetic intervention is high around the world.

Concerns of humanity, equality, and economy extend across national borders. While it can be argued that obligations are greatest to those nearest, that is a tempering factor and not necessarily a set limit to care. The National Council of Churches of Christ/USA has advocated that the benefits of biogenetic innovation should be available regardless of geography, economic ability, or race.[56] A policy statement adopted by the governing board reasons that "the whole of humankind, created by God, living under God, offered salvation by God, is a unity."[57] All peo-

---

53. Daniel C. Maguire, ed., *Sacred Rights: The Case for Contraception and Abortion in World Religions* (Oxford: Oxford University Press, 2003).

54. Dorothy C. Wertz, "Society and the Not-So-New Genetics: What Are We Afraid Of? Some Future Predictions from a Social Scientist," *Journal of Contemporary Health Law and Policy* 13 (1997): 332.

55. Chee Khoon Chan and Heng-Leng Chee, eds., *Designer Genes: I.Q., Ideology, and Biology* (Kuala Lumpur: Institute for Social Analysis, 1984).

56. National Council of Churches of Christ/USA, Panel on Bioethical Concerns, *Genetic Engineering: Social and Ethical Consequences* (New York: Pilgrim Press, 1984), pp. 4, 35. Also McCormick, *The Critical Calling*, p. 269.

57. National Council of Churches Governing Board, *A Policy Statement of the National Council of Churches in the United States of America: Genetic Science for Human Benefit* (New York: Pilgrim Press, 1986), p. 9.

ple then should have access to the benefits of biogenetic innovations. A 2002 study asked scientific experts from around the world what biotechnologies will be of most help to health in developing countries in the next five to ten years. Of the ten most-cited biotechnologies, four, such as recombinant vaccines, were based on the new genetics.[58]

New concerns at the international level might include lack of control in how such shared technology is implemented. Other governments might use the technology in ways the originating country considers unconscionable. In such cases, the first government could limit its aid, yet practically would at best probably only be able to delay the other's use. The strongest impact may be in pressure to keep up. Nations may fear falling behind the most aggressive programs. Nuclear power and weapons proliferation offer a parallel case.

A Workable Model

"It is helpful to imagine cavemen sitting together to think up what, for all time, will be the best possible society and then setting out to institute it. Do none of the reasons that make you smile at this apply to us?"[59] With such appropriate reservation in mind, a workable model for now that allows choice, yet remains thoughtful and respectful, might be that of combining the best contribution of each decision group with accountability to the others. The process might call for genetic scientists to explain what is possible, expert panels to offer long-range integrated advice, chance to set a starting point, legislatures to set a choice perimeter, physicians to enable thoughtful choices, parents to choose with caring diversity, and future individuals and generations to reverse or augment the incremental changes as appropriate to them. The resulting society could develop considerable variety from one group to another. Robert Nozick has called such a process a utopia of utopias.[60] A process would be in place, not a set ideal, for people to make their own choices, within those limits so universally felt by society to be required. The bal-

58. Abdallah S. Daar, Halla Thorsteinsdottir, et al., "Top Ten Biotechnologies for Improving Health in Developing Countries," *Nature Genetics* 32 (October 2002): 229-32.

59. Robert Nozick, *Anarchy, State, and Utopia* (New York: Basic Books, 1974), pp. 313-14.

60. Nozick, *Anarchy, State, and Utopia*, pp. 297-332.

ance would be constantly tested by practical choices, changing circumstances, and contributing judgments. Extensive literature has already developed addressing the integration of moral and religious belief, politics, and law, in our pluralistic society.[61]

Our current system of medical care for minors might be a case in point. Parents have considerable latitude in where and how they seek medical care for their children, yet the law requires a socially perceived basic minimum of certain essential care.[62] Parents are held responsible to meet that minimum. When parental choice disregards the child's needs, society, often clumsily, can intervene as minimally as necessary. A degree of genetic intervention could someday be required as the law now forces vaccination or more dramatically a blood transfusion for an infant that would die without it. When the social consensus of a basic minimum conflicts with what the parents think is best, the clash is a tragic one as seen in the deaths of children followed by the criminal prosecution of parents.[63] The balance of competing interests would require constant testing and renegotiation.

Another case is education. Parents are given considerable latitude to shape a child through education they believe best for the child, yet the government holds parents accountable for requirements the society overwhelmingly considers necessary. Our social consensus requires a minimum of a certain amount of education. All children to function in

61. John R. Pottenger, *Reaping the Whirlwind: Liberal Democracy and the Religious Axis* (Washington, D.C.: Georgetown University Press, 2007); Robert Audi and Nicholas Wolterstorff, *Religion in the Public Square: The Place of Religious Convictions in Political Debate* (Lanham, Md.: Rowman and Littlefield, 1997); Ronald F. Thiemann, *Religion in Public Life: A Dilemma for Democracy* (Washington, D.C.: Georgetown University Press, 1996); Stephen L. Carter, *The Culture of Disbelief: How American Law and Politics Trivializes Religious Devotion* (New York: Doubleday, 1994); Michael J. Perry, *Love and Power: The Role of Religion and Morality in American Politics* (New York: Oxford University Press, 1991) and *Morality, Politics, and Law* (New York: Oxford University Press, 1988). For a more sociological emphasis, see James Davison Hunter, *Culture Wars: The Struggle to Define America* (New York: Basic Books, 1991).

62. There are related issues of how involved parties exercise their role. For example, government can enter through numerous means such as taxation or forgiveness of taxes, criminal law, providing information or facilities. Note James F. Childress, *Priorities in Biomedical Ethics* (Philadelphia: Westminster, 1981), p. 101.

63. For an explanation and defense of the beliefs and practice of followers of Mary Baker Eddy in this regard, see *Christian Science: A Sourcebook of Contemporary Materials* (Boston: Christian Science Publishing Society, 1990).

our society should receive the opportunity to learn basic skills such as how to read and write. How parents achieve that goal is open to varying degrees, whether through homeschooling, public schools, professional tutoring, boarding schools, or other means.

People could advocate that genetic intervention be prohibited or limited to certain types of intervention. If by persuasion such reservation became part of the broad societal consensus, it could be enforced by society. Allowing considerable range of such decisions does not assume ethical relativism. Hopefully the test of publicity and limits where there is broad societal consensus would constrain rank abuse while allowing the diversity of response that would be most helpful. Consensus adjustment on appropriate limits would likely occur over time.

Would human beings thereby have the wisdom to choose well in an informed, accountable process? The stakes would be high and implementation would best be in increments. As Paul Ramsey warns, "Mankind has not evidenced much wisdom in the control and redirection of his environment. It would seem unreasonable to believe that by adding to his environmental follies one or another of these grand designs for reconstructing himself, man would then show sudden increase in wisdom. If genetic policy-making were not miraculously improved over public policy-making in environmental and political matters, then access to the Tree of Life (meaning genetic management of future generations) could cause grave damage."[64] With such due caution in mind, diversity and group protection could be served by widely disseminating the power to choose genetic intervention to those who receive it and to parents on behalf of their children. The community goal would be one of improvement, not perfection, in a structured but adjustable process, not the application of a unanimous and enforced ideal. So constructed, the process could support the autonomy and diversity of parents and recipients within the minimal constraints of broad societal consensus.

64. Paul Ramsey, *Fabricated Man: The Ethics of Genetic Control* (New Haven: Yale University Press, 1978), p. 96.

Expectations

It has been suggested that if a gathering of cows is a herd, of whales a pod, of geese a gaggle, of crows a murder, and of lions a pride, maybe ethicists together should be called a worry. Ethics serves an important purpose when it warns us of pride, but it should also warn us of the danger of apathy. What not to do is important, but so is being reminded and encouraged to do what we should. Christian ethics is neither lawless nor legalist. It is about being set free through and in Christ to live as God created us to live. Human genetic intervention is one part of how we can fulfill our capacity, calling, and relationship to bear God's image in God's garden.

This is always in the context that only God is the Creator. We are just creative and accountable creatures. The full picture of who God is and what God is doing is beyond our comprehension, but God does invite us to be part of God's kingdom. It is a privilege to contribute by God's grace and direction. We may plant a seed, or at a later point water a seed that has already been planted. What we do "is a step along the way, an opportunity for the Lord's grace to enter and do the rest. We may never see the end results, but that is the difference between the master builder and the worker. We are workers, not master builders; ministers, not messiahs."[1] There need not be any wishful thinking

---

1. These wise and powerful words are often attributed to Oscar Romero, as in Valdir Raul Steuernagel, "To Seek to Transform Unjust Structures in Society (i)," in *Mission in the Twenty-first Century*, ed. Andrew Walls and Cathy Ross (Maryknoll, NY: Orbis, 2008), p. 76. Doris Goodnough of Orbis Books says that according to her research they were actually first composed by Ken Untener for a homily in 1979 and never written or spoken by Romero.

for earthly genetic utopia. The point is to be faithful in this aspect of given and called human life, as in every other aspect of life.

Genotype is not phenotype, and phenotype is only part of life. Even perfect genes could never offer us complete bodily health or other utopic dreams. For that matter, salvation is about reconciliation with God, neighbor, and all that God has made, not just physical wholeness. The worthy pursuit in this case is not godhood or perfection, rather simply trying to pass on at least as good as we have received, and if possible, wherever we can, to start the next generation a little better off than we did. If, from the full perspective of the Christian tradition, an instance of genetic intervention is safe, a genuine improvement, increases the choice of recipients, and the best use of our finite resources, that genetic intervention may be an expression of love for God, one another, and the rest of creation entrusted to us. For such opportunities to serve we should be responsible and thankful.

Acknowledgments

I have appreciated the opportunity to test ideas in this book during invited lectures at professional associations including the American Academy of Religion, American Scientific Affiliation, American Society of Human Genetics, Carolina Medical Center, Canadian Scientific and Christian Affiliation, Conference Board of Canada, and the Philadelphia Society; seminaries including Garrett, Gordon-Conwell, McMaster, and the Toronto Schools of Theology; and college/universities including Arizona State, Calvin, Catholic University of America, Eastern Mennonite, Indiana Wesleyan, Oxford, Queens, Seattle Pacific, and Wheaton, but particularly across the campus of McMaster University. Guiding graduate students at McMaster as most of mine prepare to be pastors, physicians, or professors, time and again affirms the maxim that the teacher learns the most.

Dr. Laurie Peterson has been the first person to read each chapter of this work. Professors Dave Leal of Brasenose College, Oxford University and David Gushee of Mercer University each graciously read through an early draft of the whole. McMaster Divinity College funds one of my Ph.D. students as a research assistant. Patrick Franklin has had always apt questions and comments, meticulously checked page proofs, and expertly prepared the indices. I look forward to reading *his* books in the years to come.

At this point in the publishing process at Eerdmans, I am aware of Michael Thompson's early interest in the project and Jon Pott's decision to carry it. Tom Raabe caught points in the writing and documentation that needed attention, and Victoria Fanning is spreading the word about the book's publication. There are undoubtedly many more colleagues at Eerdmans that are expertly contributing to all the facets of producing and disseminating this work. The book is far better from their efforts. Heartfelt thanks to all.

Author Index

Subject Index

Abortion: avoiding disability, 134-35, 183; germ-line intervention preferable to selective abortion, 146-47; prenatal testing leading to, 183; recognizing when a human person is present, 167-69, 183, 184

Abraham, 67, 137, 150

Adam and Eve, 20, 24, 27, 66; like children in the garden, 8, 87; to till and keep the garden, 27-28

Adoption: lauded in the Christian tradition, 136-38; as model for becoming part of God's family, 93, 137-38; significant contribution of parents to the child's biological survival, 140

Anthropic principle, 15

Artificial reproduction techniques (ART), 138-40; insemination, 102n., 138-39; psychological studies of, 93, 139-40

Ashkenazi Jewish community: embraced genetic screening, 216

Atheism: relation to evolution, 2; response to Feuerbach, 50

Attention deficit disorder (ADD), 101, 175

Autonomy: family autonomy important but not absolute, 228, 238; protecting, 152-55; tension with societal consensus, 204, 217; undergirding liberal society, 164, 225, 227

Basic prudential function, 115, 120; distinguished from species-typical functioning, 109-10, 113

Beneficence: can mask self-interest, 223; as enabling genuine improvement, 164; toward future generations, 148; undergirding liberal society, 164, 225

Birth control (or contraception), 68, 141; Roman Catholic perspective on, 92-93

Body: changing of, impacts soul, 76; genetic intervention alienating to, 129; humans based on same bodily systems as animals, 20; increasing immunity to disease, 83, 172; Jesus' resurrection body, 181; mediates current human life, 81; not just a tool but part of who we are, 83; not the purpose of human life, 80, 135; pain as a safeguard, 174; and soul, 65-98, 168; temporality of, 78-79; time of "formation," 169; valued by God, 48

250

Scripture Reference Index